About the Author

Malcolm Gluck is the busiest wine writer there is. He is wine correspondent of the *Guardian* where his weekly column, *Superplonk*, has run for six years in the newspaper's Saturday magazine. He writes a monthly column in the *Scottish Sunday Post*, has a weekly wine column in the *Sunday Express*, and is consultant wine editor of *Sainsbury's Magazine*, 1994's Magazine of the Year.

He is preparing for BBC 2 a series of TV programmes on wine to be broadcast during autumn 1996. He also finds time to deal with a voluminous post bag and to play with his two young children.

He dislikes oysters, neckties and stuffy, overbearing wine critics who 'put themselves above the interests of the readers they serve'.

Superplonk 1996

Malcolm Gluck

CORONET BOOKS
Hodder and Stoughton

First published in Great Britain as
a Coronet paperback original in 1995

Typeset by Palimpsest Book Production Limited,
Polmont, Stirlingshire
Printed and bound in Great Britain by
Mackays of Chatham PLC, Chatham, Kent

Hodder and Stoughton
A division of Hodder Headline PLC
338 Euston Road
London NW1 3BH

To John Orland, in fond memory

CONTENTS

INTRODUCTION

Just as this book is released for sale, that modern abomination known as *beaujolais nouveau* follows hard (or rather I should say soft and gooey) on its heels. I spent a painful few days in the region a year ago and feel keen to share the experience with readers; not in an effort to win your sympathy but in an attempt to shine a light into that cosy and mysterious nook of the wine writer, the all-expenses-paid trip.

Wine writers lead a cruel life, cruelly misunderstood and scorned. Our teeth rattle in our heads from the ceaseless cataract of wine acid which pours over them; our stomachs swell like incipient dirigibles from the fruit and alcohol; and our income, often at the mercy and bareknuckled whim of newspaper and magazine editors, is liable at any moment to shrink dangerously. Indeed, many of those in the wine trade, whose sometime pleasure but oft-time pain it is to entertain us, tell jokes about us behind our backs.

What do you call, they will sneeringly posit, a person who spits a lot and has no visible means of support? A wine writer. Even the legendary Circle of Wine Writers is not sacred to the wits who retail wine. The Circle of Wine Wankers, one PR person employed by a well-known high street wine chain calls it. I am a member of this Circle – though I achieved this status not without some amusing difficulties of my publisher's making because my seconder for membership discovered, late in the day to his horror, that the front cover of the very first *Superplonk* book bore some resemblance to an obscure and long-neglected tome of his own. Thus he belatedly withdrew his secondment, indeed opposed membership, on the barmy grounds that this alleged plagiarism on Faber & Faber's part (the publishers of *Superplonk* prior to Hodder & Stoughton) rendered its hapless author ineligible.

The Circle, then, is an eccentric one. But then, making a living by writing about wine is an eccentric undertaking. Few of its practitioners acquire anything remotely resembling wealth (Hugh Johnson being a notable exception); most exist within shouting distance of the – albeit well-buttered – breadline. Some wine writers eke out an invisible but crust-provisioning existence doing consultancy work for wine producers, or a restaurant chain, or cobbling together the odd leaflet for a regional wine promotional board. Some send despatches to wine magazines abroad. Others write magnificently researched, but wildly uneconomic, works on the diet of a particular vineyard's worms with the generous support of a salaried husband or wife. And some members break away and form shapes of their own.

A while back, Young and not-so-Young Turks who used to be Circle members, and some of whom still are, formed a rebel group and in defiance of circularity called itself, in superb fifth form fashion, the Octagon. It is widely believed that the impoverished adherents of this sect possess a special handshake and slobber scarce New World wines over each other in arcane rites of fidelity.

Wine producers, though, are pleased to recognise the wine writer's poverty because it comes attached to the wine writer's publicity value. The United Kingdom is an important market for wines and the readers of the literate press enjoy reading about them. Wine-producing countries, therefore, actively encourage wine writers to visit them. I daresay a morning does not go by in the whole year, Christmas morning perhaps excepted, in which a group of wine writers is not huddled at Heathrow, sipping coffee or muttering over the Moet, waiting to take off for vineyards abroad.

Normally, these trips are a delight and the writer returns enhanced in knowledge and increased in girth (wine producers being heavily addicted to thrice-daily feasting). However, once in a while one lands on Devil's Island during Torquemada's tour of command when the air ticket distinctly said Sydney or Bordeaux or, in my case, Lyon.

My chief torturer was one Madame Roche. Lucretia Borgia could have honed her skills watching Madame Roche at work. Quite how this ingenious woman managed to slip me the poisonous toadstool when there were six of us tucking into the platter of *champignons sauvages* which accompanied the magnificent Charolais beef I do not know. The lunch she prepared in the kitchen of her tiny cafe (eight tables) in the village of Marchampt, just up the road and up the hill from Quincie-en-Beaujolais, was astonishing for a final bill of 600 francs since it not only included half-a-dozen fat slices of the most luxurious beef I have ever tasted but also generous portions of an *hors-d'oeuvre* consisting of a superb rough pate, charcuterie and crudite plus four *pots* of home-made beaujolais wine. A *pot* is the old beaujolais measure equalling 64cl, roughly one pint, and though the Roche wine was subtly oxidised and roundly despised by Mr Christopher Murphy, the Marks & Spencer wine buyer who had invited me to accompany him on this short trip to witness the blending of the 1994 *beaujolais nouveau* for the store, I found it delicious because it was fresh and lively. It was also unchaptalised (i.e. no sugar had been added to artificially raise its alcohol level as with every bottle of commercial beaujolais). My other English host was the Norfolk-based beaujolais wine merchant and wine broker Mr Roger Harris (telephone 01603 880171 for his current list, the best beaujolais list on the planet), source of much of the great beaujolais I drank in the past. Mr Harris is M & S's agent for the store's *nouveau*. Mr Murphy's bemused cheery mien is like that of a sardonic arts don on holiday. Mr Harris faces the world behind a Venetian carnival mask scowl which easily dissolves to reveal a forceful sense of humour.

I was, of course, rendered almost insensible with sickness in the very early hours of the next morning after the Roche repast and the prospect of the trip back – car from Fleurie to the Macon TGV terminus, train to Paris Gare de Lyon, taxi to Charles de Gaulle, plane to Heathrow, minicab to London – filled me with an ineffable mixture of loathing, horror and profound despair. You may say, not without some logic on your side, that I deserved all I got. What was I doing in the Beaujolais region in the first place? Beaujolais as a drink has filled me with loathing, horror and profound despair for a decade and a half; Madame Roche was only providing the food to match. Ironically, a sympathetic soul from one of the local co-ops claimed that my *maladie* was not due to a poisoned mushroom whatsoever but a result of all the beaujolais I had been tasting. 'Our *nouveau* blender feels ill every year about this time after he has been through so many different *cuves* of beaujolais,' he told me, in an astonishing display of frankness. I felt unable to explain that were that blender to feel as wretched as I did then he would have renounced his profession years ago.

Certainly, I may never touch another drop of beaujolais as long as I live – research purposes excepted. I will certainly have great difficulty in letting my lips again near another mushroom, wild, tame, cooked how you will. And now that I am well again (the ten pounds in weight that I lost during my illness spurring me to keep my middle from spreading too generously in future), I can see that the portents of my disaster were writ large and clear. I had enjoyed a passionate affair with beaujolais from 1967 until 1979 and yet in 1994 the earth was moving before I reached Heathrow (a landslide at the airport causing a two-mile tail-back on the approach road). I should also have guessed something odd was in the air when once in France I encountered a Frenchman who despised garlic (Thierry Coulon, the charming export director of the Cellier de Samsons wine co-operative). I should have been suspicious at the meeting with Franck Duboeuf, scion of beaujolais' most famous broker Georges Duboeuf, in *Le Chapon Fin* restaurant when a French couple whom I initially took for American tourists ordered and uncritically drank a bottle of red Mouton Cadet. In thirty years of eating and drinking in France I had never seen a single French person order anything but the wine of the region and certainly never an overpriced branded bottle. It was a sign. That man and wife knew what they were doing when they ignored the scores of beaujolais on *Le Chapon Fin*'s wine list and decided even the most feebly fruity bordeaux was a better bet. Just as Georges knew what he was about when he named his son after the national currency.

Money rules beaujolais. It is the very first thing that anyone talks about. The instant that Mr Murphy and Mr Duboeuf met the conversation was about the imminent demand by the grape growers for more dosh. An oenologist who happens to be passing is greeted and introduced and he immediately adds to this fund by saying, 'In 1989 some of the growers got so greedy they put signs on their vines saying that if you're not prepared to pay so many thousand francs then don't bother to call.' I daresay in 1955, when Franck's dad first got going in earnest as a beaujolais broker, and *Le Chapon Fin* was his first restaurant customer, money talked rather more slowly but now its speech has become racier and more powerful with every harvest. Georges Duboeuf now presides over an empire – including a vast investment in a local waxworks and wine museum catering for thousands of tourists a year which is housed within the local disused railway station and built on a scale to rival the most ambitious Disneyland extravaganzas of certain Californian wineries. Beaujolais is no longer simply about wine; it has become a branch of show business. Monsieur Duboeuf's company exports world-wide. He employs scores of people. His name appears annually on more than 20 million beaujolais bottles (15 per cent or so of the region's total production). He is *le roi du beaujolais*, the king, the very soul, of beaujolais – an accession to power and spirituality confirmed many times by the people I met throughout my three-day visit, and it is he who offered me the one great wine I drank during those seventy-two, increasingly hellish, hours.

This wine was a 1989 Moulin-a-Vent. It smelt like a Volnay.

It tasted like a mature Nuits-St-Georges from a low-yielding vineyard, made by extremely caring hands. It totally contradicted British burgundy buffs who would doubtless agree with Mr Anthony Hanson when he wrote, in the first edition of his great book on Burgundy, that 'aging never transforms the product of the gamay grape into something of a comparable quality to an aged pinot noir'. Mr Murphy may well negotiate bottles of this robust beauty onto his shelves (probably at around £10 a bottle, a price well worth paying). This experience proves, if further proof were really needed, that grape varieties are capricious and misunderstood entities.

As indeed are methods of vinification. In Beaujolais, legend says it is the *maceration carbonique* system which gives the wine its uniquely fresh and fruity structure. But no one I met and no wine I tasted during my visit was made wholly by this method. Even at Chateau Thivin, one of the richest and fruitiest of the Cote-de-Brouilly appellation, where on a pitch-dark rainy November night and wearing only a short-sleeved shirt and waistcoat above my trousers, I am to be found, hand in hand with owner and wine-maker Claude Geoffray, examining vines (my *maladie* yet to fully strike) claimed to be 110 years old, the wine is *semi-maceration carbonique*. Is this the 'traditional whole-bunch fermentation' approach this Chateau's publicity material claims is the method used? Yes and no. And even at Thivin, a conscientious winery with some claim to make characterful wine, they add sugar – even when the grapes are sufficiently ripe to reach the levels of alcohol necessary to gain *appellation controlee* certification.

The method of producing wine by the carbonic maceration method was a Beaujolais innovation which became widespread after the First World War (a particularly cruel war for many Beaujolais villages – as many as 80 per cent of growers were slaughtered as conscripts). Before that date the wine known as beaujolais must have been very high in acid and only the best and lowest-yielding of the cru wines, Fleurie, Brouilly, Morgon, Chiroubles, Julienas, St Amour, etcetera, would have been sufficiently fruity to be palatable to drinkers today. In those days the wine was drunk within the region itself; even as recently as twenty years ago when I asked the sommelier at a three-star Michelin restaurant north of Lyon, less than thirty miles from the Beaujolais region, if there might be a nice little beaujolais tucked away within his much-vaunted burgundy wine list he said sneeringly, 'Absolutely not. We do not sell such things. Besides, they are Rhone wines and would not be among the burgundies.' This last geographical quibble aside (technically correct but not necessarily how wine commentators see it – in Anthony Hanson's Burgundy book he includes the Beaujolais region within his remit), I wished I had possessed enough French to tell that sommelier that before he was born beaujolais in pint *pots* watered the palates of every patron of every bistrot in Lyon and his words to me were doubtless causing to spin in every local grave an outraged former beaujolais drinker.

The dreadful modern international phenomenon called *beaujolais nouveau* was known in those days only in the region itself where it began, largely in Brouilly, as a way of providing those Lyon cafes and restaurants with cheap, low in alcohol (8–9 degrees, not the 12 degrees of the modern concoction), brilliantly fresh and fruity wine available some months after harvest and served poured into *pots* straight from the 215-litre barrel (never bottled). This was how I first met chilled *beaujolais nouveau* in late November in Paris in 1967 and I fell in love with it instantly. By this date it had been fashionable among Paris bistrots for some years to ape their counterparts in Lyon, the gastronomic capital of the country (more prestigious than Paris which is merely the political one), by serving the young red wine from the barrel, but the custom had spread no further. It is possible to chart the modern-day success of beaujolais from that day in the thirties when Gabriel Chevalier published his famous novel, revolving around the comic antics of a priest and a pissoir, which takes place in a fictitious Beaujolais village called *Clochemerle* – which translates prosaically as 'bell of the blackbird'. Beaujolais is now built entirely from

7

successful fictions like Clochemerle. Many is the tourist who searches unsuccessfully on map and down single-track lane to find this non-existent hamlet; such a traveller will fail equally spectacularly to find a beaujolais made entirely from the *maceration carbonique* method or one unsugared. The only other unchaptalised beaujolais I tasted on my visit apart from Monsieur Roche's was cajoled out of the Cave Co-op du Bois d'Oignt co-op. It was used exclusively to refresh the workers. It was not available for sale. I enjoyed drinking it. 'Of course, it hasn't the body to be transportable for sale,' I was assured. I didn't press the point further.

Now the point about the so-called beaujolais method of wine-making, this *methode maceration carbonique*, is that, uniquely, the pressing of the grapes does not take place prior to fermentation but afterwards. Most other wine-making methods involve a pressing and the fermentation of the resulting gunge – with skins in the case of red wine, without skins in the case of white (although certain whites are permitted to luxuriate in contact with their skins from periods ranging from a few hours to some days). The beaujolais method involves hand-picked grapes; machines cannot, yet, do the work (and so when the time comes, as surely it must, when the poor of Eastern Europe and other areas find greater economic movement than their annual trek to pick beaujolais grapes, the region, like the Moselle, will find no one to attempt the tedious job of picking unless schoolchildren become forced labour). Whole berries are crucial to the process; a machine would break the skins. These berries are put into a tank from which all oxygen is removed and carbon dioxide is introduced (and also some sulphur). It is the enzymes contained within each berry rather than the yeasts naturally present on the grape skins which are the vital factor in the fermentation process here. It is, of course, difficult to see how 100 per cent whole berry fermentation is possible; the weight of the grapes towards the top of the tank naturally crushes the grapes at the bottom and this fruit, the sugar in which is greedily seized upon by the enzymes and by the yeast, is turned into ethyl alcohol in the normal way, leaving only the upper layer of berries to ferment wholly. Nevertheless, any tank of grapes, left to fizz merrily away from anything from a few days to a few weeks, could be accurately described to have undergone the carbonic maceration method. Tannin is largely but not entirely excluded in this process. It results in fresh, supple, young-tasting fruit which, for *nouveau* wine, is intended to be drunk within a few months. Those beaujolais which would be intended to age would contain more tannins allowing their fruit to develop over time and they would also be aged in barrel or tank for considerably longer than any *nouveau*.

However, no one in the Beaujolais region attempts to practise pure carbonic maceration any more (if they ever did). It is, at best, described as semi-carbonic maceration and all *nouveau* is made this way. The whole berries may either be left alone to ferment for a while before being pressed and the juice, inoculated with an artificial yeast rather than relying on any wild strains, taken off to ferment in the normal way, or the juice could be a mixture of pressed must and whole berries (and maybe some stalks in a cru wine intended to last a few years). 'I'd rather depend on indigenous yeasts,' Thivin's Claude Geoffray admitted, a mite regretfully, 'but I cannot.' It is possible that modern vineyard practices, such as spraying against diseases and pests, reduce the effectiveness of the wild yeasts and render them incapable of seeing the fermentation through to the right level of alcohol and dryness. But then what is the right level of alcohol? Modern beaujolais wine-makers want their wines to be as much as 50 per cent stronger than their forefathers' – hence the addition of sugar to the ferment to increase the final alcohol level. This practice is called chaptalisation after a Napoleonic minister of agriculture, Jean Chaptal, who conceived the idea as a way of making his country less dependent on imported cane sugar; the sugar in beaujolais coming from beet. It is known as *soleil en sacs* – sunshine in bags. This widespread use of chaptalisation conceals much of the regional differences between the crus, blurring the typicity of each, which wild yeasts would also bestow given the chance, and sugaring and artificial yeasting both contribute to the richness of modern beaujolais as well as being solely responsible for its greater alcoholic strength compared to years ago. That beaujolais owes much of its modern taste to a root vegetable is an irony especially poignant when one sees the region as I saw it, with the brilliant golds and ambers of the shrivelling leaves staked out on the wet soil throwing up a magnificently colourful rebuke to the dark, glowering skies of late autumn. I am entirely of the view that much modern-day beaujolais could be made, and be widely accepted by uncritical drinkers, simply by using gamay grape concentrate imported from anywhere you like. Such sublimely beautiful vineyards! Such fat, smug, smooth wine! Much local energy is expended maintaining the fiction that the latter is characterful because of the beauty and unique *terroir* of the former; if this energy were to be actually directed at improving the quality of the grapes and their subsequent handling after harvest rather than improving the smoothness of the lie then maybe we might get beaujolais which tastes like it used to taste.

Beaujolais nowadays is pre-eminently a smoothie. That is its overriding characteristic. It is what drinkers all over the world like about it. How can anyone deride a sales objective which aims to give the product's purchasers what they crave? The Beaujolais region is just like any other modern factory. The word used most by Monsieur Duboeuf senior during my tasting with him, concerning the vinous characteristic he most reviles, is *corse* – coarse. No wonder beaujolais is the ultimate restaurant wine because no matter what the label says, Fleurie or Regnie or Beaujolais-Villages, it is the same smooth wine. And it tastes smooth and rich the moment the cork leaves the bottle. From a region devastated by disease and war Beaujolais has become a superb business success story to sit alongside the same modern exponents of commercial wizardry like Gallo, Sony, Marks & Spencer and Microsoft. It has to be viewed in this light. A wine like *beaujolais nouveau* succeeds in spite of being despised by British trade buyers – like Steve Daniel of

Oddbins who once told me, 'I wouldn't sell it unless I had to. I'm uncomfortable with it. We shift 3,000 cases in a weekend and I'm glad to see the back of it.' Nick Dymoke-Marr, wine buyer with Asda, told me that he gave his stores a choice as to whether they stocked *beaujolais nouveau* '94 and only sixty-five out of 200+ stores wanted it. He didn't force it on them. 'If anything I discouraged them,' he said to me. 'I told them that I felt that our normal offer of wines across the range offered much better value for money than *beaujolais nouveau* and I recommended that they got behind our offers like our Merlot del Veneto at £1.99, which was wonderful light fruity wine at an unbelievable price. It's very difficult with *beaujolais nouveau* to offer the same value for money.'

The *nouveau* wine is of no interest to the intelligent wine drinker (but then neither is cru beaujolais, a tiny proportion of bottles aside) and it should not be considered as a serious wine any longer by wine critics. It should be treated like Lambrusco – ignored except on those rare occasions when a great individual example hits the shelves (like the Duboeuf 1989 Moulin-a-Vent if sufficient exists to make it a commercial reality for M & S which I very much doubt).

Anyone who visits Georges Duboeuf's waxworks with its animated talking vines, Hovis theme-tune muzak, and wax dummies quickly realises that this is the new soul of beaujolais and nothing now can change it. I salute Monsieur Duboeuf as a great showman and retailing genius who, were he British, would now be significantly ennobled and an admired adviser to Conservative prime ministers. Nothing can surely better embody the results of this genius nor so pertinently capture the new soul of the wine than the 1994 *nouveau* razzmatazz which included, at the Design Centre in London's Islington, a bathroom exhibit which had the new wine plumbed into a sink tap. Whether the wine ended up down throat or plughole obviously made little difference to anyone – the profit from its manufacture having already been banked.

I lost ten pounds as a result of my visit to Beaujolais. More importantly, I also lost all my illusions about a former love. I'm glad I made the trip. I feel much better all round.

How this Guide Works

Each supermarket in this Guide is separately listed alphabetically. Each has its own introduction with the wines logically arranged by country of origin, red and white (including roses). Each wine's name is as printed on its label.

Each wine is rated on points out of 20. In practice, wines scoring less than 10 points are not included although sometimes, because a particular bottle has really got up my nostrils and scored so lamentably I feel readers might be amused by its inclusion, I put in a low-pointer. In last year's book I wrote that over the past five years this miserable vinous underclass had assaulted my palate in steadily decreasing numbers and that the rise in the overall quality of wines was reflected in the rating figures. This year, I must make that six years. Higher ratings appear more frequently but not necessarily higher prices. I have been forced, in the interests of fair ratings, to tack on a further half-point such has been the increase in the quality of fruit without the usual concomitant upping of prices.

I continue to be the only wine writer who genuinely rates wines on a value-for-money basis (the only one, in all likelihood, who even thinks in such terms). I expect expensive wines to be good but I do not always expect good wines to be expensive. Thus, a brilliant £10 bottle may not offer better value than a £3 wine because, although the pricier wine is more impressive it is not, in my eyes, anywhere near three times as impressive. I am increasingly disappointed by wines costing over £10 a bottle and this goes double for those costing over £20.

The full scoring system, from my initial tasting and scoring point of view, works as follows:

20 Is outstanding and faultless in all departments: smell, taste and finish in the throat. Worth the price, even if you have to take out a second mortgage.

19 A superb wine. Almost perfect.

18 An excellent wine of clear complexity but lacking the sublime finesse for the top, yet fabulously good value.

17 An exciting, well-made wine at an affordable price.

16 Very good wine indeed. Good enough for any dinner party. Not expensive.

15 For the money, a great mouthful with real style.

14 The top end of everyday drinking wine. Well-made and to be seriously recommended at the price.

13 Good wine, not badly made. Not great, but very drinkable.

12 Everyday drinking wine at a sensible price.

11 Drinkable, but not a wine to dwell on.

10 Average wine (at a low price), yet still a passable mouthful. Also, wines which are expensive and, though drinkable, do not justify their high price.

9 Cheap plonk. Acceptable for parties in dustbin-sized dispensers.

8 Rough stuff. Feeble value.

7 Good for pickling onions.

6 Hardly drinkable except to quench desperate thirsts on an icy night by a raging bonfire.

5 Wine with all its defects and mass manufacturing methods showing.

4 Not good at any price.

3 A palate polluter and barely drinkable.

2 Rat poison. Not to be recommended to anyone, even winos.

1 Beyond the pale. Awful. Even Madame Roche wouldn't serve it to an English wine writer.

From your viewpoint, the wine buyer's, the rating system can be compressed like this:

10, 11	Nothing nasty but equally nothing worth shouting from the rooftops. Drinkable but not exciting.
12, 13	Above average, interestingly made. A bargain taste.
14,15,16	This is the exceptional stuff, from the very good to the brilliant.
17, 18	Really terrific wine worthy of individual acclaim. The sort of wine you can decant and serve to ignorant snobs who'll think it famous even when it is no such thing. Often a bargain price.
19, 20	Overwhelmingly marvellous. Wine which cannot be faulted, providing an experience never to be forgotten.

Prices

I cannot guarantee the price of any wine in this Guide for all the usual trite reasons: inflation, economic conditions overseas, the narrow margins on some supermarket wines making it difficult to maintain consistent prices for very long and, of course, the existence of those freebooters at the Exchequer who are liable to up taxes which the supermarkets cannot help but pass on to the consumer. To get around this problem a price banding code is assigned to each wine:

Price Band

1	2	3	4
A Under £2.50	B £2.50 – £3.50	C £3.50 – £5	D £5 – £7

5	6	7	8
E £7 – £10	F £10 – £13	G £13 – £20	H Over £20

This year, all wines costing under £5 (i.e. A–C) have their price band set against a black background.

STOP PRESS!

Although this is the most thoroughly researched and up-to-date wine guide available, some retailers introduce a few Christmas wines just as this book is going to press. It has always irritated me that these wines, in the past, have escaped my net. But no longer! Thanks to a bend-over-backwards publisher and a printer of equally untypical flexibility you will find a Stop Press section at the end of this book. Here are the last-minute bottles – wines I tasted only after the bulk of this book was already printed.

Acknowledgements

I would like to acknowledge the fact that without the help of Linda Peskin I would be unable to put this book together; without Felicity Rubinstein and Sarah Lutyens I would be deprived of advice and encouragement; and without the continuous critical support of readers of Weekend Guardian *I would be lonely and adrift in an ocean of anodyne wavelessness.*

ASDA

You get a nice echo in the new wine-tasting room at the store's Leeds headquarters. It's like being in a broom cupboard. 'Had to make myself unpopular to get it put in,' said Philip Clive apologetically. 'Buyers mustn't put themselves on a pedestal here.' But no sooner was the room in than Philip was out – on his bike down south to work for a small chain of wine shops having decided that Asda was no longer for him. Before Asda's wine buyers had a room in which to gargle and splutter in private, the departed Philip (replacement: Alistair Morrell who's come across from Booths of Preston) and his colleague Nick Dymoke-Marr presumably tasted wine sat at their desks – the loo roll buyer peering at them enviously across the way – and slobbered into their waste bins. No wonder Asda has a hard time competing with the big boys; or, rather, did. I reckon it's now given up (in spite of aiming to sell 4.5 million cases of wine this year). It is, surely, no longer running after Tesco's coat tails; it's nipping at Kwik Save's heels. And not doing a bad job of it. Earlier this year, the Consumers' Association found Kwik Save to be Britain's cheapest supermarket for groceries with a basket of 31 items costing £25.30. But Asda was only 50p behind.

This tells us a lot about the new Asda. And there is a new Asda. It can't expand like crazy with new branches (the total number of stores in the chain is currently 203 which includes five Dales discount stores and so it is way behind Tesco and Sainsbury's), therefore it has to do all it can to work out novel ways to improve the stores it has got. To this end, the staff at head office now wear red caps – but only up to two hours a day. Any longer and you might be thought antisocial or, worse, a bit of a dreamer. But that's

Asda's contribution to office cogitation, for if you're wearing your cap it tells everyone else you don't want to be disturbed. Beats protracted sit-ins in the loo, I suppose.

Mr Dymoke-Marr is still beavering away acquiring interesting wines and rarely, I would think, finds time to wear any sort of cap. Last year, he procured a solidly made 15-point German riesling with, surprise surprise, ripe, characterful fruit yet with dryness and balance. I thought it a delicious aperitif which would, in a short while, develop more fully the kerosene undertone so beloved of the aficionado of the true Rhine style. By the summer of '95 it had so developed and what we have is a terrific wine for £2.99 which works both as a blaster-away of the day's blues as well as a tastebud enlivener. It is called Ruppertsberger Hofstuck Riesling Kabinett. Pity about the name. Elland Road Riesling would be a niftier monicker and might encourage more people to try it. The real name sucks but it's easier to come up with a winning National Lottery sequence than to find a set of German syllables to set the British breast aflutter. But the wine is not your usual saccharine riesling, nor is it lean and austere (and about as fleshy as Claudia Schiffer after a sauna). The 16-point half-bottle of Amarone della Valpolicella at £4.99 was also a scorcher – as corpulently fruity and velvety textured as a Dickensian squire. A quirky bottle of wine, and a personal favourite of Mr Dymoke-Marr, which rather flies in the face of his belief, as told to me, that 'Asda wines are selected with the customer in mind and are not purchased to satisfy the buyer's personal whims and quirks.'

What do these customers have in mind when they visit Asda to buy wine? The store's six top-selling wines were, recently:

1. Merlot del Veneto.
2. Hock Jakob Demmer.
3. Lambrusco la Vigna Bianco.
4. Asda Liebfraumilch.
5. Asda Claret.
6. Asda Lambrusco Bianco.

Liebfraumilch in fourth place? That's something to celebrate. I can't say I'm always over the moon about the level of fruit in those jammy Venetian merlots but now and then they hit the spot. The new Asda is attempting to be different in a couple of other areas as well. It sells a tasting pack of four different wines, in airline-size screwcap bottles, for £3.99, and this is an interesting initiative.

However, this is a minor notion set alongside the store's decision to change the way the world is run. Taxonomically, the store's gone topsy-turvy. Instead of the conventional classification of wines by country, the bottles are now arranged on their shelves sweet to dry with stops in between. The reds run from A (light, easy drinking) through to E (full-flavoured); the whites 1 to 9 – from the driest, through the medium-sweet, to the sweetest. This may seem, on the surface, customer-friendly – certainly to the new, cut-price 1990s customer Asda now perceives itself to be going for, in contrast to the high-flying yuppies the store's livery and layout were designed for back in the 1980s. (It was to catch the eye of these trend-setters that Asda hired an adventurous label designer. As a result, the store's wine labels were once the whackiest on the block. But now? Who knows? My bet is that the labels will conform more to the new Asda customer's desire for up-front value.)

Asda's new way of arranging its wines on shelf may, or may not, win plaudits from customers, but I wonder how many wine writers will like it? Especially wine-guide writers like me. How can anyone armed with a list of wines arranged by country of origin, as in wine guides, find it pleasing to find their way around shelves organised by the amount of sugar, or the amount of *perceived* sugar, in each bottle? This criticism applies equally to a wine mentioned in a column. When I dropped in on an Asda store in Yorkshire I noticed one customer in some disarray as he tried to find the Chablis mentioned in the newspaper article he was carrying. He found it. Eventually. But then Yorkshiremen are famed for their persistence. Normal mortals may find the Asda system off-putting.

Why has Asda decided to fly in the face of received wisdom? Why are their wine shelves now out on a limb? Mr Dymoke-Marr was most eloquent in explaining the decision to plough their new furrow.

'We are very aware,' he told me, 'that a lot of our customers are buying Liebfraumilch and Lambrusco but not necessarily because that's all they want to try. A lot of customers feel a little frustrated. They can see the range of wines there but they really don't know where to start. And they don't want to take a risk and end up with something in their shopping basket that they don't enjoy. So we asked customers: what can we do to help you?'

And back came the answer in the form of a question. 'Had we ever, said our customers, considered merchandising wines of similar tastes in groups together?' said Mr Dymoke-Marr.

But who decides whether a wine is dry, half-dry, off-dry, semi-sweet or sweet? Surely the customers don't decide these matters also? Are scientifically calculated residual sugar levels the key factor?

'It's driven by that mainly, yes. But also of course the acidity comes into it. Residual sugar level in a wine is the technician's way of doing it. We're more interested in what it tastes like. Because that's exactly what our customers want to know . . .'

Mr Dymoke-Marr, a young man whose generosity of manner and girth allied to his ruby pallor and saucy, rumbling chuckle give him a demeanour as country squireish as his Amarone, pauses – conscious, perhaps, that what is under discussion here is a revolution which his competitors are unanimous in denouncing (Victoria Wine tried a similar idea in the 1980s but abandoned it).

He fingers a generous sideburn and takes me on a tour of the New World according to Asda. 'While research showed us that a sweetness and dryness guide was reasonably understood, a lot of customers weren't fully aware of its presence or usage. The best method, surely, would be to divide the wines into taste groups, but we would have to do it in such a way that it was clearly flagged in store. Hence we've got these additions to the dividers, these bus-stop signs, which work whether you've come from that direction or that direction. When you're standing here . . .' and he taps a bottle of Bordeaux blanc . . . 'you know you're looking at dry white. And to build on that, we've re-written all the shelf-edge descriptives. We've made them an awful lot simpler, with one-line descriptions as to the style of the wine and then a contemporary suggestion as to what sort of food it will go with.'

He points to the shelf descriptions of Asda's South Australian Semillon Chardonnay. This wine says of itself that 'It's a light, ripe and fruity white' and can be served with 'Chinese and Indian dishes'.

'Isn't that really practical?' he urges. 'And for those people for whom country of origin is a factor – but not the key factor, we think, with our customers – we do put the country of origin on as well.'

Very nice of you, Nick. Very nice of you to think that we wine guide Johnnies aren't completely redundant – even if to fit in with Asda's new scheme of things we ought to list the store's wines differently. Indeed, I did think of doing that for this edition of *Superplonk* but how do I know if my assessment of a wine's sweetness/dryness is the same as theirs? I suppose the only way to develop a cohesive system would be for Asda to label all its wines with an extra label, just for me, indicating into which sections they will slot in the store. But then I would need to have a new computer software system designed just for Asda's entry in *Superplonk,* since other supermarkets do not, at the moment, have any intention of classifying their wines likewise. I am in a quandary. I want to be as customer-friendly as I can but then Asda's new system is hardly wine guide-friendly, is it? Also, is it very friendly towards Asda's employees who have to fill the shelves? I asked Mr Sean Clayton, who oversees the wine shelves at one Asda store, if his life had not been made more difficult by the new initiative? He shook his head.

'It really makes no difference. You get used to where they are on the shelf and you just stick them on. And we're asking all the own-label suppliers to put the sweetness guide or fullness guide on the outside of the carton,' he told me.

How about when a customer is trying to find a wine he can't see?

'With the new system, it's easy for me to direct a customer to a particular section, like a dry or a medium-sweet or a sweet section.'

'And don't forget,' chips in Mr Dymoke-Marr, 'that Sean's helpers now find it easier to deal with customers' queries. Any colleague can now give advice.'

You mean customers only think about wines as dry or sweet? They don't say, I'm looking for an Australian white, but I'm looking for a dry wine or a sweet wine?

'Yes,' said Mr Clayton with fervour. 'Style rather than where it comes from is more important to them. It doesn't matter if it's from Australia or South Africa or wherever. It's the style they're interested in. Customers used to keep away from wine because they didn't understand it but now it's more accessible to everybody.'

'More accessible; not making an issue of it; making it easier for people to enjoy their bottle of wine. That's what it's all about, isn't it?' says Nick. 'Customers don't need to learn about wine in order to buy it. They don't need to do that with any other products here in the store, do they?'

On this basis, if Asda goes into the used car business then presumably all vehicles will be arranged from slow to fast, two doors or four. Country of origin and extras are irrelevant. The question in my mind is, except when it comes to meeting the most basic needs of the most basic wine drinker, has Asda got it all wrong? Indeed, is Asda treating its more sophisticated wine-buying customers as crudely as the parent who carefully writes Right on one of his five-year-old son's shoes and Left on the other? This, of course, begs the question as to whether Asda has any sophisticated wine-buying customers. It certainly makes me wonder if many buyers of this book, or any other conventionally classified wine guide buyers for that matter, shop there. (If there are, I'd be more than pleased to receive letters from such readers, care of Hodder & Stoughton, with their views on the matter.) But then I think of that Amarone at £4.99. *That* wine, a half for a fiver for heaven's sake, could only be bought by crazed wine lovers.

'This new system is not yet cast in tablets of stone,' says Nick. 'If we get feedback from customers or from Sean or his colleagues saying "We don't think you got it quite right", we'll change it. These are early days.'

But surely it's affected how he now buys wine for the store?

He'll commit himself no more than a cautious: 'We expect to be buying our wines differently in the future because of this.' And since he'll probably flog four and a half million cases this year, he can expect to receive a comfortable degree of cooperation from those from whom he buys his wines or expects to buy them in future. Interestingly, when asked which countries he expected to provide the most exciting additions to his range over the next few years, Mr Dymoke-Marr said 'France' (meaning the Languedoc-Roussillon), 'Australia, South Africa and Chile' (all very predictable) but then he added 'Greece and Portugal'. I think Greece and Portugal offer massive potential, particularly for the red wine drinker looking for bargains. Just where Retsina fits in the sweet-to-dry scheme of things I can't quite figure out.

Nevertheless, it is worth making the point here that Asda's revolution does demolish one of the most tangibly irritating aspects of supermarket wine buying and this is the so-called 'range gap' which often drives professional buyers barmy before they fill it. They lie awake all night thinking 'I've got a gap in my Italian range' or 'What am I going to do about the hole in my Californian?' and often they are forced to fill it with a wine from that country irrespective of its merits.

It will also help the poor German wine grower. Not to mention the downtrodden, misunderstood English. If buyers see wines from Germany among the very dry bottles and wines from England rubbing shoulders with the fruity crowd then they might be inclined to give both a try – on the grounds that they have always thought of German wines as being impossibly sweet and English wines as being unpalatably tart.

Maybe Asda *is* on to something.

Asda Stores Limited
Asda House
Great Wilson Street
Leeds
LS11 5AD

Tel 0113 2435435
Fax 0113 2418146

SEE STOP PRESS SECTION AT END OF BOOK FOR LAST-MINUTE ADDITIONS TO THIS RETAILER'S RANGE.

AUSTRALIAN WINE

RED

Berri Estates, Cabernet Sauvignon/Shiraz
1992

Sweet finish to the dry fruit. Balanced, full (yet not overblown), perfect style of fruit for all manner of grilled meats.

Goundrey Windy Hill Cabernet Sauvignon
1989

Interesting aroma and mature fruit.

Hardys Nottage Hill Cabernet Sauvignon
1993

Touch disappointing on the finish now this wine's aged a bit.

Hardys Nottage Hill Cabernet Sauvignon/
Shiraz 1993

Controlled soft spice laid on smooth blackcurrant fruit. Delicious, firm, well-styled.

Mount Hurtle Grenache Shiraz, Geoff
Merrill 1994

Lively, full of zippy, brambly fruit flavours.

Oxford Landing, Cabernet/Shiraz
1992

Penfold's Rawson's Retreat Bin 35
Cabernet Sauvignon/Ruby Cabernet/Shiraz
1993

12 C

Soft and rather expressionless.

Penfolds Kalimna Shiraz Bin 28 1992

To be poured into jugs at sausage-and-garlic-and-olive-mashed-potato parties and the cataractic torrent of this brambly, velvet fruit left to get on with it.

Peter Lehmann Vine Vale Shiraz 1993

Builds up for something amazing (aroma, fruit on the tongue etcetera) but the finish is a touch soggy in the middle. In spite of this niggle it's a delicious, well-priced bottle deserving its rating.

Rowanbrook Cabernet Sauvignon Reserve 1993

Lively, well-flavoured fruit briskly merged with tannins. Good food wine.

South Australian Cabernet Sauvignon 1989

South Eastern Australia Shiraz Cabernet 1992

Stowells of Chelsea Shiraz Cabernet (3 litre)

Rich fruit with earthy undertones. Has a long, meaty finish with a firm, purposeful balance of fruit and acid.

AUSTRALIAN WINE   WHITE

Goundrey Estate Langton Chardonnay 1993

Goundrey Langton Semillon/Sauvignon Blanc Mount Barker Classic 1993   `13` `C`

Hardys RR 1994   `10` `C`

Hardys Nottage Hill Chardonnay 1994   `17` `C`

Best vintage yet. Lovely textured, oily fruit, never overdone or blowsy and a buttery, melony finish of surefooted delivery. Terrific value for such classy drinking.

Hardys Stamp Series Grenache Shiraz Rose 1994   `12.5` `B`

Upfront pong of artificial soft fruit but the finish is dry and flavourful.

Jackdaw Ridge 1994   `14` `B`

Delicious smoked fish wine.

Mitchelton Marsanne 1993   `12` `C`

Mitchelton Un-Oaked Marsanne 1993   `14` `C`

Rich and fruitily riveting. Lovely grilled chicken wine.

Oxford Landing Chardonnay, 1994   `15` `C`

Rich, nicely buttered and broad. Lots of character.

Penfold's Rawson's Retreat Bin 21 Semillon/Chardonnay 1994   `15` `C`

Great clash of soft mango/melony fruit and pineapple acidity. Slightly exotic, generous, bold, delicious.

Penfolds Bin 202 Riesling 1994   `13` `C`

Can you have bags of delicacy? (This wine is described by Asda as having it.) It has small pockets of it, to my mind.

South Australian Chardonnay 1994, Asda   `13.5`   `C`

Has a buzz and some bite. You won't, however, be stung by the price.

South East Australian Semillon Chardonnay 1994, Asda   `10`   `B`

Turning a bit flat on the finish after a good start.

South Eastern Australian Semillon Chardonnay 1993   `15`   `B`

Stowells of Chelsea Semillon Chardonnay (3 litre)   `14`   `G`

Presence and lift, style and purpose – this fruit knows where it's going. Good with food and mood.

BULGARIAN WINE   RED

Bulgarian Country Red Cabernet/Merlot, Burgas   `13.5`   `A`

Apple edge to the blackcurrant fruit. Very good value for pasta parties.

Bulgarian Vintage Premium Merlot 1994   `13`   `B`

Merlot 1990   `11`   `B`

Oriachovitza Cabernet Sauvignon Reserve 1991   `17`   `B`

Quite staggering for the money. Soft, jammy fruit (with hints of dry seriousness lurking on the edge) and so wonderfully gluggable.

Suhindol Cabernet Sauvignon/Merlot 1991 `13` `B`

BULGARIAN WINE WHITE

Bulgarian Country White, Lyaskovets `12.5` `A`
Bit thin.

CHILEAN WINE RED

Chilean Cabernet/Merlot 1994, Asda `12.5` `B`
Touch cough-mixture-like.

Cono Sur Cabernet Sauvignon 1993 `14` `C`
Solid performer if not a hugely exciting one. Will age well
over the year.

**Rowanbrook Cabernet Sauvignon,
Mataquito Valley 1990** `15` `C`

Rowanbrook Cabernet/Malbec 1994 `16.5` `B`
Blackberries! Blackberries!! Blackberries!!! What a lovely bottle
of hedgerow fruit.

Terre Noble Chilean Merlot 1994 `15.5` `C`
The colour of crushed blackcurrants (freshly morning-crushed,
that is, by athletic peasants), this wine is a gentle giant.
Aromatic, very handsomely flavoured, serious, complex, it will
be great with roast foods.

CHILEAN WINE   WHITE

Chilean Sauvignon Blanc 1994, Asda   `13`   `B`
Some freshness and nutty fruit here.

Rowanbrook Chardonnay Reserve 1993   `13.5`   `C`

Santa Helena Rose 1994   `15`   `B`
One of the fleshiest roses around for the money. Lovely fruit.

ENGLISH WINE   WHITE

Denbies English White Wine 1992   `13.5`   `B`
The nearest thing to an English sancerre I've tasted. Alas, with the current states of sancerre that isn't saying a great deal. Nevertheless this is still a respectable wine.

FRENCH WINE   RED

Beaujolais, Asda   `10`   `B`
Flabby.

Beaujolais Villages Domaine des Ronzes 1994   `13`   `C`
A beaujolais with tannin! Put it down until the year 2050 and your grandchildren can auction it at Sotheby's.

Cabernet Sauvignon VdP d'Oc, Asda   `14.5`   `B`
A junior league claret-style wine of softness and charm. Bargain. Tasty, deep, bright-edged.

Cahors, Asda
13 B

A wine for burnt sausages.

Chateau d'Arcins, Haut Medoc 1992
13 D

Chateau de Cabriac, Corbieres 1991
14 B

Drinking brilliantly now, this vintage, having been softened and opened up.

Chateau de Parenchere AC Bordeaux Superieur 1993
12 D

Chateau du Bois de la Garde, Cotes du Rhone 1992
14.5 C

Gentility triumphing over rusticity with no loss of character. Lovely bottle of wine.

Chateau Haut Saric 1994
13.5 B

Young and a touch raw but will soften over the next 6 months (ie between June and December 1995) to become a minor Bordeaux classic (15 points +) for the money.

Chateau La Ramiere, Cotes du Rhone 1993
15 C

Brilliant controlled earthy fruit. Smashing chilled with salmon or with bangers and fried greens.

Chateau Plaisance AC Cotes de Bourg 1990
13 C

Chateau Vieux Georget 1990
11 C

Chateauneuf-du-Pape, Chateau Fines Roches 1992
13.5 E

Delicious (if you look the other way at the pricing).

Chevalier d'Aymon Oak Aged 1993 `13.5` `C`

Most attractive wine for grilled and roast meats.

Claret, Asda `14` `B`

If you want soft, ripe, approachable claret at a rock-bottom price, this is your bottle.

Cotes du Roussillon, Asda `13` `B`

Some brisk grenache fruit here, gently peppery and rustic.

Domaine de Barjac Vin de Pays du Gard 1993 `12.5` `B`

Soft and juicy.

Domaine de Grangeneuve, Coteaux du Tricastin 1993 `14` `C`

Impressive hauteur here. Has brisk, savoury fruit.

Fitou, Asda `13.5` `B`

Hints of depth and richness. Very soft.

Fleurie Domaine Verpoix 1993 `11` `D`

Some attractive fruit here. The price lets it down.

Le Vigneron French Red (3 litre) `11` `E`

Mas Segala Cotes du Roussillon Villages 1994 `16.5` `C`

Wonderful.

Mausejour Bordeaux Rouge 1993 (half bottle) `14` `A`

Almost interesting claret for the solo luncher: plenty of dry tannins mingling with the rich fruit.

Merlot, Vin de Pays d'Oc, Asda `13` `B`

Morgon, Michel Jambon 1993 `12.5` `D`

Pinot Noir Les Saulthiers, VdP de l'Aude 1993 `10` `C`

Pinot Noir Vin de Pays Producteurs de Limoux 1992 `10` `C`

Red Burgundy 1992, Asda `10` `C`

Saint-Laurent Vin de Pays de l'Herault 1993 `15` `B`

Lovely chewy tannins, coal-edged and rich. Great wine to keep for a year or two or to drink now with spicy sausages.

Santenay, Foulot, Chateau Perruchot 1993 `11` `E`

St Chinian, Asda `13.5` `B`

Bargain, serious fruited wine. Dry and rich.

St Emilion, Asda `13` `C`

Stylish, dry, good weight of fruit.

Stowells of Chelsea Vin de Pays du Gard (3 litre) `14` `F`

Delightful smooth fruit with flavour and balance. A lovely touch – a distant echo, really – of earth.

Syrah, Vin de Pays des Collines Rhondaniens, Asda `13` `C`

Vin de Pays des Cotes de Gascogne `12` `C`

FRENCH WINE
WHITE

Blanc de Blancs, Asda `11` `A`

Burgundy 1993, Asda `10` `C`

Chablis 1993, Asda `10` `D`

Chablis Premier Cru Les Fourchaumes, 1993 `10` `F`

Outrageous. A tenner? A delicate, attractive wine but so are so many other whites at Asda at a third of the price.

Chardonnay, Vin de Pays d'Oc, Asda `12` `C`

Chateau Fondarzac Entre Deux Mers 1994 `13.5` `C`

Clean and flavoursome.

Chateau le Desert Bordeaux Sauvignon 1994 `13` `B`

Not quite as dry as its name suggests or so barren of fruit.

Chevalier d'Aymon Graves Blanc 1994 `14.5` `C`

Classy touch of wood nicely integrated with the fruit. Delicious with or without food.

Cotes du Roussillon, Asda `12` `B`

Domaine Baud Chardonnay, VdP du Jardin de la France 1994 `13` `B`

Fresh and gently lemony. Good value.

Domaine des Deux Roches St Veran 1994 `13.5` `D`

Always one of the best St Verans, this vintage is a good one. Expensive.

Domaine St Francois Sauvignon Blanc
1994   `13` **B**

Fortant Cabernet Rose, VdP d'Oc 1994   `13` **C**

Rather fugitive fruit here. But crisp and useful with grilled fish.
One of the better roses around.

Fortant Sauvignon Blanc Vin de Pays
d'Oc 1994   `15` **C**

A superb nutty, subtly creamy sauvignon blanc with the
cleanness to lift a black mood plus the flavour to live with
trout (smoked).

Laperouse Blanc Val d'Orbieu & Penfolds,
VdP d'Oc 1994   `14` **C**

Delicious. A marriage of sun and freshness which makes for an
invigorating tipple.

Le Pigoulet VdP du Gers 1994   `15` **B**

Bright, breezy, fresh, nutty. A bargain.

Le Vigneron French White (3 litre)   `12` **E**

Macon Vinzelles Les Cailloux Blancs 1994   `12` **D**

Curious softness here.

Mausejour Bordeaux Blanc 1994 (half
bottle)   `13.5` **A**

Young, fresh, perky, very attractive shellfish wine.

Montagne Noire Chardonnay, VdP
d'Oc 1994   `12` **C**

Citrus notes rather flattened by the wood rather than enhanced.
Maybe time will smooth this kink.

Montagny Premier Cru Domaine de Montorge 1993 `12.5` `D`

Muscadet de Sevre et Maine Sur Lie, Domaine Gautron 1993 `10` `C`

Muscat Cuvee Henry Peyrottes `15` `B`

Pouilly-Fume, Domaine Patrick Coulbois 1993 `10` `E`

Lot of money. Bad value.

Sancerre La Porte du Caillou H. Bourgeois 1992 `12` `E`

Sauvignon de Bordeaux, Asda `11` `B`

Stowells of Chelsea Vin de Pays du Tarn (3 litre) `12` `F`

Sound but dullish – not a lot of fruit.

VdP du Gard 'Les Garrigues' 1994 `12` `B`

GERMAN WINE WHITE

Bereich Bernkastel Mosel, Asda `11` `B`

Bretzenheimer Vogelsang Riesling Spatlese Schloss Plettenberg 1992 `12` `D`

Rather one-dimensional.

Deidesheimer Hofstuck Kabinett 1993 `10` `B`

Flonheimer Adelberg Kabinett, Rheinhessen 1993, Asda   `14` **B**

Delicious aperitif. Has an almond undertone to the cream-soft fruit.

Graacher Himmelreich Riesling Kabinett Reichsgraf von Kesselstatt, Moselle 1994   `13` **D**

Will develop well over the next 5/6 years.

Herxheimer Himmelreich Huxelrebe Beerenauslese Weingut Pfleger 1993 (half bottle)   `14` **E**

Hochheimer Holle Riesling Kabinett Geheimrat Aschrott 1993   `15` **C**

A brilliant wine to lay down for the millennium.

Mainzer Domherr Spatlese 1993, Asda   `12` **B**

Mosel, Asda   `13.5` **A**

A medium dry, engagingly fruity aperitif at a knock-down price. Fragrant and summery.

Niersteiner Pettenthal Riesling Auslese Graf Wolff Metternick 1993   `14` **D**

An expensive but truly delicious aperitif – honey on the finish but never cloying.

Niersteiner Spiegelberg Kabinett 1993, Asda   `14` **B**

I'd happily accept this as an aperitif any day.

Ruppertsberger Hofstuck Riesling, Pfalz 1992   `14` **B**

Developed brilliantly, aromatically, in bottle. It now reveals deliciously controlled, petrol-scented undertones to the fruit and finishes firm if not entirely gripping. Drink with smoked fish or exceptionally gripping episodes of *Neighbours*.

St Ursula Binger Kirchberg, Riesling Auslese, Rheinhessen 1992   14   C

Honeyed aperitif. Delicious. Go on – swallow your prejudices.

St Ursula Deidesheimer Hofstuck, Riesling Kabinett, Pfalz 1994   13   B

Attractive aperitif. And rated on this basis. With smoked salmon I'd rate it a higher experience.

Wiltinger Braunfels Riesling Kabinett, Jordan and Jordan 1994   12   D

Wiltinger Scharzberg Riesling Kabinett 1993, Asda   13   B

Delicious aperitif.

HUNGARIAN WINE RED

Hungarian Cabernet Sauvignon 1994, Asda   13.5   B

Good with cheese dishes.

Hungarian Merlot 1994, Asda   13   B

Attractive berry fruit for pizzas.

Kekfrankos 1994, Asda   13.5   B

Richly shaped with dark cherry fruit and a dry edge. Will soften over the months.

HUNGARIAN WINE WHITE

Hungarian Chardonnay 1994, Asda `14.5` `B`

What a price! A gift. And so is the fruit on the tastebuds.

**Hungarian Chardonnay Reserve Mecsekalji
1994** `12` `B`

Hungarian Muscat 1994, Asda `12` `B`

Makes an appealing little aperitif.

Pinot Blanc 1994, Asda `15` `B`

Brilliant value for money. Has varietal character plus a rich edge
to the fresh zinginess of the style.

Tokaji Five Puttonyos Havas Hill 1988 `10` `D`

Lingering but lacking depth.

ITALIAN WINE RED

**Amarone della Valpolicella Sanroseda 1990
(half bottle)** `16` `C`

Wonderful soft licorice fruit.

Barbera d'Asti Cantina Gemma 1993 `13.5` `B`

Flavour and fruit.

Barolo, Veglio Angelo 1990 `13` `E`

Keep for another 100 years before opening? Possibly.

Carbone, Aglianico del Vulture 1988 `15` `C`

Chianti 1993, Asda `12` `B`

Chianti Classico 1992, Asda `14` `C`
Earthy, authentic, rich, really brilliant with 'meaty' Italian dishes.

Chianti Classico, Quercia al Poggio 1991 `16` `C`
One for the millennium as well as a wine for right now with rich, grilled meat and vegetables. Lovely tannins and earthy fruit which is never coarse but characterful and very striking. Impressive wine at a good price.

Chianti Colli Senesi Salvanza 1994 `14` `B`
If you like soft smoochy Italians you'll love this.

Coltiva Il Rosso 1994 `11` `B`

Lambrusco Rosso, Asda `14` `A`
9 per cent alcohol gently sparkling red with real warmth and cosy fruitiness. Would be great with game dishes, or chilled with Chinese meats.

Merlot del Veneto `13` `A`
Sunny to the point of tanning the tongue. Warms the cockles most engagingly, this wine.

Montepulciano d'Abruzzo, Cantina Tollo 1994 `14` `A`
Brilliant drinking for the money. Good with pasta or just people (cannibals, please note).

Rozzano Villa Pigna 1992 `14` `C`
Smooth, satiny fruit of flavour and richness.

Sangiovese di Romagna 'Riva' 1993 `15` `A`

Best bottle of plonk I've tasted in a while. It'll sit very nicely on the dining table beside a plateful of spaghetti. Soft, gluggable to the point of indecency, this is a modern curiosity (made by a Chilean winery in Italy).

Sicilian Rosso, Asda `16` `B`

Aromatic, breezy, full, deep, rich, savoury, warm, sunny, brilliant value, this wine has astonishingly well-polished fruit. If only beaujolais was remotely such good value and so purposeful and tasty. You could serve this wine in jugs at the poshest of dinner tables and people would think some New World merlot-dominated blend was being served them.

Spanna del Piemonte, Cantina Gemma 1994 `10` `B`

Valpolicella NV, Asda `11` `B`

Cheap. And a cheerful soul.

ITALIAN WINE WHITE

Barbecue Bianco `13` `B`
Good, solid fish wine.

Bianco Del Lazio Gabbia d'Oro 1994 `14` `A`

Yes, Gabbia d'Oro with flavour! Cheap, cheerful, fruity – can't ask for much more.

Ca' Pradai Chardonnay, Bidoli 1994 `14.5` `B`

Excellent echoes of nutty apricot plus fresh acidity. Lovely little glug.

Ca' Pradai Pinot Grigio Bidoli 1994 `13.5` `B`

Tasted in late August, this wine struck the palate as one which will develop well, maybe up to 15 points or more, over Christmas '95 and spring '96.

Coltiva Il Bianco NV `13.5` `B`

Brilliant value for a brightly fruity wine.

Frascati 1994, Asda `13.5` `B`

Very attractive price. Attractive fruit. I'll wear this combination any day.

Frascati 'Colli di Catone' Superiore 1994 `11` `C`

Frascati Superiore, Asda `13` `B`

Some rich fruit here, curiously.

La Vis Trentino Chardonnay 1994 `15` `B`

Fresh as a sauvignon blanc from the New World with an Old World mature edge of rich fruit. Superb value for all manner of fish dishes.

Lambrusco Bianco, Asda `12` `A`

Fun and light, almost childish. Drink with fish fingers with sweet tomato sauce.

Lambrusco Rosato, Asda `12` `A`

Fruity and fun for young people who cannot afford the cost of real cherries.

Lambrusco Secco, Asda `11` `A`

Lugana Sanroseda Boscaini 1994 `14` `C`

Very tasty, very very tasty.

Orvieto Classico Campeto 1994 `13` `B`

Orvieto Classico Cardeto 1992 `14` `B`

As good as they get for orvieto: balanced, clean, fresh.

**Recioto di Soave Castelcerino 1990
(half bottle)** `15` `C`

Oh, what a wonderful marriage this wine makes with a bunch of grapes and a hunk of fresh cheese.

Sicilian Bianco, Asda `14` `B`

Modern, fresh, gently nutty and with a fruity finish of calm, unfussy dryness.

Soave, Asda `11` `B`

Soave Classico 'Corte Olive' Lenotti 1994 `11` `B`

MOROCCAN WINE   RED

Moroccan Red Wine, Domaine Mellil `14` `B`

Dry, rustic, excellent for small Bacchic orgies with sausages.

NEW ZEALAND WINE   RED

**Cooks Cabernet Sauvignon/Pinot Noir,
Gisborne 1993** `11` `C`

Weird marriage of opposing grape varieties. Like Dudley Moore mud-wrestling with Camille Puglia.

NEW ZEALAND WINE — WHITE

Cooks Chenin Chardonnay, Gisborne 1994 `13` `C`

PORTUGUESE WINE — RED

Bela Fonte Estremadura 1994 `14` `B`

Simple, soft, ripe, very fruity, delicious chilled and poured over parched tongues.

Dao 1992, Asda `15` `B`

PORTUGUESE WINE — WHITE

Bela Fonte White Estremadura 1994 `10` `B`

Belafonte Portuguese White 1994 `12` `B`

Not exactly an island of fruit in the sun.

Vinho Verde `13` `B`

ROMANIAN WINE — RED

River Route Romanian Pinot Noir 1994 `12.5` `B`

Curious pinot. Has as much varietal impact as shoe leather — which its chewy fruit resembles.

Romanian Cellars Pinot Noir/Merlot
1990   16 B

Brilliant combo with deep chocolatey fruit undercut by a
blackcurrant figginess which finishes with a soft, rich, velvet
texture. Good with spicy sausages and mash.

ROMANIAN WINE   WHITE

River Route Sauvignon/Muscat 1994   12.5 B

Good with grilled mackerel.

SOUTH AFRICAN WINE   RED

Cape Red, Asda   14 B

Rich and rolling, the serious, meaty fruit. This wine is imposing
for the money.

Fairview Estate Shiraz 1994   15 C

Briskly developing aroma and flavour the moment it is opened,
this is rich, dry and very food-friendly.

Landskroon Estate Pinotage 1994   14 C

Soft, not overly spicy, and plenty of flavour. Finishes soft and
jammy. A beginner! Moving up from beaujolais.

Woodlands Pinot Noir, Western Cape
1994   11 D

SOUTH AFRICAN WINE   WHITE

Cape White, Asda   `12.5` `B`

Peachy, juvenile.

Fairview Estate Dry Rose 1995   `14.5` `B`

An utterly delicious rose with true depth of flavour (and class) to go with all sorts of food, along with the freshness to be quaffed as a rose is surely designed – naked on a bearskin rug in front of a roaring fire.

Fairview Estate Gewurztraminer 1995   `11` `C`

Fails to convince on the finish. Is it, perhaps, too early to judge properly this early bottling? I'd lay it down for two years.

Newlands Field Chenin Blanc, Western Cape 1995   `17` `B`

Are you ready for this? It's rich with a burst-on-the-tongue fruitiness which turns curiously nutty and almost sourly honeyed at the finish. It's got to be one of the best white wines for the money in the world. Complex, riveting, and at all Asdas.

Spes Bona Chardonnay, Van Loveren 1993, Robertson   `14` `C`

Delicious, stylish, fruity and well-crafted. Good fruit, not over-rich or gawky. Nice balance. Touch of mint perhaps, but this passes for elegance.

Van Loveren Sauvignon Blanc 1995   `14` `B`

Simple, delicious, delicate, fresh and half the price of sancerre.

ASDA

SPANISH WINE   RED

Bodegas Campillo, Rioja Crianza 1989   `16` `C`

Lovely vanilla edge to soft fruit which is plummy with subtle
echoes of blackcurrant. Delicious.

Don Darias   `15` `B`

The Old Don seems a bit thinner than when I last encountered
him but he's still hale and hearty and full of vanilla-ey fruit.

Leon 1989, Asda   `14` `B`

Six years old and bright, dry, fruity and in fine, food-friendly
fettle.

Navarra, Asda   `13` `B`

Ribera del Duero Senorio de Nava 1989   `15` `D`

Good for AD 2000 and 1995. Masses of dry fruit of considerable class.

Rioja 1991, Asda   `13.5` `B`

Bit muted and smooth-cheeked, but easy to drink.

Stowells of Chelsea Tempranillo La
Mancha (3 litre)   `15` `F`

A bright, cherry/plum dry wine of really good fruit, balance and
a really attractive finish.

Terra Alta Cabernet/Garnacha 1994   `16` `B`

Simply a brilliant fruity bargain.

Torres Coronas 1991   `14` `C`

Valencia Red, Asda 13 A

Soft and fruity. Well, sort of . . .

Vina Albali, Valdepenas 1990 13 B

SPANISH WINE WHITE

Bela Fonte Medium Dry White Estremadura 1994 12 B

La Mancha, Asda 12 A

Moscatel de Valencia, Asda 16 B

Brilliant pudding wine. Rich and honeyed enough to appreciate on top of Everest.

Valencia Dry, Asda 13.5 B

Crisp, nutty, good value. Good with shellfish.

USA WINE RED

Arius Neif Californian Red Wine 1993 12.5 D

Expensive soft fruit.

Quivira Dry Creek Valley Cabernet Cuvee 1991 14 D

Better than many a barolo it reminds me of. A different cabernet to be sure, with polish, complexity, flavour and the weight to go beautifully with mushroom risotto. Will age brilliantly to AD 2000 and beyond.

Sebastiani Cabernet Franc 1994   14   C

Lovely dry edge to the strawberry, blackberry fruit. Delicious with food, delightful without.

Sebastiani Merlot   13   C

Delicious, soft fruit.

USA WINE   WHITE

Arius Californian Chardonnay 1993   14   C

Tasty, well fleshed out with flavour, balanced and stylish.

August Sebastiani's White Zinfandel 1994   12.5   C

Sweetish fruit but fair flavour. Rated at £2.99 only. Not worth £3.99.

Californian White, Asda 1994   11   B

Sebastiani Chardonnay   13.5   C

Absolutely nothing wrong with this – except it's a quid more than it should be.

Sebastiani Semillon/Chardonnay 1994   14.5   C

Delicious blend of grapes. The best Sebastiani white on sale.

FORTIFIED WINE

Fine Ruby Port, Asda   12   D

Great in gravies.

Fino Sherry Quinta Osborne y Cia `15` `D`

Bone-dry perfection. Salty, clean and superb.

Late Bottled Vintage Port 1989, Asda `14` `D`

Value and richness not always the same bedfellow where port is concerned. A bargain.

Stanton & Killeen, Liqueur Muscat, Rutherglen `15` `D`

Like tawny port with molasses. Brilliant with a slice of Christmas cake.

Tawny Port, Asda `14.5` `D`

Vintage Character Port, Asda `14` `D`

Has the fine acidity under the fruit to suit all manner of cheeses.

SPARKLING WINE/CHAMPAGNE

Asti Spumante, Asda `13` `C`

Screams with fruit! Try it after the meal before you jump into bed together (or just flop in front of the TV set).

Barramundi Australian Brut `16.5` `D`

My sparkling wine of the year (if I was a big enough clot to introduce such categories into this book). I love the dazzling fruit! I love the dazzling label!

Blanquette Methode Ancestrale `13` `C`

Granny will love this.

Cava, Asda `14` `C`
Good value, dry, classically styled.

Champagne Brut, Asda `13` `F`
Lovely lemony aperitif.

Champagne Rose Brut, Asda `14` `F`

Chandlers Point Australian Brut `14` `C`
Lemony and crisp. Good value.

Feist Belmont Sekt (Germany) `12` `C`

Nicholas Feuillate Blanc de Blancs Chardonnay Champagne `14` `G`
A rich yet delicate edge to this expensive champagne. Authentic classic style with assertive sparkling chardonnay plumpness. For very special occasions.

Scharffenberger Brut (USA) `14.5` `E`
Touch lean for the fatness of the price.

Varichon et Clerc Sparkling Chardonnay `14` `C`
Soft and peachy, this makes an excellent aperitif. But champagne it ain't.

Victoria Park Pinot Noir/Chardonnay (Australian) `15.5` `D`
Has elegance and finesse. A clean, crisp bubbly with a soft fruit undertone plus hints of lime. Delicious. A bargain.

BUDGENS

Budgens has two fewer stores than it did in 1920. This cannot, by even the most generous of commentators with the most benign of temperaments, be considered spectacular growth. Yet it had been going for forty-eight years in the twenties (making it a business of greater vintage even than Sainsbury's). There have been, since those early days, four different owners and occupiers – the last of which, Germany's largest retail outfit REWE, purchased a significant minority shareholding in 1993 and proceeded to institute severals ideas of its own. One of these, a so-called Penny Market off-shoot, was, according to wine buyer Tony Finnerty, 'an absolute flop' and he blamed much of this failure on German ideas simply not working in the British market.

But no one can gainsay Mr Finnerty's success. Turnover of the wine department was, at ex-till prices, £9m during the tax year '94 to '95. 32 per cent up on the previous year's total. But the interesting thing is that the increase in the total number of cases of wine sold, 392,668 in the '94/'95 year, represents only a 12.5 per cent increase. What does this tell us? Why am I risking your propulsion into the arms of Morpheus by trotting out these tedious statistics? It shows how cheaply Budgens flog vino, dear reader. And this is a subject I care mightily about. Margins are slim at Budgens. The average price paid by its customers for a bottle of wine is £1.91p on the basis of the figures above. £1.91p. How do they do it? Beats me. And if you're wondering why I haven't asked Budgens how they do it the answer is that I can't actually *find* any £1.91 wines on Budgens' shelves to taste, so the matter – or should I say the mystery – is largely academic.

But it does demonstrate that the skinflint would do well not to ignore Budgens' ninety-eight central and southern English stores. In the list which follows this introduction, the wines go from under £3 to something over £5. Pausing only to remark my regret at not nabbing a £1.91p wine for you, I pass on the joys, and otherwise, of this list as drunk and rated by me.

What sort of individual buys wines at Budgens? I suspect when I ask a retailer which are its top six best-selling wines that the question is considered as being of interest to me solely as a wine writer who's concerned, naturally enough, with what wines are the most popular. But my real motive for asking this question is that it tells me a great deal about the sort of people who shop at the place.

Budgens' top-selling wines are:

1. Spanish Red.
2. Budgens Liebfraumilch.
3. Budgens Claret.
4. Bordeaux Blanc Sec.
5. Cotes du Rhone rouge.
6. Budgens Niersteiner.

These top-selling wines reveal, by my guesswork, that Budgens' regular customers are older non-car-owning women and young mothers plus a sprinkling of male pensioners. Irregular customers will use the store chain strictly because of convenience, not as first choice.

If any such people do read *Superplonk*, I hope they will, when they find this magical £1.91 bottle of wine, contact me via Hodder & Stoughton. This is a wine I have to taste.

Budgens Stores Limited
PO Box 9
Stonefield Way
Ruislip
Middlesex
HA4 0JR

Tel 0181 422 9511
Fax 0181 422 1596

AUSTRALIAN WINE RED

Brown Brothers Tarrango 1993   15   C

All-singing, all-dancing fruit. A sort of joyous Aussie beaujolais.

**Flinders Creek Shiraz/Cabernet/Merlot
1992**   13.5   C

Jacob's Creek Dry Red   13   C

AUSTRALIAN WINE WHITE

Brown Brothers Dry Muscat Blanc 1993   13.5   C

An intriguing aperitif. Or you could try splashing it behind
your ears.

Flinders Creek Semillon 1993   12   C

Hardys RR Medium White 1993   11   C

Quite why Hardys puts its name to this dull wine is one of life's
exceedingly tedious mysteries I have no interest in solving.

AUSTRIAN WINE WHITE

Winzerhaus Gruner Veltliner 1993   14   C

With its engaging rich edge to the ripe fruit, this is a well-
balanced and well-made wine.

CHILEAN WINE   RED

Underraga Pinot Noir 1993   `12` `C`

ENGLISH WINE   WHITE

Lamberhurst Vineyards Monarch, Medium   `12` `B`
For a patriot wishing to trade up from Liebfraumilch, this wine
has charms.

FRENCH WINE   RED

Abbaye Saint Hilaire, Coteaux Varois 19923   `14` `C`
Brisk tannic edge here. Be great with a Christmas roast fowl.

Chateau Bassenel, Minervois 1993   `12` `C`

Chateau de Malijay, Cotes du Rhone 1993   `13.5` `C`

**Chateau la Gorlonne Cotes de Provence
1993**   `14` `C`
Perfectly delicious, lightly chilled. Has style and richness, a dry
edge, and it slips down very easily.

Chinon, Les Bernieres 1993   `13` `C`
Pleasant.

Claret   `10` `B`

Costieres de Nimes Fontanilles 1993 `13` `C`

Touch austere. Needs more time in bottle? Like as not.

Cotes du Rhone Villages `13` `C`

Cotes du Rhone Villages 1994 `12.5` `C`

Crozes Hermitage 1993 `11` `C`

Faugeres, Jean Jean 1993 `13` `C`

Geminian Cabernet Sauvignon, Vin de Pays d'Oc 1993 `12` `C`

Geminian Merlot Vin de Pays d'Oc 1993 `12` `C`

Apples and plums. Very dry.

Le Haut Colombier, Vin de Pays de la Drome 1992 `13` `B`

Touch of sweet fruit to it. It's a really Rhone-style structure and feel.

Tuilerie du Bosc, Cotes de Saint-Mont, 1993 `14` `C`

Class for the claret and roast beef lover.

Vin de Pays des Coteaux de l'Ardeche, 1991 `12` `B`

Nice dry cherry fruit.

FRENCH WINE WHITE

Blanc de Blancs Cuvee Speciale `11` `B`

Bordeaux Blanc 1992 `15` `B`

A solid, fruity, well-made bargain. Lots of melony fruit and freshness. Remarkable price for the level of fruit on offer.

Chateau le Gardera, Bordeaux Blanc 1992 `13` `D`

Corbieres, Blanc de Blancs, 1992 `12` `B`

Basic rather than brilliant.

Cotes de Provence Rose `10` `C`

Domaine de Villeroy-Castellas Sauvignon Blanc 1994 `13` `C`

Not at all bad with a creamily sauced fish dish.

Domaine l'Argentier Terret, CdP Cotes de Thau 1993 `14` `C`

Ripe, rounded fruit, well-polished and deep. Very forceful style of wine.

Geminian Sauvignon Blanc, Vin de Pays d'Oc 1993 `13` `C`

Keen and fresh. Good shellfish wine.

Gewurztraminer, Gisselbrecht 1989 `14` `C`

Expensive but lovely. Spicy lychee fruit plus clean acidity.

Le Bonnefois, Vin de Pays de Cotes de Gascogne 1991 `13` `B`

Delicious fruit. Very good value.

Les Chasseignes, Sancerre 1993 `10` `E`

Listel, Domaine de Bosquet-Canet `11` `C`

Muscadet sur Lie, Domaine du Bois Breton 1992 `9` `C`

Pinot Blanc Gisselbrecht `12` `C`

Tuileries du Bosc, Cotes de Saint-Mont, 1992 `13` `C`

Fruit which doesn't turn crisp on the finish.

Vin de Pays des Coteaux de l'Ardeche 1993 `13` `B`

Agreeably fruity and firm.

GERMAN WINE RED

Dornfelder 1993 `13.5` `C`

Try its soft, unGermanic fruitiness.

GERMAN WINE WHITE

Baden Gewurztraminer Reserve, Badischer Winzerkeller 1991 `12` `C`

Some spicy fruit here.

Bereich Bernkastel 1993 `11` `B`

Flonheimer Adelberg Auslese 1993 `12` `C`

Klusserather St Michael Kabinett 1992 `12` `B`

Some attractive touches here make this a good aperitif.

Longuicher Probstberg Kabinett   11 | C

Schmitt vom Schmitt Niersteiner Spatlese 1992   11 | C

Schmitt vom Schmitt Pinot Blanc Rheinhessen 1992   14 | C

Forget the fact that it's German. Think of it as Swiss or Alsatian. A delicious, dry wine of sound class and weighted fruit.

HUNGARIAN WINE   RED

Cabernet Sauvignon   13 | B

Hungarian Cabernet Sauvignon 1994   12 | B

Hungarian Merlot 1993   10 | B

Merlot   12 | B

Nagyrede Rouge 1993 (half bottle)   11 | A

HUNGARIAN WINE   WHITE

Chateau Megyer Tokaji Furmint 1993   10 | C

Dull. So dull it is hard to credit why anyone would bottle it, let alone ship it, shelve it, and pay £3.99 to let it slip down the throat.

Hungarian Chardonnay 1993   10 | B

Nagyrede Selection Blanc 1993 (half bottle) `11` `A`

Sauvignon Blanc `10` `B`

ITALIAN WINE RED

Merlot del Veneto, Pergola di Vento `12` `B`

ITALIAN WINE WHITE

Frascati 'Casale de Grillo' 1994 `13.5` `C`
Expensive for the breed but a very solidly fruity, well-made frascati with more than a touch of good breeding.

Lugana, Villa Flora 1994 `13.5` `C`
Expensive for a trebbiano but it is very sound.

Tocai del Veneto, Pergola del Vento `13` `B`
Bargain fruity tippling.

NEW ZEALAND WINE RED

Montana Cabernet Sauvignon 1993 `13` `C`

PORTUGUESE WINE RED

Alta Mesa Estremadura 1994 `14` `B`

Simple, soft, ripe, very fruity, delicious chilled and poured over parched tongues.

Dao Dom Ferraz `13` `B`

Great fast-food wine. But then Mr Ferraz is an incredibly fast driver.

Leziria Tinto `14` `B`

Still a brilliant pasta wine for the money. Has a rich edge to its fruit, balance and a good depth of flavour.

Tinto de Anfora 1988 `14` `D`

One of the classiest and most satisfying wines of Portugal, and in a great vintage not available everywhere (it has been replaced by the '89). Made from satin and figs by an Australian.

PORTUGUESE WINE WHITE

Alta Mesa Medium Dry White Estremadura 1994 `12` `B`

Leziria Medium Dry White, Almeirim `14` `B`

SOUTH AFRICAN WINE   RED

Table Mountain 1994   13   B

Some flavour and fruit here.

SOUTH AFRICAN WINE   WHITE

Clear Mountain Chenin Blanc   14   C

Tasty little wine. Is 'little' condescending? I apologise. I mean it is not complex. But it is soft and full, satisfyingly fruity and attractive.

SPANISH WINE   RED

Gran Condal Rioja, Gran Reserva 1987   12   D

Marques de Caro Reserva 1988   11   B

Raimat Tempranillo   14   D

Utterly ravishing wine of deep richness and suave fruit.

Vina Albali 1987   14   C

Real quality fruit, rich and personality-packed.

USA WINE — RED

Sutter Home Merlot 1992 `13` `C`

Good with rich food.

USA WINE — WHITE

Glen Ellen Proprietor's Reserve Chardonnay 1993 `14` `C`

California dreamin' of making it under four quid and succeeding.

Inglenook Charbono, Napa Valley 1985 `13.5` `C`

Getting a bit crotchety round the edges, this wine, but it's a formidable customer with a savoury casserole.

Sutter Home White Zinfandel Rose 1992 `12` `C`

Chilled, very chilled, with oysters and lemon. Might work.

SPARKLING WINE/CHAMPAGNE

Espuma Prima (Spain) `11` `B`

Good ice-cold with ice-cream in the Gobi desert in mid-summer. Only 5 per cent alcohol.

Flinders Creek Brut (Australia) `12` `C`

Good fruit, good price, good structure . . . until the finish. It doesn't have one. Pity.

Flinders Creek Brut Rose (Australia) 14 C

Bargain rose with a fresh finish of cherry and strawberry. Dry.

Lindauer, New Zealand 13 D

Good fizzer.

Seaview Brut 15 D

Where available for under £5, one of the best sparklers on the market: stylish, refined, and quite delicious.

CO-OP

The Co-op has patiently explained its distribution system to me but *A Brief History of Time* is a simpler exposition – about, it must be admitted, a simpler subject – and so tipplers in search of certain of this sprawling retailer's wines will, I daresay, continue to find black holes instead of full shelves. Arabella Woodrow and Paul Bastard, who together run the company's wine-buying department, explained the problem thus:

'The Co-op isn't the name of a company like Sainsbury's or Tesco,' Ms Woodrow said. 'It is a quasi-political organisation if you like, comprising of a number of different societies all of which subscribe to the Co-op ethos. But they are all independent companies and we at the Co-operative Wholesale Society don't purchase for the whole of the Co-operative movement. If you write in your column or your book that the wine is at the Co-op it doesn't necessarily mean it's in every Co-op.'

I nodded sympathetically. 'It's largely regional,' she went on to explain. 'If a reader is in Cornwall, for example, those areas are served by the CRS – Co-operative Retail Services – and we don't buy wines for them. Those stores may well take some of the Co-op label wines which are available to the whole movement. Indeed, you will find the majority of Co-op labels in the majority of stores. It's the *other* wines you recommend that have been causing the most problems.'

The other wines, I murmured, I see. Ms Woodrow continued. 'There are forty different Co-operative Societies and only about 60 per cent of the sales are controlled by us. One of your readers who lives in a region that we don't happen to serve can look in every local Co-op and won't necessarily find the wine he or she is looking for. But if they were to look fifty miles away they might find them in all the Co-op shops. That's the problem.'

She sighed. I sighed. She carried on:

'Our sphere of influence is increasing all the time and this means the likelihood of your readers finding the wine you're recommending is increasing. You must remember that the whole of the Co-operative movement comprises about 2,500 stores. Many are very small.'

Mr Bastard seized on this point.

'In Sainsbury's,' he said, 'I think they've about five different space plans. Five different sizes of capacity for the range of wines they sell. Do you know how many different space plans we have?'

I said seventy-five since it seemed a suitably absurd figure. I waited for Mr Bastard to snort.

But he didn't. He smiled wanly. And he nodded – like one man with a broken leg nodding sympathetically to another man with a broken leg in the casualty unit of the local hospital.

'We have seventy-two different space plans, actually. They cover everything from half a metre's worth of wine space to 0.66 metres, 0.71 metres, 1.22 metres, 1.33 metres . . .'

He paused to allow the full nightmare of this scenario to sink in.

'The reason for this is because over the years we have taken over different Societies, some of them working on metreage, others on yardage, others in three-feet sections . . .'

Had he ever felt like telephoning the Samaritans, I wanted to ask.

'It's historical, Malcolm. We have every possible size of shelf space for the wines because we've taken over Societies rather than building stores to a set formula. The other thing of course is that the Co-op does try to be all things to all people. We don't just operate at the hypermarket end of the market. We also run small convenience stores and late stores. We sell to a very wide range of people.'

Get the situation, dear reader? Notwithstanding the alienating aspects of seventy-two different space plans (even Professor Hawking ended up with fewer options in space than that), I shall continue to push the Co-op's case, bottle by bottle, only pausing to regret that not only may I frustrate some readers but also fail to bring to their notice bargains sent too late for publication. The Co-op's Cava, a brilliant 16.5 point bubbly on offer for an astonishing £3.89 in the spring, failed to make its way into my *Superplonk* column, where I would have dearly loved it to shine, because I received a sample to taste too late for inclusion. This is another knotty problem the Co-op is sorting out, with the help of its energetic PR person Ruth Chadwick.

The Rosemount Estate Range Shiraz 1993, only to be found at Leo's Co-op stores, has, however, made it into print, and if you found a bottle you had cause to rejoice. This 17-pointer was vividly fruity with touches of chocolate and cassis and soft spice. It cost £5.99. Two new Co-op wines more widely distributed are also cause for serious celebration and are still available. Long Slim Red Cabernet/Merlot 1993 (16 points, £3.59) and Long Slim White Chardonnay/Semillon (15.5 points, £3.49) sound for all the world as if they are Australians, but they come from Chile. The red is a brilliantly rich, dark, fruity beast with a dry catering chocolate edge; the white offers masses of flavour crisply wrapped in stylish acidity. The name Long Slim may provoke derision, but I have a hunch the producers of this wine wanted an Aussie-sounding name. Largo Delgado doesn't sound half so intriguing. There was a time when wines, from wherever they came, all hankered after cod French monickers to confer putative excellence. Those days are, it seems, long gone. Farewell, then, *Parfum de Chauve-Souris Blanc* (made from grape concentrate in Huddersfield). Welcome, Alice Springs' Big Red (made from grenache and carignan in the Languedoc).

Little need, in circumstances like this, for the wine buyers to travel to the vineyards. The vineyards will come to them. 'I had one day last year when I went abroad and visited a vineyard!' Mr Bastard revealed to me with a measure of regret.

Ms Woodrow gets abroad more often. I once caught sight of her in Romania and she once successfully ran a marathon of 26 miles around the chateaux of Bordeaux only pausing now and then en route to sample the wines (which she claimed she spat out). Of the Co-op's top six best-selling wines, however, only one comes from Bordeaux and they are all own-label:

1. Liebfraumilch.
2. Lambrusco Bianco.
3. Valencia Red.
4. Claret.
5. Portuguese Rose.
6. Corbieres Rouge.

This is the only retailer to have a pink wine in its best-sellers list. I cannot for the life of me conjecture what this tells us about the nature of the person who buys wine at the Co-op. When I asked Mssrs Woodrow and Bastard what sort of drinker they thought patronised its wine shelves, I was told, 'It's not fair to generalise, except to say that the customers who buy our wine are thirsty people!'

In other words, 'We don't know any more than you do. ' I was also told that 'We try to cater for the interests of a diverse range of shoppers and to offer a good choice and value for money for all.'

Note that 'all'. Is the Co-op a classless establishment? I wish it was. The Co-op is rather like State Education, the British Film Industry and the National Health Service – somehow they all seemed rather better in the good old days. And the good old days are gone and weren't particularly good at that. I would love to shop regularly at the Co-op – especially if the divi was still widely in operation. I can still remember my parents' divi number from four decades ago. Even this idea Tesco has pinched and turned into a modern plastic discount card for regular shoppers. But the Co-op is slowly coming into the twentieth century (perhaps too late to actually *make* the twentieth century but we can hold out hope that the twenty-first century might see it make it) and is, it is rumoured, looking at an 'experimental scheme' to reintroduce the dividend idea in late 1995.

The group revamped its superstore range 'to include many new wines which offered a better, more balanced selection', so I was told, and many of these new wines are not simply own-labels. In particular, the Co-op expanded its range of Southern French and Australian wines. Thirteen new store openings are planned during this year and next and in addition many superstores are 'to be refurbished'. The modern EPOS system will also be extended to many more check-outs, which means shorter queue times and, in theory, a faultlessly computed bill. The Co-op is somewhat behind its competitors in this area.

It is also, as far as the wine department is concerned, still not up with the big boys when it comes to generating new ideas off its own bat. It cannot, yet, widely initiate own-label wine projects built totally around its own needs and specifications, it can only hope to find such wines already made, or capable of being blended, and it is not, as yet, the originator of flying wine-maker ideas, but it does take these wines when they are generally available.

None of this detracts from the Co-op's greatest retail strength. This is surely in offering wines which are damn good value for money above all else. The core range, around £3 in price, has some highly satisfying wines, and if only the Co-op's vast resources were tightly focused and accurately energised then we would begin to see own-label Co-op wines among the top-selling branded wines in the country.

The group is, if Mr Tony Blair's notion of the 'community' does become the dominant political theme of the next elected parliament, better placed than any to be the retailer which best exemplifies this philosophy. Could, then, the Co-op movement be the retailer of the future?

It's about time the Co-op gave Tesco and Sainsbury's something to think about.

Co-operative Wholesale Society Limited
PO Box 53
New Century House
Manchester
M60 4ES

Tel 0161 834 1212
Fax 0161 834 4507

Australian Red, Co-op

From the Co-op comes a pair of young hopefuls grown in the Murrumbidgee irrigation area of New South Wales. Australian Red has a cherry side to its fruit, making it suitable for light chilling and drinking with salads.

Chateau Reynella Cabernet/Merlot 1992

A dazzlingly misleading wine. It aromatically sets you up for tar and violets, soothes the tongue with satiny, cassis-like fruit, then wallop . . . the long arching upper cut of rich fruitiness pierces the throat with such exquisite force it leaves a linger.

Co-op Jacaranda Hill Shiraz/Cabernet 1993

Ripe plums with a touch of red earth.

Co-op South Australian Cabernet
Sauvignon 1993

A lot of good characterful fruit here. Plum and blackcurrants, a hint of tannin and a solid, decisive structure.

Hardys Nottage Hill Cabernet Sauvignon/
Shiraz 1993

Controlled soft spice laid on smooth blackcurrant fruit. Delicious, firm, well-styled. Also available in half bottles.

Kasbah Shiraz/Malbec/Mourvedre, Alambie
Wine Co 1993

Juicy fruity finish on the soft fruits makes this a food wine – chilled with fish, more temperature with meat and vegetables, and cheese dishes.

Kingston Estate Shiraz/Mataro, Murray Valley ` 14 ` **C**

Aromatically intriguing, fruitily soft and flavourful, good firm finish. Very good value.

Vine Vale Shiraz ` 14 ` **C**

Famous bruising Aussie style.

AUSTRALIAN WINE WHITE

Butterfly Ridge Sauvignon Blanc/Chenin Blanc ` 15.5 ` **C**

Brilliant blend of flavours and marriage of styles. Has structure, texture and balance. Lovely controlled exoticism to the fruit with buttery pineapple undertones. Delicious.

Co-op Australian White ` 14 ` **B**

Has some bite and freshness, suggesting semillon in its make-up perhaps, and is a simple fish wine. At heart, a simple quaffing wine.

Co-op South Australian Chardonnay 1994 ` 15 ` **C**

Buttered bread, sprinkled with the faintest touch of lemon. Delicious.

Hardys Nottage Hill Chardonnay 1994 ` 17 ` **C**

Best vintage yet. Lovely textured, oily fruit, never overdone or blowsy and a buttery, melony finish of surefooted delivery. Terrific value for such classy drinking.

Jacaranda Hill Semillon/Chardonnay 1994 ` 13 ` **C**

Mite subdued.

Moondah Brook Chenin Blanc 1994 `13.5` `D`

Complex, weird, slightly overpriced. But delicious in the right circumstances: will readings, late night horror films on TV, reading the Michael Winner column in the *Sunday Times*.

BRAZILIAN WINE
RED

Amazon Cabernet Sauvignon `13.5` `C`

Interesting, highly drinkable curiosity.

Amazon Chardonnay `11` `C`

A touch confectionery fruited and sweet to finish. Good soft wine for those looking to move up from Liebfraumilch.

BULGARIAN WINE
RED

Co-op Cabernet Sauvignon `11` `B`

Co-op Suhindol Merlot/Gamza `12` `B`

BULGARIAN WINE
WHITE

Co-op Preslav Chardonnay `11` `B`

Co-op Welchriesling and Misket `12` `B`

CHILEAN WINE   RED

Carmen Reserve Merlot 1994   `16` `C`
Classy merlot for under a fiver: rich, subtle, leathery softness, dry brambly flavour and a classic lingering finish. Very good value.

Chilean Red   `15` `B`
Cabernet sauvignon-dominated, non-vintage blend of style, class, flavour and firm balance. Dry, fruity, very good value.

Co-op Chilean Cabernet Sauvignon   `15` `B`
Coffee and chocolate fruit.

Long Slim Red Cabernet Merlot 1993   `16` `C`
Brilliant rich, dark fruit with dry catering chocolate edge. Serious yet fun. It is a terrific wine for the money.

Santa Carolina Merlot 1993   `14` `C`
A classy mouthful of smooth, polished, gently tannic fruit. Great with cheese dishes.

CHILEAN WINE   WHITE

Chilean White   `16` `B`
Superb value for money: modern, fresh, aromatic, fruity, classy. Brilliant glug or with all sorts of poached and grilled fish.

Long Slim White Chardonnay/Semillon 1994   `15.5` `B`
Masses of flavour crisply packaged. Real style here. Great grilled chicken wine.

Peteroa Sauvignon Blanc 1993 `14` `B`

Excellent balanced fruit and acid. Terrific shellfish wine.

ENGLISH WINE WHITE

Co-op English Table Wine `14` `C`

Excellent as before – but pricey. Still worthy of support.

Denbies English Table Wine 1992 `13` `C`

Three Choirs New Release 1994 `12` `B`

Fragrant, summery bouquet redolent of elderflowers and a hint of strawberry. Ripe fruit with a sweet edge. Not as crisp or as exciting as previous vintages. Too much residual sugar?

FRENCH WINE RED

Barton & Guestier Margaux Tradition 1992 `13` `E`

Classy, without a doubt. But is it worth nine quid? Hum . . .

Beaujolais Villages Domaine Granjean 1994 `12` `C`

Chateau Barbeau, St Chinian 1993 `14` `C`

Tannic grip to the fruit gives it terrific casserole compatibility.

Chateau Cissac 1983 `11` `E`

Chateau Cissac 1987 `10` `E`

Chateau Laurencon, Bordeaux Superieur 1993 `12` `C`

Chateau Les Hauts de Pontet, Pauillac 1991 `13.5` `E`

Bold, subtly chocolatey, rather expensive.

Chateau Moulin de Pez 1990 `15.5` `E`

Brilliant tannic structure – it's what the Medoc should always be about if it has to charge eight quid for a wine. This is classy stuff, impactful, gripping, lingering. Roast meat, meet thy maker!!

Chateau Pierrousselle Bordeaux 1994 `13` `C`

Exceeding dry. Put down for 2/3 years.

Chateauneuf-du-Pape, Cellier des Princes 1991 `10` `E`

Co-op Anjou Rouge `12` `C`

Co-op Bergerac Rouge `13` `B`

Co-op Cahors `14` `C`

Made by the highly regarded Rigal brothers who are negociants as well as making their own wine at Chateau St Didier in Parnac. This wine is blackcurrant and coal tar and is well dry yet has soft fruit – indeed the smiling softness of the fruit is curiously counterpointed by a typical scowl of Cahors dryness, and the whole adds up to a pleasantly balanced personality.

Co-op Claret `12` `B`

Also available in half bottles now.

Co-op Corbieres `11` `B`

Co-op Costieres de Nimes `13` `B`

Earthy, soft, dry, edgily nutty with blackcurrant and plum fruit. Good value.

Co-op Cotes du Luberon `13` `B`

Attractive, gentle charcoal/rubber bouquet, plus a good dollop of cheering fruit. Good value.

Co-op Cotes du Rhone `11` `B`

Co-op Cotes du Roussillon `15` `B`

Dry, earthy edged (rich tannins) and wonderfully purposeful and fruity. A really good food wine. Has bite and character and rustic charm.

Co-op Cotes du Ventoux `11` `B`

Co-op Fitou `12` `B`

Co-op Medoc `12` `C`

Co-op VdP Merlot 1994 `14` `B`

Rich and good value. Even throws in some handsome tannins.

Co-op VdP Syrah 1994 `13.5` `B`

Co-op Vin de Pays de l'Aude `11` `B`

Co-op Vin de Pays de l'Herault Rouge `12` `B`

Co-op Vin de Table Red (1 litre) `11` `B`

Cote de Beaune Villages, Jules Vignon 1992 `11` `D`

Crozes Hermitage Louis Mousset 1991 `11` `C`

Domaine de Conquet Merlot, J & F Lurton 1994 `13.5` `C`

Domaine de Hauterive, Cotes du Rhone Villages 1992

`13` `C`

Good earthy stuff.

Domaine des Combes Syrah, VdP d'Oc 1993

`12` `B`

Light, dry, with a faint cherryish edge.

Domaine Serjac Grenache VdP d'Oc 1994

`14` `C`

Good earthy grenache character. Great with grilled bangers.

Gamay, VdP des Coteaux de l'Ardeche 1994

`13.5` `C`

Fruitier, more appealing and better priced than so much beaujolais.

Mediterre Rouge, VdP d'Oc

`14` `B`

Soft, simple, fruity red without a hint of rustic coarseness.

Medoc Vieilles Vignes 1993

`12` `C`

Too dry for me.

Minervois Domaine les Combelles 1991

`14` `C`

Dry and full of savoury flavour. Excellent with roast Sunday lunch.

Montbazillac Domaine de Haut Rauly 1993 (half bottle)

`13.5` `C`

With a plate of blue cheese and biscuits this wine would be wonderful.

Morgon, Les Charmes 1992

`11` `D`

St Emilion, Bernard Taillan (half bottle)

`13` `C`

Vacqueyras, Cuvee du Marquis de Fonseguille 1993 `14` `D`

A handsome bottle of wine. Delightfully bristly at the edges but it is deliciously fruity and full with an ineffable serious tone.

FRENCH WINE WHITE

Chardonnay Fleur du Moulin, VdP d'Oc 1993 `15` `C`

A rolling, rich edge to fruit which could be almost buttery. Good acid balances this out. A solid chardonnay for the money.

Chateau Pierrousselle Entre-deux-Mers 1994 `12.5` `C`

Co-op Alsace Gewurztraminer `14` `C`

Lychee and grapefruit to the nose, mulled fruit, richly edged, for the mouth, spicy tickle in the throat. An interesting aperitif, or to drink solo with a book, or for mild Chinese food.

Co-op Alsace Pinot Blanc `13` `C`

Co-op Anjou Blanc `13` `B`

Co-op Bergerac Blanc `11` `B`

Co-op Blanc de Blancs `11` `B`

Co-op Bordeaux Blanc Medium Dry `12` `B`

Co-op Cotes du Roussillon Blanc `10` `B`

Co-op Premieres Cotes de Bordeaux `11` `B`

Co-op Rose d'Anjou `12` `B`
A pleasant little rose.

Co-op VdP d'Oc Chardonnay `12` `C`

Co-op VdP de l'Herault Blush `11` `C`

Co-op Vin de Pays des Cotes de Gascogne `12` `B`

Co-op Vin de Pays des Cotes des Pyrenees Orientales `13` `B`

Domaine du Clos du Bourg, Touraine Sauvignon 1992 `15` `B`
Delicious nutty fish wine yet with enough depth of dry, leafy fruit to be enjoyed on its own.

Hermitage Blanc, Les Nobles Rives 1992 `13` `F`
True Rhone dry white earthiness and class but what a price!

Les Pavois d'Or, Sauternes (half bottle) `13` `D`
Sweetie for puds – or just fruit.

Mediterre Blanc, VdP d'Oc `13` `B`
Some attractive fruit here.

Muscadet sur Lie Domaine de la Haute Maillardiere 1994 `13` `C`
Not a bad muscadet at all, this specimen. Touch pricey compared with New World equivalents.

Sancerre, Domaine Raimbault 1993 `12.5` `D`
Sound rather than sensational, and overpriced. Most sancerres are these days.

Vignerons des Remparts, VdP Sauvignon Blanc 1994   `13` `C`

Vouvray, Domaine des Perruches 1994   `13.5` `D`

Interesting. Has a distant echo of earthy honey to its medium dryness. Try it with Chinese food.

GERMAN WINE   WHITE

Bad Bergzaberner Auslese 1993   `13` `C`

Almond essence on the finish. I'd drink it in AD 2000.

Co-op Baden Dry   `13.5` `B`

Dry, fruity, clean, well-priced. Not a lot you can add to that.

Co-op Bernkasteler Kurfurstlay 1994   `12` `B`

Pretty aperitif wine.

Co-op Dornfelder   `13` `C`

Drink it chilled with grilled salmon or mackerel.

Co-op Hock Deutscher Tafelwein   `11` `A`

Co-op Liebfraumilch   `10` `A`

Co-op Morio-Muskat   `13` `B`

A delicious aperitif.

Co-op Mosel Deutscher Tafelwein   `11` `B`

Co-op Muller Thurgau   `11` `B`

Sweetish – good with Chinese food.

Co-op Niersteiner Gutes Domtal 1994 `13` **B**

Co-op Oppenheimer Krotenbrunnen 1994 `12` **B**

Co-op Piesporter Michelsberg 1994 `13` **B**

Delicious lemon-prickle aperitif wine.

Co-op Rudesheimer Rosengarten 1994 `13` **B**

Chilled as an aperitif? Or a TV soap opera glug? Possibly. Possibly.

Devil's Rock Riesling 1994 `12` **C**

Smoked salmon wine.

St Ursula Galerie Pinot Blanc 1993 `14` **C**

A creamy-edged, nutty pinot of most attractive fruit. Excellent fish wine.

St Ursula Galerie Riesling, Pfalz 1993 `13` **C**

Good fish wine.

Westhofener Bergkloster Auslese, St Ursula 1992 `14` **C**

Rich, gently honeyed. Try it as a complex alternative to Liebfraumilch with a bunch of grapes and a piece of cheese.

GREEK WINE   RED

Boutari Red `12` **B**

Chilled, with a smoked eel and smoked pork stew, this might be OK.

GREEK WINE   WHITE

Boutari White   `11` **B**

HUNGARIAN WINE   RED

Chapel Hill Cabernet Sauvignon, Balaton 1992   `13.5` **B**

Co-Op Hungarian Red Country Wine, Balaton Region   `12` **B**

Hungaroo Merlot 1992   `14` **B**

An extremely quaffable merlot of soft, yet tannic, savoury fruit. Most agreeable.

HUNGARIAN WINE   WHITE

Chapel Hill Oaked Chardonnay, Balaton 1994   `13` **B**

Some soundly fruity flavour here, and value.

Co-op Hungarian White Country Wine, Nagyrede   `14` **B**

Delicious fruit for the money. Gooseberry/melon/musky peach. Good with food or solo.

Gyongyos Estate Chardonnay 1993   `13` **B**

Losing freshness.

Hungaroo Pinot Gris 14 B

Waxy weight to the fruit which will improve in bottle and the
apricot edge deepen, between now and the spring of 1996. Great
smoked fish wine.

ITALIAN WINE   RED

Bardolino Le Canne, Boscaini 1993 15.5 C

A riot of typefaces on the unusual mauve-coloured label. A riot
of flavours in the bottle. Light but impactful, this has swirling
juicy fruit with a dry, serious edge. Delicious.

Co-op Barbera del Piemonte 11 B

Co-op Cabernet del Veneto 14.5 B

A lovely fruity wine, excellent lightly chilled, which compares
with a simple beaujolais of the old school. Bargain.

Co-op Chianti 10 B

Co-op Merlot del Veneto 13 B

Cherries! Who'll buy my sweet cherries?

Co-op Montepulciano d'Abruzzo 1993 14.5 B

Joyously fruity bargain which is not as jammy as some examples;
nevertheless it is thick enough to spread on toast.

Co-op Sicilian Red 13 B

Excellent rubbery fruit with a candied cherry finish. Soft, fruity,
subtle vivacity. Delicious with rabbit stew.

Co-op Valpolicella 12 A

Country Collection Puglian Red 15.5 B

Cherry/plum fruit and considerable verve and style. Dry, fruity, very flavourful and frisky.

Le Volte Ornellaia 1993 12 E

Overpriced novelty.

Principato Rosso Valdadige 14 B

A blend of schiara, lambrusco and merlot. Dry yet ripe, with a light cherry fruitiness which is never frivolous but rather serious in the length and richness of the finish, this is not only a marvellous pasta, pizza, and risotto wine but something which could stand up to much posher fare (although that said, I must say I regard risotto as one of the poshest treats imaginable, and a first-class example made with mushrooms with a bottle of Principato would make me a happy man any day of the week).

Sangiovese di Toscana, Fiordaliso 1994 16 C

Wonderful sweet fruit finish in this deliciously dry red gives it a superb versatility with food (anything from red meats to rice dishes).

Sanroseda Valpolicella Classico 1992 14 C

Real rich fruit here – not to be confused with the thin valpols of old.

Vino da Tavola Trebbiano, Co-op 8 B

ITALIAN WINE WHITE

Chardonnay del Piemonte, Alasia 1994 13.5 C

Good fruit and flavour.

Co-op Bianco di Custoza
`12` `C`

Nice-ish weight of fruit, fair-ish balance, fresh-ish finish. If you like your wine with lots of ish, this ish for you.

Co-op Bianco Verduzzo del Veneto 1994
`14` `B`

Real flavour and subdued richness here.

Co-op Chardonnay Atesino
`11` `B`

Co-op Frascati Superiore
`11` `B`

Co-op Orvieto Secco
`12` `C`

Co-op Pinot Grigio del Veneto
`10` `B`

Co-op Sicilian White
`11` `B`

Rather fruitless.

Co-op Soave
`10` `B`

Frascati Villa Catone 1994
`11` `C`

Lazio Country White
`11` `B`

Soave Monteleone, Boscaini 1994
`14` `C`

A very sound soave with a balance of fruit and acid which is a lesson in poise to most soave, which is deadly dull.

LEBANESE WINE   RED

Chateau Musar 1977
`13` `G`

£20? An eight-quid wine at best. It has a refined muscularity, immensely dry, perfectly mature, and it's wonderfully aromatic with its cigar-box scents and fruit. Strictly for the nut who loves old books with musty leather covers.

MOLDOVAN WINE   WHITE

Kirkwood Chardonnay   `14` `B`

Flavour and style. Not a huge dollop of fruit but a convincing
glassful of it.

NEW ZEALAND WINE   WHITE

Forest Flower Fruity Dry White 1994   `13` `C`

PORTUGUESE WINE   RED

Co-op Bairrada Tinto 1991   `12` `B`

Co-op Douro Tinto 1991   `13` `C`

Co-op Vinho de Mesa Santos   `15` `B`

Typical baked figs and earth aromatically which completely belie
the creamy fruit flavour. Delicious. Astoundingly good value.

Duas Quintas Douro 1991   `14.5` `C`

Lovely rich fruit with lots of class and flavour. Stylish, mature,
deliciously accomplished. A polished performance.

**Quinta da Pancas Cabernet Sauvignon
1992**   `16` `D`

Impressively smooth and subtly chocolatey. Has wonderful
fruity presumption which it carries off to a rich, dry finish.

PORTUGUESE WINE WHITE

Co-op Bairrada Branco 1993 `13.5` `B`

Fresh and clean with a minerally prickle. Tasty with shellfish.

Co-op Portuguese Rose `10` `B`

Co-op Vinho Verde `11` `B`

ROMANIAN WINE RED

Classic Pinot Noir 1990 `15` `B`

Brilliant cherry fruit, dry, bright and weighty without being overripe.

Dealul Mare Cabernet Sauvignon Special Reserve 1985 `15` `B`

Rich, delicious, bright-berried softness. Great fruit and great price.

Feteasca Neagra Special Reserve 1991 `14` `B`

Superbly fruity pasta wine. Delicious chilled. Class in a glass for relative peanuts.

Pinot Noir Prahova 1993 `15.5` `B`

What a thundering bargain! Fruity, dry, superbly structured, it has flavour, tannins and balance. Terrific casserole wine.

SOUTH AFRICAN WINE — RED

Co-op Cape Red — 15 B

Distinctive fruit, rich and rolling without being overripe or blowsy, and there is an attractive dry edge of real class. Drink chilled like beaujolais (or rather, like beaujolais used to be). Brilliant soft fresh aromatic fruit. Bargain.

Kumala Cinsault/Pinotage — 16 B

Burnt rubber fruit of great charm. Distinctive, soft, deliciously well formed and stylish! Exceptional depth of flavour and lingering-finished fruitiness.

Rustenberg Cabernet Sauvignon 1991 — 13 D

SOUTH AFRICAN WINE — WHITE

Co-op Cape White — 15 B

Bargain. Most attractive dry peach fruit with subtle acidic backcloth providing modernity and freshness. Really terrifically tasty for the money.

Huguenot Hills South Africa White — 12 B

Kumala Chenin/Chardonnay — 13.5 B

Modern pear-drop undertones. Good with a tuna salad.

Namaqua Colombard 1994, Co-op — 14 B

Delightful fresh fruit. Washes off the weary traveller's dust as effectively as it clears the throat for further portions of fish and chips.

SPANISH WINE   RED

Campo Rojo, Carinena   14.5   B

Thundering bargain. An edge of earthy tannins to the mature
plum fruit makes this a solid food wine (cheese dishes and
stews).

Co-op Rioja Crianza   12   C

Co-op Tempranillo Oak-Aged   15   B

Brilliant value fruit, tinged with vanilla, bright, dry, savoury.

Co-op Valdepenas   11   B

Co-op Valencia Red   12   A

Now available in 3 litres as well.

Marques de Parada Garnacha, Calatayud
1994   14   B

Flavourful, food-friendly fulsomeness – a bargain.

Pozuelo Crianza 1990   14   C

Dry and vaguely rich, like a middle-aged playboy whose age is
impossible to guess.

Santara Cabernet/Merlot, Conca de
Barbera 1994   14   C

Fresh to finish but will develop brilliantly in bottle between now
and the spring of 1996. Rich and soft.

Torres Gran Sangredetoro 1989   13   D

Vina Pomal Rioja Crianza 1990   13.5   C

Ripe and very ready for a chorizo sausage.

SPANISH WINE WHITE

Berberana Carta de Oro Blanco Rioja 1991 12.5 C

Co-op Moscatel de Valencia 16 B

Marmalade and toffee caramel – rich and exciting. Fabulous value for the Christmas pud.

Co-op Valencia White 14 A

Good level of fruit – balanced. Now available in 3 litres as well.

Co-op Valle de Monterrey, Vino de la Tierra 14 A

A deliciously fruity, well-balanced white with a touch of melon (excellent fish 'n' chip wine).

USA WINE RED

California Ruby Cabernet (Co-Op) 14.5 B

Bargain dry fruit – curiously plummy and cherryish, but attractive. Brilliant pasta wine.

USA WINE WHITE

August Sebastiani's White Zinfandel 1994 12.5 C

A rose wine of sweetness and plainness. Rated at £2.99 only. Not worth £3.99.

Barefoot Cellars Gamay/Zinfandel   `12` `C`
Sole food wine? More a fish stew brew.

Co-op California Colombard   `11` `B`

Stowells of Chelsea California Blush (3 litre)   `10` `F`
Barbie-doll fruit, great for Barbie dolls.

SPARKLING WINE/CHAMPAGNE

Barramundi Sparkling (Australia)   `16.5` `D`
I'd try it just for the label! And I'd drink it for the sheer pleasure of the delicately fresh fruit – so much better than more expensive champagnes. A bubbly to get married for!

Co-op Cava   `14` `C`
Bargain – whistle-clean and fault-free.

Co-op Sparkling Saumur   `13` `D`
Clean and classic.

De Clairveaux Champagne NV   `13.5` `F`
Attractive fruit here, really attractive. Pity about the price. (If it was under a tenner we'd really be in business.)

Liebfraumilch   `10` `C`

Pinot di Pinot (Italy)   `12` `D`

Sparkling Chardonnay (Italian)   `11` `C`

Veuve Honorian Champagne Brut NV   `12` `E`

KWIK SAVE

One of the stimulating facts of life I've become acquainted with since I started writing the *Superplonk* column in the *Guardian* is the indefatigable epistolary prowess of its readers. I have to employ a secretary just to help me to deal with my post bag now and then, and Kwik Save, now and then, is often the cause of a reader deciding to write to me. Kwik Save, for mercy's sake! I bet the readers of *The Times* or the *Telegraph*, not to mention the *Independent*, have no idea what a Kwik Save is. Unlike the readers of *The Times*, say, who require needling to send off a letter ('I am appalled to learn' is a pet opening and 'It is to be regretted that' is another favourite standby), one glance at the *Guardian*'s published letterpage any day of the week will show you that its contributors require no sense of moral outrage or desire to spleen-vent in order to fire off a letter; they send the things in as a matter of conversational course – for all the world as if they were engaging in nothing more remarkable than an earnest chinwagging with the neighbour next door. Is it, then, any surprise that such literate, friendly folk should feel obliged to tell me of the constant supply of bargains they avail themselves of at this retailer? One chap told me he'd saved a fortune on his daughter's wedding by going to Kwik Save and picking up a load of excellent sparkling wine going cheap.

   This last word is Kwik Save's by-word. Its customers, for the most part, feel an attack of hives coming on at the mere thought of spending more than three quid on a bottle of wine and so there is a concentration of wines around this price level. Its top-selling wines are all under £3 and the top three are Liebfraumilch, Hock and Lambrusco Bianco (at

5 per cent alcohol). Last summer, Rouge de France, 'a very light, slightly sweet red table wine' in the wine buyer's own words, was in the number 4 spot but this was pushed out at Christmas by the non-vintage Lovico-Suhindol Bulgarian Country Red Cabernet/Merlot. At festive times, the Lambrusco Light (3 per cent alcohol) and the Lambrusco Rose (at 5 per cent alcohol) make the best-sellers list, too.

Doesn't sound to you like the sort of place to find quizzical, thirsty, ink-stained *Guardian* readers thronging? Ah, how little you know, madam, about the world of the bargain hunter.

Listen to the words of Kwik Save's consultant wine buyer, Angela Muir:

'Kwik Save stores tend to be sited in heavily populated urban areas. A much higher proportion of their customers walk to the stores than would be the case with most supermarkets. Many of them often shop for a basketful every other day rather than a trolleyful every week or fortnight. The layout of the off-licence operations also encourages people to nip in for one or two items in passing without having to go through the checkout queues. We therefore have a lot of relatively less well-off customers who count very carefully what, if anything, they spend on a bottle of wine, and tend to choose by habit rather than interest. These customers are now gradually being joined by additional customers who never thought of buying wine in Kwik Save before. They spread their purchases fairly evenly across the range. A number of these relatively well-off customers would have come to Kwik Save purely to stock up on known brand-name groceries such as detergents in the past.'

Crafty, eh? Red wine sales at Kwik Save have risen by almost 30 per cent over the past year and it is undoubtedly these newer customers who are responsible for this. Kwik Save has also joined the very new movement away from phoney French names for wines. And being crafty is important here, too.

Earlier this year, the company introduced a new range of wines which enjoy a name which sounds Australian but is a simple translation from the French *alouette*. Skylark Hill

Vermentino (£2.89), Skylark Hill Merlot (£2.79), and Skylark Hill Very Special Red (£2.99) are smartly packed to appear like innocent New World beauties but they are in truth non-vintage Vin de Pays d'Ocs. The vermentino grape, known also as malvoisie in Corsica and other places, is grown in a couple of Italian regions and it is a newcomer to the list of officially approved varieties of the Languedoc. It aroused sufficient excitement in my breast for me to rate it 12 points. It is pleasant, inoffensive, gently fruity and soft. The merlot rates 14 for it has a good depth of flavour, with an attractive subtly bitter background, and it has sufficient character to go with grilled vegetables and meats. However, it is the Very Special Red which most lit up my palate. Its name is no lie. It has delightfully rich fruit with a subtle tannin element, and the swirling flavours of the wine give it a serious aspect as well as a twinkle-in-the-eye gluggability. It rates 16 points.

'Our aim is to provide really good-value everyday drinking pleasure,' says Ms Muir. How well has Kwik Save demonstrated, over the past three years, the accuracy with which it has fulfilled this aim! It has almost 1,000 licensed outlets and whilst not all carry the full range it is reckoned that 60 per cent now carry most of it. This complete range is not large, under 100 wines, but it is meticulously selected to meet criteria which may not please the snob but is right up my alley. Not all the wines are high raters, but there is no doubt that 'working to probably the tightest parameters imposed on a high street wine selecting team anywhere', in Ms Muir's terms (by which she means the prices she must bring the wines in at), the result is one of the best-value ranges of inexpensive wines on sale anywhere.

'. . . I suspect that a number of (competitors') ranges would offer the consumer far less of a gamble if they were pruned down as ours is,' says Ms Muir and since, on the evidence of the list which follows, this shorn state also means good fruit at good prices, there is a lot of sense in what she says. She goes on: '. . . the majority of our customers still buy known names. While we can and do tempt them with alternatives, we feel that we cannot let them down if they do choose to stay with the familiar. We therefore do a lot of work on the bread-and-butter lines to keep them as drinkable as possible so that they live up to expectations. We nag Lambrusco producers if their wine is too flat; we nag Liebfraumilch producers when they put too much sulphur dioxide in the wine; we nag claret producers if their wine becomes too mean and astringent.'

Ms Muir, you're a very successful nag. Keep it up.

Kwik Save Stores Limited
Warren Drive
Prestatyn
Clwyd
LL19 7HU

Tel 01745 887111
Fax 01745 882504

SEE STOP PRESS SECTION AT END OF BOOK FOR LAST-MINUTE ADDITIONS TO THIS RETAILER'S RANGE.

ARGENTINIAN WINE — WHITE

Gauchos Blanco White Wine, Mendoza `10` `A`

AUSTRALIAN WINE — RED

Butterfly Ridge Cabernet Sauvignon/Shiraz 1993 `12.5` `C`

Pelican Bay Red `13` `B`

AUSTRALIAN WINE — WHITE

Angove's Chardonnay 1994 `13.5` `C`
Gentle varietal impact but very soundly put together and flavoursome.

Pelican Bay Dry White `12` `B`

Pelican Bay Medium Dry White `12` `B`

BULGARIAN WINE — RED

Cabernet Sauvignon, Burgas Bulgarian 1990 `15` `B`
Juicy fruit but has a serious side. Great roast food wine for lots of guests.

Iambol Merlot/Pamid 1992, Bulgarian Vintage Blend 13 A

Lovico Suhindol Cabernet Sauvignon/ Merlot Bulgarian Country Wine 14.5 A

Smooth, ripe, rich, delightfully cheap.

BULGARIAN WINE WHITE

Bear Ridge White 1994 13.5 B

Very very tasty – and very very tastily priced.

Preslav Vintage Blend Chardonnay/ Sauvignon 1994 14.5 B

Superb wine for the money. Serious fruit with a gentle citric edge. Great with shellfish.

CHILEAN WINE WHITE

White Pacific Chardonnay/Semillon 1994 13.5 B

Rich-edged, soft fruit.

White Pacific Sauvignon 1994 14 B

Astonishing bargain. Not varietally convincing but who gives a heck with fruit at this price?

FRENCH WINE RED

Cabernet Sauvignon 1993 VdP d'Oc 10 B

Cabernet Sauvignon VdP d'Oc 1994   `12` `B`
Mouthful of pure tannin. Needs milk and sugar?

Chateau Fontcaude 1993, St Chinian   `15` `B`
Lush, soft fruit. Delicious style.

Claret Cuvee VE   `11` `B`
Authentic stalky fruit.

De Belfont Cuvee Speciale 1993   `13` `B`
A pleasant softie with an appealing, easy style. It finishes a bit flat, that's all.

Fortant de France Grenache VdP d'Oc 1994   `13.5` `B`
Very well packed with dry, well-flavoured fruit.

Merlot Domaine Resclause 1993, VdP d'Oc   `14` `B`

Minervois   `12` `B`
Dryish style.

Pinot Noir Domaine St Martin, VdP d'Oc Virginie 1994   `10` `C`
Might soothe a sore throat.

Rouge de France, Selection Cuvee VE   `12` `A`

Skylark Hill Merlot, VdP d'Oc   `14` `B`
Good depth, a touch bitter, but has fruit and flavour and will be great with grilled sausages.

Skylark Hill Very Special Red VdP d'Oc NV   `16` `B`
Lovely rich, subtly tannic fruit with swirling flavour, serious-edged style and rich food compatibility.

**Steep Ridge Grenache/Shiraz, VdP
d'Oc 1994** `13` `B`

Vin de Pays de l'Herault `13` `A`
Soft and friendly. It works.

FRENCH WINE   WHITE

Blanc de France `14` `A`
Lots of melony fruit well put together.

Bordeaux Sauvignon, Cuvee VE 1994 `10` `B`

**Domaine Fontenille Marsanne, VdP d'Oc
Virginie 1994** `14.5` `B`
Serious bargain here for its real rich-edged nutty marsanne
(grape variety) fruit.

**Domaine la Gravenne Sur Lie, VdP d'Oc
Virginie 1994** `13` `B`

**La Fondation de Donatien Rose de
Loire Sec** `14` `B`
Simple, faint cherry echo on clean fruit.

Muscadet 1994 `10` `B`

Rose de France Selection Cuvee VE `9` `A`

Rose de Syrah, VdP d'Oc Virginie 1994 `12` `B`

Skylark Hill Chardonnay VdP d'Oc `15.5` `B`
Astounding varietal fidelity. Lovely, rich, rounded fruit, dry-
edged yet fruity. Has structure, depth and real class. Big bargain.

Skylark Hill Vermentino VdP d'Oc NV `12` `B`

Pleasant, inoffensive, gently fruity, soft.

Steep Ridge Chardonnay/Sauvignon VdP d'Oc 1994 `13` `B`

Sound, very sound.

Stowells of Chelsea Vin de Pays du Tarn (3 litre) `12` `F`

Sound but dullish – not a lot of fruit.

VdP des Cotes de Gascogne, Plaimont 1994 `12` `B`

Vin de Pays de l'Herault `13` `B`

GERMAN WINE   WHITE

Hock Deutscher Tafelwein, Rhein, K. Linden 1994 `10` `A`

Liebfraumilch, K. Linden 1994 `10` `A`

Morio Muskat, Pfalz 1994 `10` `B`

Piesporter Michelsberg, K. Linden 1994 `11` `B`

Zimmermann Kabinett, Pfalz 1993 `14` `B`

Great aperitif – or drink with shellfish.

HUNGARIAN WINE — RED

Hungarian Merlot 1993 `12` `A`

HUNGARIAN WINE — WHITE

Chateau Megyer Furmint, Tokaji 1994 `12` `C`

Hungarian Chardonnay 1993, Balaton Boglar `11` `B`

Hungarian Chardonnay 1994 `13` `B`
Fresh, sound, some flavour.

Hungarian Country Wine 1994 `11` `A`

Pinot Gris Asznar-Neszmely 'Rich' Cuvee 1994 `14` `B`
Distant peachy edge to the dry fruit gives this wine varietal purity and style.

ITALIAN WINE — RED

Arietta Montepulciano d'Abruzzo 1994 `13.5` `B`
A bargain parcel of fruit, simply tied together it's true, but attractive chilled.

Cadenza Red, VdT `12` `A`
Simple, drinkable, cheap. It may be enough.

Country Collection Puglian Red, VdT 13 B

Immensely soft and simple and attractively priced.

Il Paesano, Merlot del Veneto 13 B

Light and juicy. Fun.

Montepulciano de Molise, Cantina Clitarna 1993 15 B

Oh, what a bargain of edgily dry, jam-packed fruit. Great with pasta or more serious savoury dishes.

Valpolicella, Cantina Sociale di Soave 1994 11 B

ITALIAN WINE WHITE

Cadenza Medium Dry White 12 B

Concillio Atesino Chardonnay 13.5 B

Fails to reach 14 only by a whisker – it's a clean wine nevertheless and admirably modern.

Country Collection Puglian White VdT 14 B

Fresh, clean, lemony. A lovely summer thirst-quencher – also good with simple foods.

Frascati Superiore, Villa Pani 1994 11 B

Gabbia d'Oro 10 A

Soave, Cantina Sociale di Soave 1994 11 B

MACEDONIAN WINE — RED

Macedonian Merlot 1993 `11` `B`

Macedonian Country Red 1993 `11` `A`
Drinkable, but on the basis of this basic qualification one can understand Alexander the Great's enthusiasm for trying to conquer the rest of the civilised world.

PORTUGUESE WINE — RED

Alta Mesa Estremadura 1994 `14` `B`
Simple, soft, ripe, very fruity, delicious chilled and poured over parched tongues.

Villa Moresco Tinto `13` `B`
Tasty mid-week tippling for bangers and mash.

PORTUGUESE WINE — WHITE

Rosado Vinho de Mesa `10` `B`

SOUTH AFRICAN WINE — RED

Clearsprings Cape Red, Simonsvlei `14` `B`
Some good, clean, well-polished fruit.

Landema Falls Cinsault/Cabernet Sauvignon `14.5` `B`

Ripeness and flavour to the savoury-edged fruit give this wine bargain appeal.

Silver Hills Red `11` `B`

SOUTH AFRICAN WINE WHITE

Clearsprings Cape Medium White, Simonsvlei `13` `B`

Residual sugar gives it the fruit.

Landema Falls Colombard/Chardonnay `15.5` `B`

Lovely, lushly fruity bargain with a crisp undertone and soft melon overtones. Brilliant buy.

Silver Hill White 1994 `13` `B`

Great price. Convincing, dry fruit.

SPANISH WINE RED

Flamenco `11` `A`

Suit wild parties.

Pedro Rovira Garnacha/Cabernet, Tarragon 1994 `15` `B`

Real flavour, softness, brightness, style. Almost dizzily rich for the money.

Promesa Tinto 1994

Dark cherry fruit, dry yet soft. Lovely little glug for the money.

SPANISH WINE WHITE

Castillo de Liria Moscatel, Valencia

Brilliant pudding wine for the money. Also, well chilled, an effective aperitif.

Don Fadrique Cencibel, La Mancha 1994

Dry, bright, with a delicious textured finish on the fruit.

USA WINE RED

Barefoot Cellars Cabernet Sauvignon, California

Rough but smooth. A John Wayne of a wine. Fruity, bold, cheap.

California Cellars Red, Mission Bell Winery

Fruity, big-hearted, soft, very ripe. Connoisseurs will choke on it.

USA WINE WHITE

Barefoot Cellars Chardonnay, California 1994

Hint of lemon to the soft fruit gives the wine some style – at a great price.

California Cellars White, Mission Bell Winery
13 B

Some flavour and a little style here.

SPARKLING WINE/CHAMPAGNE

Champagne Brut, Louis Raymond
13 E

Lemony, light style.

LITTLEWOODS

Littlewoods is a very large and very profitable company (it has 30,000 employees) which is all owned by a single family. This family, called Moores, is neither little nor wooden and it is into football pools, mail order catalogues and, of most relevance here, stores – some of which sell wine. Just how animated and extensive the Moores are was revealed by the newspaper coverage given earlier this year to the hiring, allegedly by the family's top ruling brass, of various gumshoes, sleuths and flatfoots to spy on certain members of the executive management of the company in an effort to amass incriminating evidence against them. It was reported that Mr Prodip Guha, one in line to the Chief Executive position himself, was given the boot after being captured on film talking to a journalist. A *journalist*, begorrah! The very devil himself!

Well, I have news for the Moores family. This journalist has had secret meetings with one of its executives, wine buyer Mr Ian Duffy, in the offices above the Littlewoods branch in Oxford Street and, furthermore, Mr Duffy has been instrumental in passing on valuable information to me. I freely admit to this and so does, I am quite sure, Mr Duffy himself. No need to despatch a private dick, Mr and Mrs Moores. Let me reveal all that I know.

Littlewoods' six top-selling wines are:

1. Liebfraumilch.
2. Valencia white.
3. Lambrusco.
4. Hock.
5. The store's own-label champagne.
6. Bucks Fizz.

This clears up for good the answer to one of retailing's great riddles. And this is: just who visits Littlewoods stores and buys wine there? The answer, through the medium of divination by wine statistics (a more reliable method of arriving at the irrefutable truth than astrology, phrenology or the study of chicken entrails), is that women, and women only, are Littlewoods customers and these women work, drive, have children, husbands (who may or may not work), enjoy a manageable level of mortgage debt, and whose favourite TV programmes are *Barrymore* and the *National Lottery Live*. Littlewoods is the only retailer in this book whose top-sellers list is exclusively white. It is also significant that a champagne makes the list (and a good one it is) as well as the diluted, fruit-based bubbly Bucks Fizz. Stretched out on the sofa with an effervescent glass in one hand and Barrymore beamed in and beaming on the goggle-box at the other, is surely the fate of the Bucks Fizz drinker, whilst the champagne is reserved for the Lottery broadcast when, who knows, Lady Luck may be smiling. Littlewoods customers are incorrigible gamblers and the company caters for such tastes in many ways, though not, ironically, with its wines. Mr Duffy knows what his customers like and is not given to exotic experimentation. It is a sign of the times that this can be said and yet Mr Duffy can stock an Australian range fully twenty-five wines strong. He also launched New World ranges this spring from Chile, South Africa and California. Romania, Bulgaria and Hungary as well as the less fashionable areas of France are other countries Mr Duffy is looking at most closely. Undoubtedly the greater emphasis on food in Littlewoods stores, or some of them at any rate, over the past two years has helped wine sales. The incorporation of the Iceland franchise in Littlewoods foodhalls has, in Mr Duffy's words, 'changed our customer profile to younger women who are more likely to buy table wines than any other type of alcoholic drink'.

'We intend,' Mr Duffy informed me revealingly, 'to continue to increase space with our wine range at the expense of beers and spirits. We will also start to open Cornerstore units within our stores with the intention of having wine offers in all 129 branches.'

He confidently asserts that 'Based on results so far I anticipate a 250 per cent increase in wine sales over the full year.'

This from a man buying wine for a company specialising in football pools, mail order catalogues and stores selling a great many things to put *on* the body.

There has to be a message in here somewhere for the struggling wine merchant as he comes to terms with the same market conditions which have so resoundingly and unpleasantly smacked in the chops the estate agent and the electrical retailer.

Far be it from me to point out what this message is. If it isn't obvious then he shouldn't be in the business he's in in the first place.

Littlewoods Stores Support Centre
Atlantic Pavilion
Albert Dock
Liverpool
L70 1AD

Tel 0151 242 6000
Fax 0151 242 6390

**Andrew Garrett Black Shiraz, McWilliams
Vale 1993**

Curious. Must be the only wine to have a rival retailer's name, Marks & Spencer, on the back label. This is not sufficient recommendation – the wine is rich, deeply so, but it has a ripe edge which only food will ameliorate. Mexican chilli is about its mark.

Angoves Misty Moorings Australian Red

Soft, very soft.

**Hardy's Nottage Hill Cabernet Sauvignon/
Shiraz 1993**

Controlled soft spice laid on smooth blackcurrant fruit. Delicious, firm, well-styled.

Hardy's Shiraz/Cabernet Sauvignon 1994

Rolling soft fruit well supported by acids and tannins: firm, delicious, decisive.

Jacobs Creek

Orlando Jacobs Creek Shiraz/Cabernet 1993

Orlando RF Cabernet Sauvignon 1991

Dry, rather serious.

**Wolf Blass Yellow Label Cabernet
Sauvignon 1993**

Big and bonny – but very dry-edged and wrinkly in the corners. Food has to accompany it.

AUSTRALIAN WINE WHITE

Andrew Garrett Fume Blanc 1993 15 D

Lime and pineapple with a heavier fruit of some exotic but unknown breed in the centre. Delicious.

Angoves Misty Moorings Australian White 13.5 B

Well-fruited, well-priced.

Hardy's Padthaway Chardonnay 1993 16 D

Oily fruit bursting with flavour, dry rich fruit and rolling texture.

Hardy's RR Medium White 1993 11 B

Hardy's Semillon/Chardonnay 13 B

Hardy's Stamp Semillon/Chardonnay 1993 13 C

Hardy's Nottage Hill Chardonnay 1994 17 C

Best vintage yet. Lovely textured, oily fruit, never overdone or blowsy and a buttery, melony finish of surefooted delivery. Terrific value for such classy drinking.

Orlando RF Chardonnay 1993 14.5 D

A good fiver's worth of rich fruit – gently woody, buttery and well-balanced.

Wolf Blass South Australian Chardonnay 1994 14 D

Try it with fish curry or chicken tandoori – or both.

BULGARIAN WINE   RED

**Bulgarian Classic Cabernet Sauvignon
1991**   `14` `B`

Nice burnt edge to the fruit. Very dry but very effective with
meaty casseroles.

CHILEAN WINE   RED

Chilean Cabernet Sauvignon 1993   `14` `B`

Dark, dry and tannin-edged. Must be drunk with food –
lamb chops.

CHILEAN WINE   WHITE

Chilean Sauvignon Blanc 1994   `13.5` `B`

Tasty and poised. Touch of class for relative peanuts.

FRENCH WINE   RED

Beaujolais, Littlewoods   `8` `B`

Chateau d'Aigueville Cotes du Rhone 1993   `13` `C`

Chateau Grand-Jean, Bordeaux 1989   `13` `C`

Juicy, yet dry. Good with bacon dishes.

Claret, Littlewoods `12.5` `B`

Some flavour here.

Corbieres NV, Littlewoods `12` `B`

Cotes du Rhone, Littlewoods `13` `B`

Some deep, dark fruit here. Great with sausages and mash.

**Cotes du Roussillon Villages 1993,
Littlewoods** `13.5` `B`

Rustic and ready for anything. Cheese dishes would be good.

French Red Table Wine `11` `B`

Vin de Pays de l'Aude Red `10` `B`

Vin de Pays Pyrenees Orientales Red `12.5` `B`

FRENCH WINE WHITE

Bordeaux Blanc, Littlewoods `10` `B`

French Dry White Table Wine, Littlewoods `8` `B`

Plain as plain can be. Possibly plainer.

**French Medium White Table Wine,
Littlewoods** `2` `B`

Difficult to imagine how grapes came to end up so sublimely awful.

**Muscadet de Sevre et Maine 1993,
Littlewoods** `10` `B`

117

Premieres Cotes de Bordeaux, Littlewoods `12` `C`

Worth a go with blue cheese.

Rose d'Anjou, Littlewoods `12` `B`

Pleasant warm evening tippling.

Vin de Pays Pyrenees Orientales White `10` `B`

Vin de Table Dry White `10` `B`

Vin de Table Medium, Littlewoods `10` `B`

GERMAN WINE   WHITE

Bereich Niersteiner Rheinhessen 1990, Littlewoods `12` `C`

Sweet aperitif.

Hock, Littlewoods `7` `B`

Liebfraumilch Rheinhessen 1990, Littlewoods `8` `C`

Piesporter Michelsberg 1993, Littlewoods `11` `C`

St Johanner Abtei Auslese Rheinhessen 1993 `13.5` `C`

You will find this wine, served with duck and cherry sauce, quite terrific.

HUNGARIAN WINE   RED

Cabernet Sauvignon, Szekszard 1993   8   C

The least varietally impactful cabernet sauvignon I've ever tasted. This wouldn't matter if there were other compensations, but . . .

Hungarian Merlot, Eger 1990   10   B

HUNGARIAN WINE   WHITE

Gewurztraminer   10   B

Hungarian Chardonnay, Badacsony Region 1993   5   C

To be drunk with chargrilled donkeys' hooves with mustard sauce.

Hungarian Sauvignon Blanc, Zemplen 1993   9   B

ITALIAN WINE   RED

Chianti Il Borgo   10   B

Valpolicella Il Borgo   11   B

ITALIAN WINE — WHITE

Frascati, Il Borgo `8` `C`

Lambrusco White, Il Borgo `8` `B`

Soave Il Borgo `11` `B`

PORTUGUESE WINE — RED

Bairrada `13` `B`

Borges Bairrada Reserva 1989 `10` `C`
Flat. Gone. Popped its clogs.

ROMANIAN WINE — RED

Romanian Cabernet Sauvignon 1985 `15` `B`
Gamy and rich with dried strawberry fruit. Delicious.

Romanian Classic Merlot 1990 `12` `B`
Feeling its age. But useful with food.

Romanian Classic Pinot Noir 1990 `13.5` `B`
Fresh and fruity, not at all arthritic, and good with rice dishes.

ROMANIAN WINE   WHITE

Transylvania Pinot Gris 1992   `14` `B`

Lovely, bright and breezy aperitif.

SOUTH AFRICAN WINE   RED

Great Trek Pinotage   `15.5` `B`

Vibrant fruit so resounding with flavour it bruises the buds. Has oodles of jammy flavour and a soft, swinging style to it. A jazzy wine. Try it chilled, as an alternative to beaujolais, with baked beans on toast.

SOUTH AFRICAN WINE   WHITE

Great Trek Chenin Blanc   `14` `B`

Excellent price for such firm-footed fruit. Good with chicken dishes.

SPANISH WINE   RED

Carreras Cabernet Sauvignon   `10` `B`

Marques de Caceres Rioja 1991   `14` `C`

Calm, polished, dry, very attractive. Not a coarse note anywhere.

Rioja Romancero Crianza 1990 `14.5` `C`
Light vanilla trimming to the sound fruit makes this an excellent companion to chillied food – including light Indians.

SPANISH WINE   WHITE

Carreras Chardonnay `10` `B`

Carreras Sauvignon Blanc `9` `B`

USA WINE   RED

**Eagle Ridge Cabernet Sauvignon,
California 1992** `15` `B`
Bargain. Has a serious hint of tannic blackcurrant fruit and a rich finish. Good with Sunday's roast. Very dry.

Eagle Ridge California Red NV `14` `B`
Excellent fruity pasta plonk.

USA WINE   WHITE

Eagle Ridge California Chardonnay 1993 `12` `C`

SPARKLING WINE/CHAMPAGNE

Asti Spumante, Martini `10` `D`
Terribly sweet young thing.

Cavalino Sparkling Moscato (Italy)　6　

5 per cent alcohol and quite horrible. Probably best poured over ice-cream.

Champagne Brut Francois Daumale　13.5　F

Light, with a soft yet unmistakable lemon edge.

Marques de Monistrol 1991　13　D

Old-fashioned style with an earthy edge.

Monsigny Champagne, Littlewoods　11　F

MARKS & SPENCER

I sometimes take this supermarket's products to a competitor's wine tasting and no one bats an eyelid. To be sure, one of the more sharp-eyed women present – able to recognise a perfectly formed male body sporting the sharpest up-to-the-minute gear – might say, 'That's a nice shirt', but no one sees the St Michael label on the back of the collar or, for that matter, imprinted on my socks or sewn into my underpants, and the emblem has long worn off the inside of my brown suede shoes. And whatever you might be thinking (the Tesco introduction may put the thought into your nasty, suspicious mind), I can tell you that I have paid for every single one of these garments out of my own pocket. There is something rum, there is no doubt about it, to be including the nation's number one bra and knicker retailer in a wine guide, but then Marks & Spencer, which began life in 1884 on a Leeds market stall run by a Russian immigrant who spoke no word of English other than 'thanks', is a rum supermarket altogether. Even referring to it as a supermarket in the first place gets up the collective and very sensitive nostrils of its upper management, and I suspect they would be far more comfortable if I referred to it as a religion. But even the fertile imagination of L Ron Hubbard never conceived of so convincing and metaphysically thrilling an idea as M & S, and, what's more, the store does not need to stop people on the street to drum up business. It merely has to hang out a sign.

Can you believe this list of its six top-selling wines (as it was earlier this year)?

1. Lambrusco Bianco.
2. Oudinot Champagne.
3. Chablis.
4. Italian Chardonnay.
5. Montepulciano d'Abruzzo.
6. Classic Claret.

If anyone needed confirmation that the store has a massive, loyal female clientele (with any other shop you'd say 'customer base', but clientele, with its chic drawl, suits M & S better) then there is the evidence. It is also evidence that these women are immensely well-heeled; Oudinot Champagne is £10.99 a bottle. This makes M & S unique. It is the only store in this book to have an over-a-tenner bottle amongst its top sellers. It is equally remarkable that the Chablis, a £6.99 wine, is in there at number 3. It is also worth commenting that its number 1 wine is dry, not sweet, therefore we can further conjecture that these loyal, well-heeled women are experienced tipplers. The more you enjoy alcohol, even in the moderate levels inherent in wine, the drier you want it to be for everyday enjoyment because your sugar tolerance level drops and sweet wines are less attractive. It is significant, in this context, how many other retailers in this book list sweet white wines in their best-sellers lists. If you ask the store, it will say (as do all of them) that its customers come from all walks of life, but as far as the wine customers are concerned the walk is surely wall-to-wall carpeted with a Golf GTi at the very least in the garage.

'White burgundy is the rock of our business,' says wine buyer Chris Murphy. You can't get more Golf GTi than that (not at £6.99 a bottle you can't). Mr Murphy spends a lot of days a year in Burgundy but still finds time, with his colleague Jane Kay, to gradually build up a New World portfolio, and in Australia they have found some cracking bottles as well as increasing its representation from South Africa and, launched last year, four Chileans, some of which are truly outstanding. The introduction of a mail order wine business and the purchase of special so-called 'Fine Wine' parcels have also broadened and deepened the range. Ms Kay in particular has also been involved in trying to solve the problem of corked wines by working on developments of a foolproof plastic substitute, and this is now in place in a dozen M & S wines. I was told that 'We anticipate that the majority of our wines up to £3.99 will have the plastic cork' at some time in the future.

I must say I find it difficult to think of any other wine retailer which concerns itself more with its suppliers' businesses on the ground, but then this is undoubtedly a primary commandment of the M & S religion which demands that quality is something which can be controlled only at source of supply not at point of sale. A streak of retail genius runs through M & S and as with all successful geniuses it is application which is as important as inspiration, and no retailer applies itself so assiduously to making sure its products please. Hence its special concern with eliminating the occasional corked wine. I daresay it is only in the wine area that faulty M & S products ever occur to any appreciable extent (since 5 per cent of all wines sold are, in my considered view, corked to a greater or lesser degree), and this inconsistency is anathema to the M & S religion which aspires if not to the unclimbable peak of perfection then at least to such a small percentage of faulty goods as is bearable. If all wines had plastic corks then that 5 per cent of faulty wines, millions of bottles a year, would disappear. I have little doubt that if all the M & S customers who encountered a corked wine and merely shrugged it off as just one of those things were instead to complain vociferously, the store would act so quickly and so impactfully that the cork industry in Portugal wouldn't know what had hit it. It is, after all, only the acceptance of corked wine as being 'in the nature of the beast' that we, or rather some of us, tolerate the situation at all. Certainly the store acted instantly a little while back when certain bottles of Italian wine on its shelves were found to be contaminated by a fungicidal chemical (but in such fractional amounts that you would have needed to consume, in one sitting, ten thousand bottles in order to feel any ill effects). All the supplier's bottles disappeared from sight rather soon after the discovery, and other retailers, notably Sainsbury's, Tesco and Safeway, also carried out tests (but apparently found nothing amiss). This was an irritating ripple of such minor proportions – leaving aside the somewhat larger implications for the image of Italian wine-making in general – that it left not a blot on the escutcheon of integrity that customers see as the M & S hallmark (the shield of St Michael indeed).

I read somewhere that in a 1994 survey of young people the store was more trusted as an institution than either Her Majesty's Government or the Church of England. Considering that it is also regarded by financial commentators as the nation's most profitable retailer (profits currently running at around £800 million annually), this is an enviable position. It employs over 60,000 people and has 285 British branches. But it also has a considerable number of stores in other parts of Europe (including France, Belgium, Spain and the Netherlands). It is likely to set up in Italy in the near future but probably not before it has moved into Germany.

M & S has been the acceptable face of capitalism for a long time. I am compelled to remark, on the evidence of my visits to wine producers in Eastern Europe, that without this kind of commercial culture in a modern society, without the wide participation of people in it either as producers or as consumers, many other things of wide cultural significance are smothered. M & S should expand into Moravia, Slovakia, the Czech republic, Hungary, Bulgaria, Romania, Moldova, not to mention all the states of the CIS, forthwith.

Fat chance. If the current wine shelves are anything to go by, on which at time of writing stands just one Eastern European wine (the 1990 Bulgarian Cabernet Sauvignon Svischtov at £2.99), then this part of the world has little attraction for the store either as a place to build branches or to find wine suppliers.

I have a suspicion, in fact, that this is another of the M & S religion's commandments. If a country has reliable suppliers, then it can surely produce loyal customers as well. It cannot, for example, be a coincidence that there are now seven M & S branches in Hong Kong after years of successful buying from suppliers in the region.

And now, as has been widely reported, M & S is contemplating moving into the Chinese mainland itself.

Mao is dead! Long live Chairman Marks!

Marks & Spencer
Michael House
57 Baker Street
London
W1A 1DN

Tel 0171 935 4422
Fax 0171 487 2679

SEE STOP PRESS SECTION AT END OF BOOK FOR LAST-MINUTE ADDITIONS TO THIS RETAILER'S RANGE.

ARGENTINIAN WINE RED

Trapiche Medalla Tinto 1991   15.5 D

Brooding class and style here. Throbs with flavour and fruit.

ARGENTINIAN WINE WHITE

Trapiche Medalla Blanco 1993   15 D

Expensive, but the wine has a subtle hint of smoke – almost like a malt whisky. Speyside.

AUSTRALIAN WINE RED

Capel Vale Merlot 1993   13 E

Fine Wine Stores only.

Coldstream Hills Cabernet Sauvignon 1990   11 E

James Halliday Coonawarra Cabernet Sauvignon 1992   12 F

Difficult to rate this £12 wine higher. Fine Wine Stores only.

Langhorne Creek Cabernet Sauvignon 1993   14 D

Quirky edge to the fruit. Has something individual to say for itself at least.

Lindemans Australian Shiraz 1993 | 13.5 | C

Flounces about like a young goat – gauche and uninhibited.

Lindemans Bin 37 Australian Cabernet Sauvignon 1991 | 16 | C

Has a fruity, digestive-biscuit heart to the lush, soft fruit. Lovely. Has touches of leather and yet manages to achieve massive drinkability.

McLaren Vale Shiraz 1992 | 15.5 | C

McLaren Vale Shiraz 1993 | 15 | D

A contented brew: savoury, dry, rich, very good with a pork chop. Pity it's not £4.99 but . . .

McWilliams Pheasant Gully Shiraz | 12 | C

Like cherryade – a bit.

'Rose Label' Coonawarra Cabernet Sauvignon 1992 | 15 | E

Gorgeously crunchy tannin edge to the ripe, soft fruit. Lovely mouthful of wine. Fine Wine Stores only.

Rosemount Estate Shiraz 1993 | 14 | D

Soft yet sharply in focus.

AUSTRALIAN WINE WHITE

Australian Medium Dry | 11 | C

Would work well with Chinese food.

Hunter Valley Chardonnay/Semillon 1992 | 15 | C

Hunter Valley Semillon/Chardonnay 1994 `12.5` `C`

Len Evans Chardonnay 1992 `16` `D`

Woody and rich, upfront and tasty. Very good with rich seafood dishes.

Lindemans Bin 65 Australian Chardonnay, 1993 `16` `C`

Balanced, elegant, full of fruit, which impinges on the tastebuds like crystallised melon and lemon.

McWilliams Australian Semillon/Chardonnay, SE Australia `15` `C`

Brilliant depth of flavour and crisp, tangy acids: melony, lemon, fresh. Lovely stuff.

McWilliams Pheasant Gully Colombard `13` `C`

Orange Vineyard Chardonnay 1993 `14.5` `E`

A lot of money but a lot of wine. Wonderful integration of fruit and acid wood.

Peter Lehmann Barossa Valley Semillon 1994 `12` `C`

Rosemount Estate Fume Blanc 1994 `13.5` `D`

Expensive – a touch. Sauvignon blancish – a touch.

Rosemount Estate McLaren Vale Chardonnay 1994 `13` `D`

Rothbury Estate Barrel Fermented Chardonnay 1994 `14` `D`

Excellent with moules mariniere thickened with tomato puree.

Rothbury Estate Chardonnay NV 14

Buttery-rich fruit, not overripe, with a gentle pineapple edge.
Delicious.

Rothbury Estate Chardonnay/Semillon 15 C

BULGARIAN WINE RED

Bulgarian Cabernet Sauvignon, Svichtov
Region 1990 15 B

Excellent fruit; balanced, dry, full and rather elegant.

CHILEAN WINE RED

Cabernet Sauvignon, Rapel 1993 15

Soft, highly attractive blackcurrants with a savoury edge. Terrific
roast meat wine. Dry, polished, classy and very approachable.

Cabernet Sauvignon Reserve, Maipo 1993 15.5 C

A touch of licorice to a dry, blackcurranty wine which will
develop excitingly over the next year or more. Rich style
without fatness. Very classy.

Maipo Cabernet Sauvignon Reserve 1993 14

Great, ringing fruit – like a clap of thunder on the tongue.

Rapel Cabernet Sauvignon 1993 14 C

Lots of flavour, not typical cab sauv but deliciously rich and
soft.

CHILEAN WINE   WHITE

Chardonnay Lontue 1994   `15.5` `C`

Rich-edged fruit, balanced and purposeful, Excellent grilled
chicken wine.

Sauvignon Blanc Lontue 1994   `14` `C`

Delightful breezy fruit with a touch of spicy gooseberry.

FRENCH WINE   RED

Beaujolais AC, Cellier des Samsons 1994   `12.5` `C`

Beaujolais Villages AC, G. Duboeuf 1992   `12` `C`

Beaune Premier Cru, Les Theurons 1989   `11` `H`

**Bordeaux Matured in Oak, AC Bordeaux
1991**   `14` `C`

Softer and less 'clarety' than many. Very attractive roast
joint bottle.

**Cabernet Sauvignon 'Domaine de
Mandeville' 1994**   `13.5` `C`

Dry fruit edged by exciting tannins.

Cabernet Sauvignon, Vin de Pays d'Oc   `14` `B`

Savoury dry fruit, rounded to finish. Superb roast food wine.

Chateau Cos d'Estourdel, St Estephe 1987   `13` `G`

Not a bad stab at making an Aussie-style shiraz. Touch
overpriced, though, at £19.99.

Chateau Ducru Beaucaillou 1991 `16` `G`

Violet-fruited touches. Lots of tannin. Great shape. Will be magnificent in 12/15 years.

Chateau Gazin, Pomerol 1987 `13` `G`

Chateau l'Hospitalet, Pomerol 1988 `12` `F`

Lingers on the palate less emphatically than the lost memory of £13 will linger in the pocket.

Chateau Pichon-Longueville-Baron, Pauillac 1987 `15` `G`

Brilliant in 10 years.

Chateauneuf du Pape AC, Les Couversets 1992 `13.5` `E`

Chinon Caves des Vins des Rabelais 1993 `14` `C`

Great typicity of the grape but soft and deliciously gluggable with it. Mail order only.

Classic Burgundy 1993 `11` `C`

Classic? Pshaw!

Classic Claret Chateau Cazeau 1994 `14` `C`

True classic claret at a very fair price.

Domaine de Bellefeuille Cotes du Rhone 1994 `15` `C`

Odd C-d-R in that the typical brambly/earthy fruit is enhanced by a ripe, rounded feel – a result of the method of vinification using whole branches instead of crushed berries.

Domaine St Germain Minervois 1993 `14` `C`

Lingering full-flavouredness. Great with casseroles. Mail order only.

Domaine St Pierre, Vin de Pays de l'Herault 1994

`12` `B`

Fitou, 1992

`13.5` `C`

Expressive. Of what? Oh . . . southern sun, dirty roads, grinning peasants – you know the sort of thing.

Fleurie AC, Cellier des Samsons 1994

`12` `D`

French Country Red Vignerons des Catalans, VdP des Pyrenees Orientales

`13` `A`

French Full Red, Cotes du Roussillon Villages (1 litre)

`13` `C`

Gamay, Vin de Pays des Coteaux de l'Ardeche 1993

`12` `C`

Good beginner's wine: no tannin, no acid, just gluggable fruit by the dessertspoonful.

Gold Medal Cabernet Sauvignon, VdP d'Oc 1994

`14` `C`

Flavour and depth.

House Red, Vin de Table Tresch

`12` `B`

Sweet as a fruit-drop and almost as endearing.

Margaux 1992

`13.5` `E`

Good, solid, classy stuff. Doesn't hit any high spots but it's an excellent posh dinner wine.

Moueix Merlot, AC Bordeaux 1990

`16` `D`

Aromatic, tarry, dry, blackberry and fig concentration. Brilliant wine.

Moueix St Emilion 1990

M&S have been up their old tricks taming the tannins in Bordeaux and the store has come up with a fabulous new vintage of their own-label St Emilion 1990 which is a gorgeously soft wine of beautifully rounded fruit with so little detectable tannin it bursts on to the tongue like soup, then coats it like chocolate emulsion.

Syrah Domaine des Truquieres VdP d'Oc 1994

Teeth-smashing tannins and depth of flavour. Rusticity and modern style in perfect tune.

Vacqueyras Domaine de la Curniere 1994

Lovely rolling fruit powdered by dusky tannins. Great with roast meats.

Visan, Domaine de Rastelet Cotes du Rhone Villages 1994

Brilliant lingering depth of flavour here. Fantastic classy Rhone with polish, purpose and real poshness.

Volnay, Maison Louis Jadot 1989

Some faint glimpses of class. Fine Wine Stores only.

FRENCH WINE WHITE

Bordeaux Sauvignon, Yves Pages 1994 13 B

Attractive partner here for shellfish.

Chablis Bougros, Grand Cru 1990 12 H

Fine Wine Stores only.

Chablis Premier Cru, Grande Cuvee 1990 | 13 | G |

Very full of itself. Fine Wine Stores only.

Chardonnay 'Domaine de Mandeville', VdP d'Oc 1994 | 14.5 | C |

Lovely combination of soft, rich, melony fruit with gentle citric acidity. Great style here.

Chardonnay Viognier VdP Coteaux de l'Ardeche 1994 | 12 | C |

Curious blend of two fat grapes. Not so much Laurel and Hardy here as Hardy and Arbuckle.

Chateauneuf du Pape, Les Courversets 1992 | 14 | E |

This is not everybody's cup of wine for it needs food (fish, chicken). Yet I love its earthy overtones and old-fashioned feel.

Domaine Laporte Sancerre, La Terre des Anges 1993 | 13 | E |

Tasty but possessed of a weighty price tag. Mail order only.

Duboeuf Chardonnay, Vin de Pays d'Oc | 15 | C |

Plump fruit, crisp acidity. Lovely bottle.

French Country White | 12.5 | B |

Gold Label Chardonnay VdP d'Oc 1994 | 14 | C |

Depth of flavour and style. Very attractive wine.

House White Wine, Vin de Table Tresch | 12 | B |

La Charmette, Sancerre 1993 | 9 | D |

Macon Villages, Rodet 1994 `13` `D`

Meursault Louis Jadot 1992 `12` `H`

Fine Wine Stores only.

Montagny Premier Cru 1992 `14` `D`

Very proper and purposeful. Lots of flavour and style.

Puligny Montrachet, Domaine Maroslavac-Leger 1991 `11` `G`

Rully Blanc, Les Thivaux 1989 `14` `E`

Delicious, refined, almost a treat.

Sauvignon de Touraine Domaine Jacky Manteau 1994 `14.5` `C`

Vibrancy of flavour and fruit. Very satisfying. Mail order only.

Sauvignon Domaine de l'Etang VdP d'Oc 1994 `13.5` `C`

Vin de Pays des Cotes de Gascogne, Plaimont 1994 `12` `B`

Vin de Pays du Gers White, Plaimont 1994 `13` `B`

Viognier 'Domaine de Mandeville', VdP d'Oc 1994 `15` `C`

Delicious example of the big hearty viognier grape. Real zip and fruit, style and flavour.

Vouvray AC, Domaine Pouvraie 1994 `15` `C`

Masses of flavour with a dry, honeyed finish. Great wine for Thai food.

Vouvray, Chateau Gaudrelle 1993 `15.5` `D`

Expensive but exceedingly tasty. Rich, not sweet, dry undertones of sour melon. Superb, classy, delicious. Stores and mail order.

White Bordeaux Matured in Oak 1994 `14` `C`

Classy and authentic. A really delicious wooded Graves-style wine. Great with shellfish and light chicken dishes.

White Burgundy AC, Caves de Lugny 1994 `13` `C`

Flavour and purpose. Good style.

GERMAN WINE WHITE

Deidesheimer Hofstuck Riesling, Kabinett 1992 `13` `C`

Put down for 5/6/7 years to let the petrol undertones blossom. Mail order only.

Rudesheimer Rosengarten Spatlese 1993 `13` `C`

Delicious aperitif. Mail order only.

ITALIAN WINE RED

Barbera del Piemonte `14` `B`

Bradesco Giordano NV `13.5` `C`

Interesting companion to spaghetti carbonara.

Brunello di Montalcino I Due Cipressi 1989 `15` `E`

Aromatic and rich – just like the price tag.

Chianti Classico, Basilica Cafaggio 1993 · 15.5 · D

A lot of fruit, dry and earthy, but packed with verve and vivacity. Terrific flavour. Great food compatibility.

Il Caberno Giordano 1992 · 14 · C

Subtle licorice edges to the fig and blackberry fruit. Delightful tannins underneath.

Italian Table Red, Girelli (1 litre) · 14 · C

Perfect pasta partner.

Merlot del Veneto Vedovato NV · 13 · A

Soft and squelchy with fruit.

Montepulciano d'Abruzzo 1993, Girelli · 15 · B

Delicious soft fruit, vibrant and cheering as a warm day and a plateful of cherries and raspberries.

Rubilio Casa Vinicola Calatrasi 1993 · 13.5 · C

Sangiovese Cabernet Sauvignon della Toscana, Villa Banfi 1993 · 14.5 · C

Has earthiness and softness yet the zip of the acidity wraps it up nicely.

ITALIAN WINE · WHITE

Bianco Veronese · 13 · B

Chardonnay, Vino de Tavola del Piemonte 1992 · 14 · B

**Frascati Superiore DOC, Estate Bottled
1994 Girelli**   `12` `C`

**Giordano Chardonnay, Chardonnay del
Piemonte 1994**   `13.5` `C`

Some flavour here.

Italian Table Wine, Girelli (1 litre)   `13` `C`

Pleasant, inoffensive, gently fruity.

Orvieto Classico 1994   `14` `B`

Tasty, soft, firm-edged, balanced, very good with complex salads and soups.

Pinot Grigio delle Toscana, Le Rime 1994   `12` `C`

**Pinot Grigio delle Tre Venezie, Vino de
Tavola, Girelli**   `14` `C`

Delicious: firm, fruity, balanced. A pretty aperitif.

Soave DOC 1993, Girelli (1 litre)   `13` `C`

Basic, fresh.

NEW ZEALAND WINE   WHITE

Kaituna Hills, Gisborne Chardonnay 1994   `13.5` `C`

**Kaituna Hills, Marlborough Sauvignon
Blanc 1994**   `14.5` `C`

Grassy – great with oysters.

**New Zealand Medium Dry, Averill Estate
1994**   `13.5` `C`

PORTUGUESE WINE RED

Dao Garrafeira, Caves Alianca 1989 16 C

Soft, very expressive fruit, elegant yet ripe and multi-layered.
Lovely spicy food wine – try it with curries.

SOUTH AFRICAN WINE RED

**Simonsvlei South African Cabernet
Sauvignon Reserve 1993** 12 C

Odd. Distinctly odd. It's an oddity spiced food will remove,
however, so don't be alarmed.

Stellenbosch Merlot/Cabernet 1993 14 C

SOUTH AFRICAN WINE WHITE

Cape Country Chenin Blanc 1994 14 B

Cape Country Colombard, KWV 1993 13 B

Cape Country Sauvignon Blanc 1994 13 B

**Craighall Chardonnay/Sauvignon Blanc
1993** 13 C

Madeba Reserve Chardonnay 1994 13.5 D

Madeba Reserve Sauvignon Blanc 1994 12 C

Stellenbosch Chardonnay 1993 15 C

SPANISH WINE RED

Costers del Segre DO, Raimat 1990 18.5 C

Blended specially for M & S (the merlot in the blend is not normal) and it is a stupendously perfect marriage (with cabernet sauvignon and tempranillo). Ripe, full, forward yet never showy, it has beautifully polished fruit and deep rich berry flavours of huge class. A great modern wine.

Gran Calesa Costers del Segre 1990 14 C

**Marques del Romerol, Gran Reserva Rioja
DOC 1985** 16 D

Superb vanilla undertones to the fruit. Great style. Lushness without yukkiness.

Penascal Vino de Mesa Tinto NV 14 C

Ripe and jammy with vanilla undertones.

Raimat Carretela 1991 15.5 C

Ripe, soft and very rich without being annoyingly ostentatious.

Rioja DOC, AGE 14 B

Modern, light rioja with gentle vanilla touches.

Roseral Rioja Crianza 1991 13 C

Mail order only.

Valencia Bodegas Schenk 1993 15.5 B

Brilliant vibrancy of fruit, depth of flavour, polish and bite. Absolutely smashing wine.

SPANISH WINE WHITE

Conca de Barbera Dry White, H Ryman 1994 `14` `B`
Value and flavour. Can't ask fairer than that.

Moscatel de Valencia DO `15` `C`
A Beaumes de Venise clone at nothing like a B-d-V price. Has marmalade aromas but thereafter it's all soft honey.

USA WINE WHITE

Canyon Road Chardonnay 1994 `13.5` `D`
Well, not quite chardonnay. There's also chenin blanc, French colombard and semillon in there.

Canyon Road Sauvignon Blanc 1994 `13.5` `D`

SPARKLING WINE/CHAMPAGNE

Asti Spumante DOC Consorzio `11` `D`
Usual sweet stuff.

Australian Chardonnay, Blanc de Blancs Bottle Fermented Brut 1991 `15` `E`
Delicious from nose to tail.

Blenheim Sparking Wine (New Zealand) `14` `D`
Austere, lean, clean, fine.

Brut Sparkling Vin Mousseux (France) `13` `C`

Has some decent biting freshness.

Cava (Spain) `15.5` `D`

Bargain. Light, stylish, elegant.

Champagne Chevalier de Melline, Premier Cru Blanc de Blancs `15` `G`

Superb depth and richness here. The height of fine French polishing.

Cremant de Bourgogne AC `15` `D`

Rich touch to the fruit, yet very refined over all.

Oudinot Brut Champagne `15` `F`

Bargain. Real elegance and class here.

Oudinot Rose Brut (France) `11` `F`

Prosecco (Italy) `15` `C`

Lovely, apricot edge to prettily balanced fruit and acid.

Rose Sparkling Vin Mousseux `14` `C`

An excellent value rose with a lilting touch of soft fruit to the well-formed fresh structure of the whole.

Veuve de Medts, Premier Cru Brut (France) `14` `F`

Tasty and deep without being overrich.

Vintage Champagne, St Gall, Premier Cru Brut 1988 `14` `G`

A mature, richly-edged champagne of class and style.

MORRISONS

They have some funny ideas at Morrisons. Can you imagine coating a corn cob with thick spicy batter and then deep-frying it? I thought I was chewing carpet underlay. But the platters of fresh shelled crustacea are still tasty (small portions available at 99p), the corned beef pie is refined (and sadly lacks its unique rationing era fribrosity), and the potato and onion pies are absolutely ace. But they all pale beside the five-pack of fresh-baked-on-the-premises jam-filled doughnuts. I sampled several of this store's gastronomic delights when I visited the company's brand-new store in Doncaster earlier this year, and the looks on the customers' faces as they compared the store's prices with those available locally, at Asda, Tesco and Sainsbury's, suggested that Morrisons will give each of its competitors a run for its money as thoroughly as it gives its own customers good value for theirs.

They like wine at Morrisons (not to mention possessing a broad and well-developed taste in beer and spirits). The store group's top six best-sellers are:

1. Liebfraumilch.
2. Lambrusco Bianco.
3. Soveral Portuguese Red.
4. Gabbia d'Oro Rosso.
5. Morrisons Rioja Tinto.
6. Hock.

Predictable, those whites. But the Iberian reds? This shows that the shrewd wine-buying approach of Stuart Purdie,

Morrisons' wine buyer, exactly mirrors the shrewd palates of his red wine drinkers, predominantly male. The Soveral from Portugal was a £1.99 bargain for a long time, now it's hovering around £2.20 and Mr Purdie is energetically trying to find a comparable red for the same sort of money. He'll have a hard job (he's got a hard job – he's doubled Morrisons' wine sales in the three years he's been working for them and he's done it single-handed, without so much as a personal assistant to call his own), but somewhere in the world of wine there lurks a soft, drinkable red packed with flavour which can be consistently priced the same as a packet of fags and Mr Purdie will find it. The red rioja, from the splendid Navajas family bodega, has also encountered a couple of irksome hurdles. It's crept over the three quid mark and the latest vintage (the '93), whilst well rated, is undoubtedly lighter and less rich to finish than previous ones. It really needed a great 1993 vintage to keep the faithful faithful and whilst it will retain popularity it will, unless a brilliant '94 redeems it, slowly drift down the top-sellers chart and may even drop out of the top six altogether. Such is the impossible world of the supermarket wine buyer.

Mr Purdie could have chosen a profession as a blindfold steeplejack but it was his feeling for a real challenge and a head for lows which brought him to William Morrison's and they were made for each other – indeed, like the legendary Cheesman at Sainsbury's, the magnificent Mount at Gateway/Somerfield, and the urbane Brind at Waitrose, the marriage of Morrisons and Purdie is as nigh perfect as these spiritual couplings can get.

What sort of people buy wine at the store? 'I believe,' says Stuart, 'that we cater for most customers – from students in university centres such as Leeds and Sheffield to the more mature drinker who knows his wines.'

He's pleased to report, as further evidence to support the above customer profile, that Liebfraumilch is under increasing attack as the store's number one best seller as other, more serious wines, are gaining popularity. This is a sure sign of a wine buyer attracting wine drinkers with a nose not only for a bargain but also for good wine.

What does he believe to be the special strengths of Morrisons' wine range? 'It isn't enough for us,' he says, 'to continually offer an interesting and varied range of wines from all the major areas as well as the developing wine-producing regions. We also always have available a good range of sizes in our popular lines and, of course, we pride ourselves on being price-competitive.' It is, Mr Ken Morrison the guvnor believes, important to provide the same wine in many differently sized bottles – where big sellers are concerned – so that the customer can always buy more for less. Underlying the whole Morrisons philosophy to trading is a simple mathematical formula (and not even Wittgenstein could reduce his *Tractatus* to a simple set of figures). This philosophy says that customers are a privileged species who should walk out of the store with the absolute conviction that they have shopped well and economically. Therefore, if a litre of Morrisons hock costs X then a 2-litre bottle of it should cost X times 2 minus a little bit. This is what adding value *should* mean rather than what it has come to stand for in the world of retail marketing which is often the tawdry, simplistic addition of fancier packaging wrapped around such horrific niceties as ready peeled and sliced carrots with a sachet of salt on the side at five times the price of the vegetables in their unscrubbed rawness. Value really means something at Morrisons because it believes that this is the fundamental tenet of its business beside which all else is secondary. It is true that more than one food and drink retailer has lost sight of this tenet and concentrated on fitting more lifestyle or aspirational objectives but while Morrisons does not entirely eschew this route – as is shown by the development of its Oven Fresh Pie Shop (selling sweet and savoury pies hot from the oven) and the introduction of on-site American-style shops selling popcorn, doughnuts and muffins and Flan Shops selling sweet and savoury flans – nevertheless the value is truly added by the prices being fresh and hotly competitive also.

Morrisons opened nine new stores in 1994 and the same

number this year. This brings the total in the chain to ninety. As for wine, 'We have,' says Stuart, 'developed the range in most areas, particularly France, Italy and South Africa, and all of them are performing well and showing above-average growth figures.'

Which countries does he expect to provide the most exciting additions to Morrisons' range over the next few years? 'South Africa and Chile will be of major importance from the New World. I believe Spain has some interesting possibilities too – if we can rely on respectable vintages. Southern France, I think, holds the best traditional European opportunities with some great value out of the Languedoc/Roussillon. New areas of Eastern Europe will include Moldova and, further afield, Macedonia.'

Aristotle was a Macedonian. Morrisons would appeal to the old syllogist – he could see an unequivocal bargain when it was under his nose, or in his glass, quicker than anyone.

Wm Morrison Supermarkets
Wakefield 41 Industrial Estate
Wakefield
West Yorkshire
WF1 0XF

Tel 01924 870000
Fax 01924 821250

ARGENTINIAN WINE

RED

Cousino Macul Antiguas Reservas
Cabernet Sauvignon 1990

Smooth, with a rich chocolate edge. Delightful drinking.

Trapiche Oak Cask Malbec 1990

Brilliant value: dry, classy, true depth of fruit and flavour. Great roast meat and veg wine.

AUSTRALIAN WINE

RED

Coldridge Shiraz/Cabernet 1994

Hanwood Estate Cabernet Sauvignon 1992

A deep, soupy wine of delicious softness. Not complex but effortlessly upfront and likable.

Lindemans Bin 50 Shiraz 1992

Lindemans Bin 45 Cabernet Sauvignon
1992

Attractive berry flavours and residual richness.

Penfolds Bin 35 Shiraz Cabernet 1992

Wyndham Bin 444 Cabernet Sauvignon
1992

Very deep and rich – like Pavarotti clearing his throat.

AUSTRALIAN WINE   WHITE

Coldridge Semillon/Chardonnay 1994   `11` `B`

Goundrey Riesling 1991   `13` `C`

Lindemans Bin 65 Chardonnay 1994   `15` `C`

Good as ever it was. Oily, ripe, balanced, very fruity. Lovely with grilled chicken.

McWilliams Hanwood Estate Chardonnay 1993   `14` `C`

A fruity chardonnay of innocence and charm.

Penfolds Rawson's Retreat Bin 21 Semillon/Chardonnay 1994   `15` `C`

Great clash of soft mango/melony fruit and pineapple acidity. Slightly exotic, generous, bold, delicious.

BRAZILIAN WINE   RED

Amazon Cabernet Sauvignon   `13.5` `C`

Interesting, highly drinkable curiosity.

BRAZILIAN WINE   WHITE

Amazon Chardonnay   `11` `C`

A touch confectionery-fruited and sweet to finish. Good soft wine for those looking to move up from Liebfraumilch.

BULGARIAN WINE　　　WHITE

Bear Ridge Bulgarian Chardonnay 1993　`13` `B`

Flavour here.

Debut Fume Sauvignon Blanc 1993　`13.5` `B`

Balsa wood flavouring to the fruit makes this curious – less so
with food.

CHILEAN WINE　　　RED

Cousino-Macul Cabernet Sauvignon 1989　`15` `C`

Entre Rios　`15.5` `B`

Richer and brighter than ever it was. A deliciously savoury fruit
almost Marmite-edged, and this rolls smoothly and effortlessly
over the tongue. Fabulous value.

Gato Negro Cabernet Sauvignon 1993　`14` `B`

Has a juicy middle around which a dry shroud has been
sympathetically wrapped. Great pizza wine (spicy).

Santa Carolina Cabernet Sauvignon 1992　`15` `C`

Lots of berried flavour which continues to be soft yet the tannins
are agreeably tasty.

CHILEAN WINE　　　WHITE

Entre Rios　`12` `B`

San Pedro Sauvignon Blanc 1994 `15.5` `B`

Delicious sauvignon character – good fresh fruit with undertones of ripe raspberry and melon. A perfect thirst-quencher.

Santa Carolina Sauvignon Blanc 1993 `16.5` `C`

Superb style of fruit beautifully balanced by the citric acidity. Huge style for the money.

ENGLISH WINE WHITE

Three Choirs Estates Premium 1992 `15` `C`

As good an English wine as you can get. Fresh and zippy on the tongue, backed by a faint echo of honey on the off-dry finish.

FRENCH WINE RED

Bourgogne Pinot Noir Vallet Freres 1989 `10` `D`

Cabernet Sauvignon, Chais Cuxac, Vin de Pays d'Oc `14` `C`

Soft, rich, fruity, dry. An excellent food wine.

Cellier des Dauphins Cotes du Rhone 1993 `12` `B`

Cellier la Chouf, Minervois `14` `A`

Excellent value, softly tannic, friendly wine. Daft price.

Chais Cuxac Cabernet Sauvignon `14` `C`

Deliciously approachable cabernet. Real class yet real drinkability.

Chateau Cantenac, Cotes de Bourg 1988

A far from indecent bit of claret at a very decent price.

Chateau de Lastours, Corbieres 1990

Chocolate edges to the rich fruit which is dry and complex. A balanced, full wine of depth and style, with a delicious length of flavour.

Chateau Saint Galier, Graves 1992

Dry, rich, mature. Hints at being more terrific than it actually is. But the fruit is sound and well structured.

Comtesse de Lorancy

Swirling black cherry flavours, rich, savoury. Terrific value.

Corbieres, Les Fenouillets 1993

Fleshy and softly fruity.

Cotes du Rhone A. Brillac 1993

Cotes du Rhone Villages

Some easy-to-swallow richness and flavour here.

Cotes du Ventoux J. P. Leon, 1993

Domaine du Vieux Lazaret Chateauneuf-du-Pape 1991

Expensive and not convincingly expressive of the region or the great name. It is very drinkable, however, and not unattractive – it's simply not complex enough for the £8.

Domaines Terres Noires Grenache/Merlot 1993

Pleasant. Faint touches of dirty-fingered peasant to the fruit.

155

Ginestet Bordeaux

Some typical Bordeaux austerity detectable here.

La Source Cabernet Sauvignon VdP
d'Oc 1993

Delicious blackcurrant fruit. Effective, forceful, great with stews
and casseroles.

La Source Merlot VdP d'Oc 1993

A richly endowed, mighty bargain. Lots of soft, gripping
tannins, rich meaty fruit, leathery textured. Great stuff for
the money. Will age well for at least 2/3 years.

La Source Syrah VdP d'Oc 1993

Rolling fruit of smooth texture and dry intent.

Le Millenaire Cotes du Roussillon Villages
1993

Is there an echo of chocolate in this warm, sunny red? How the
mind dreams when you get 11p change out of £3 for such a
fruity, dry red.

Le Vigneron Catalan

Can't grumble at this much reasonable fruit for the money. Also
in magnums for under a fiver – useful party size.

Louis Fontaine VdP des Pyrenees
Orientales

Margaux 1990

Medoc La Taste

Has some taste, ironically. And the tannins give it backbone
and savour.

Merlot, Vin de Pays d'Oc 1993 `12` `B`

Regnie, Duboeuf 1993 `10` `D`

Renaissance Buzet 1992 `14` `C`
Soft and rich. Delicious.

**Stowells of Chelsea Claret Bordeaux
Rouge (3 litre)** `13` `G`
A good simple quaffing claret with an agreeable echo of the dry,
tannic heritage of the region.

Tradition Coteaux du Languedoc `15.5` `B`
A new batch of this stunningly good-value wine has landed
and it's in fine form. Not as dazzling as last year's wine, it is
nevertheless still full of style and flavour.

Vin de Pays des Bouches du Rhone `13` `B`

Winter Hill VdP de l'Aude 1994 `13.5` `B`
Merlot and caignaine in soft, plummy collusion. Worthy rather
than exciting.

FRENCH WINE WHITE

Chais Cuxac Chardonnay `15` `C`
Full and rich and yet balanced. A really fruity wine for
the money.

Chateau Jougrand St Chinian 1993 `14.5` `B`
Depth, chewiness, flavour – great dry fruit here.

Chateau Saint Gallier 1993 `15` `C`

Delicious ripe fruit, very rounded and lush, with a fresh-ish finish. Very fleshy stuff.

Comtesse de Lorancy `13` `A`

Very fresh and breezy. Good fish wine.

Cotes du Rhone Blanc 1993 `12` `B`

Feels fruity. Rustic, plain and good, price apart, with fried fish.

Cotes du Roussillon Blanc 1993 `14` `B`

Terrific style for a white from this area.

Domaine du Rey Cotes de Gascogne 1994 `14` `C`

Lovely fruit and vibrancy, cool acids. Fresh, flavoursome and good value.

Domaine Terres Noires Muscat Sec 1994 `11` `C`

Domaine Terres Noires Picpoul 1994 `12` `B`

Gewurztraminer Preiss Zimmer Vin de l'Alsace 1993 `14` `C`

Much better! This label, from an excellent co-op, has been in need of improving and this vintage demonstrates greater vibrancy and concentration than before.

Ginestet Graves Blanc 1992 `8` `C`

J. P. Chenet, Cinsault Rose 1993 `9` `B`

La Source Chardonnay VdP d'Oc 1994 `14` `B`

A ripe fruitiness with a nutty edge. Excellent fish wine.

La Source Sauvignon Blanc VdP d'Oc 1994 `14.5` **B**

Flavour and fruit, style and zip – and nicely balanced. Excellent value.

La Source Syrah Rose VdP d'Oc 1994 `10` **B**

Laperouse Blanc Val d'Orbieu & Penfolds, VdP d'Oc 1994 `14` **C**

Rounded fruit flavours energetically supported by the elegance of the acids.

Le Piat d'Or `9` **C**

Interestingly, hypermarkets in the ferry ports put this under the foreign wines shelf rather than the French, and quite right. In spite of the brilliant lies of the TV commercials no Frog would be seen dead drinking this wimpish concoction – made for the British market. Morrisons is the only supermarket brave enough to send me a sample of this wine and I'm pleased it did. This wine has no character and little style.

Le Vigneron Catalan `10` **A**

Le Vigneron Catalan Rose `13.5` **B**

Softer flavour and fruit here.

Macon Villages Domaine Jean-Pierre Teissedre 1992 `13` **C**

Good stuff – excellent grilled fish wine.

Michel Lynch Blanc 1993 `13.5` **C**

A touch pricey and a touch musty.

Muscadet La Pantiere 1993 `7` **B**

Premieres Cotes de Bordeaux `13` **C**

Has some style. Good with hard cheese and hard fruit.

Rose d'Anjou Laverrine 1993 6 B

Rose d'Anjou Vincent de Valloire 1994 12 B

Toffee edge to the sweet fruit.

Terret Vin de Pays Lurton 1994 12 B

**Tradition, Gewurztraminer Preiss-Zimmer
1993** 16 C

Could this be the salvation of the gewurztraminer market? This
wine is brilliant, vibrant, complex, fresh yet exotically fruity
and full (with enough acidity to keep it fluid and rich without
cloying). A terrific £5 gewurztraminer. It has the weight to
accompany food (like complex salads) and the personality –
lively, talkative, quirky – to be excellent solo company.

**Tradition Pinot Blanc Preisszimmer
1993** 12.5 C

Vin de Pays Terret, J. Lurton 1993 13 B

Has a good old earthy edge to the fruit. Knock it back with
TV football.

Vouvray Jean Michel 1993 12 C

Sweet but not nothing: gently honeyed, rich-edged and good
with Peking duck.

Winter Hill VdP de l'Aude 1994 16 B

An ugni blanc and sauvignon blend masterminded by western
Australians near Carcassonne in Southern France. It is full
of flavour and style with a fresh edge to subtle rusticity.
Splendid glug.

GERMAN WINE WHITE

**Binger St Rochuskapelle Kabinett,
Johannes Egberts 1992** `11` `B`

Deinhard Riesling Dry 1993 `12` `C`

Humm. Neither fish nor fowl nor good with either. Pricey, to boot.

Deinhard Yello 1994 `8` `C`

**Flonheimer Adelberg Kabinett Johannes
Egberts 1993** `13` `B`

Delicious sweet-natured aperitif for summer lawns and picnics.

Franz Reh Auslese 1994 `12` `C`

Franz Reh Kabinett 1993 `11` `B`

A light Lieb-style wine.

Franz Reh Spatlese 1993 `12` `B`

Sweet but not entirely nothing. Grandma will like it.

**Herxheimer Herrlich Muller-Thurgau
Kabinett, Weinkellerei Klostergarten 1993** `10` `B`

Klusserather St Michael Spatlese 1993 `11` `B`

**Piesporter Gunterslay Riesling Spatlese
1988** `14` `C`

Another terrific aperitif. Hint of spice in this one.

Piesporter Treppchen Auslese 1988 `13` `D`

Piesporter Treppchen Kerner Kabinett 1989 | 15 | C

Delicious aperitif – or with smoked salmon.

Seafish Dry, Rheinhessen 1993 | 13.5 | B

Few wines are so well named that they do the wine hack's job for him but this is a rare exception. I can only add that it is also a good refreshing glug.

St Johanner Abtey Ortega Spatlese 1993 | 13.5 | B

Might be fine with a bunch of hard grapes and a hunk of hard cheese. Otherwise, strictly for the honey-dentured.

Stowells of Chelsea Liebfraumilch (3 litre) | 12 | F

As reasonable a proposition as you get with this beast.

Wiltinger Scharzberg Spatlese 1993 | 13 | B

GREEK WINE   RED

Mavrodaphne of Patras | 10 | B

This is basically stewed prunes made into wine. Probably rather good with Christmas pudding.

GREEK WINE   WHITE

Kourtaki Vin de Crete 1994 | 13 | B

This is firmly fruity, not flabby, and it goes very well with complex vegetable salads.

162

ITALIAN WINE

RED

Chianti Riserva Uggiano 1990 `15.5` `D`

Very elegant drinking. Soft, rich (but not overripe) character and real calm style.

Chianti Classico Uggiano 1992 `14` `B`

Flavourful, lingering, dry, controlled earthy fruit – a subtle edge of candied orange. Distinctive. Good value.

Chianti Uggiano 1993 `13.5` `B`

Dry – some weight of fruit but rather stringy. Good with pasta though.

Eclisse Rosso `14` `B`

Totally ripe damsons – never tasted them quite so ripe. Great with pizza and pasta.

Feyles Barbera d'Alba 1991 `15.5` `C`

A wine with delicious licorice hints to the soft fruit – but these are never aggressive. Delicious with cheeses or to drink solo.

Gabbia d'Oro `8` `A`
Ugh.

Grave del Friuli Merlot 1993 `13` `A`

La Casona, Bardolino Classico 1993 `14` `B`

Soft, ripe cherries, lovely to drink slightly chilled with all sorts of fish and meat dishes.

Montepulciano d'Abruzzo Cortenova 1993 `14` `B`

Splendid little bargain. Pizzas will love its softness, give and warmth – like an old woolly sweater.

Morrisons Valpolicella 12 B

Sangiovese di Romagna 13 B

**Vigneti Casterna Amarone della Valpolicella
Classico 1988** 15 D

Cloyingly rich, herby fruit with baked undertones, seems hardly
to possess any acids so smooth is it. Great with roast meats
with herbs.

**Vigneti del Sole Merlot del Veneto,
Pasqua 1993** 11 B

ITALIAN WINE WHITE

Eclisse Bianco 14 C

Some rich edge to the earthy fruit here. Attractive, easy
drinking.

Est! Est!! Est!!! 10 B

Gabbia d'Oro 7 A

It tastes like dilute apple juice without the fruit. I've tasted
bottles of this wine a year apart and found my notes almost
word for word the same so obviously the producer of this
miracle of mediocrity has found a formula and he's sticking to it but then the same can be said of a serial killer.
Ugly.

Orvieto Classico Uggiano 1994 13.5 B

Basic but excellent with fish dishes.

**Stowells of Chelsea Chardonnay
(3 litre)** | 13.5 | G |

Some weight to the fruit, and balance. A pleasant glug.

Trebbiano del Veneto | 10 | A |

MOLDOVAN WINE   WHITE

Hincesti Chardonnay 1993 | 12 | A |

Getting a bit creaky in the joints.

Hincesti Sauvignon Blanc 1993 | 15 | A |

Bargain. Bit poky on the fruit but a bargain fish 'n' chip wine.

MOROCCAN WINE   RED

Moroccan Red Wine | 16 | B |

Touches of Colombian coffee for this superbly rich, leather-touched wine which slips down superbly.

PORTUGUESE WINE   RED

Borges Bairrada Reserva 1989 | 10 | B |

Flat. Gone. Popped its clogs.

Dao Meia Encosta 1990 | 13 | B |

Dry figgy fruit. Good with grilled sausages.

Soveral Tinto de Mesa

Clodfuls of sock and fruit.

PORTUGUESE WINE WHITE

'M' Portuguese Rose

So much better than Mateus at the price and zippier in the fruit department.

Vinho Verde

ROMANIAN WINE RED

Cabernet Sauvignon Reserve 1985

For lunch one Sunday I decanted this 16-point wine and served it to a well-heeled American wine buff. He was bowled over by its lovely dry dusty aroma and fruit and he was touched that I had opened some ancient 5th growth claret specially for him. When I revealed its true provenance and stunning under-three-quid price tag, he admitted he wouldn't have been less surprised to learn that Sylvester Stallone was dating Margaret Thatcher.

Cabernet Sauvignon Special Reserve 1986

The '85 was quite a remarkable bottle. The '86 is not so deep and mature in outlook, nor so dry, but what it lacks in aroma and seeming age it makes up for with a biting vibrancy of fruit which is cherrified and delicious. Not a typical cabernet but an immediately drinkable one.

Classic Pinot Noir 1990   15   B

Brilliant cherry fruit, dry, bright and weighty without being overripe.

Pietroasa Vineyards Young Merlot 1994   14.5   B

Good with pies, tripe and even roast ape (if you read such omens into the vineyard's name). It certainly is a versatile young red with vigour and bite and lots of young fruit.

Romanian Cabernet Sauvignon 1985   16   B

Still brilliant old stuff.

Romanian Cellarmasters Feteasca Negra and Cabernet Sauvignon   13   B

Good value for food-related orgies.

Romanian Pinot Noir Reserve 1990   16   B

Lots of flavour and style here for relative peanuts. Has youth, flavour and oomph.

ROMANIAN WINE   WHITE

Classic Sauvignon Blanc 1993   13   B

Simple, fruity, refreshing. Not classic? Hardly. But fine with fish and chips.

Romanian Cellarmasters Chardonnay and Feteasca Regala   14   B

The perfect quaffer at this price and it even has enough fruity oomph to go with food.

Romanian Chardonnay 1993   14   B

Has nimble balance and good fruit.

Romanian Late Harvest Chardonnay 1985 `14` `B`

Brilliant with hard cheese and fruit.

SOUTH AFRICAN WINE   RED

Bainskloof Pass Cabernet 1994 `12` `B`

Fair Cape Cinsault 1992 `13` `B`

Fair Cape Pinotage 1992 `14` `B`

Better than most beaujolais and less money.

K.W.V. Shiraz 1990 `14` `C`

SOUTH AFRICAN WINE   WHITE

Bainskloof Pass Chenin Blanc 1994 `10` `B`

Fair Cape Chenin Blanc 1993 `10` `B`

Fair Cape Chenin Blanc 1994 `15` `B`

Fresh, fruity, a touch spicy and exotic (only a touch). Puts most dry vouvrays to shame for the money.

Fair Cape Sauvignon Blanc 1993 `12` `B`

Fair Cape Sauvignon Blanc 1994 `12` `B`

Stowells of Chelsea Chenin Blanc (3 litre) `14` `F`

Comes out bright and clean – here is fruit and zip and real style.

SPANISH WINE RED

Carreras Dry Red, Valencia 1987   15 A

A thundering great bargain: dry, fruity, balanced and flavoursome. Excellent pasta and pizza wine.

Corba, Campo de Borja 1994   13 B

Juicy fruit fun.

Jaume Serra Tempranillo 1991   15 B

Earthy, rich, fresh-edged, terrific.

Mosen Cleto Campo de Borja 1989   13.5 B

Distressed bottle possessed of an unreadable label and a useless weight around its neck – this sums up the generally hopeless nature of the presentation. Rough? It's indescribably naff. But the fruit inside is much in better shape, though it is very ripe and juicy. It will probably go well, decanted, with grilled hunks of tuna and black bean salsa.

Navajas Rioja 1993   14.5 B

A light, gentle wine which dances deftly without any exotic movements but is nevertheless, with its soft raspberry/strawberry-like fruit, very put-downable and friendly. Not for rich food.

Navajas Rioja Reserva 1986   14 D

Lots of vanilla-edged fruit. Soft, luxurious, delicious – hints of chocolate and wild strawberry – but this is a light airy assemblage in tone for rich food.

Raimat Abadia 1991   15 C

Truly delicious and stylish. Notes of savoury fruit, vibrant, bold, yet soft and characterful – true class for under a fiver.

Rioja 1992

Solana Cencibel 1993 15.5 C

Brilliant presentation on the label, as good as the fruit in the bottle: vivid, soft, flavourful, generous soft fruit yet dry, beautiful tannins – a superb wine.

Stowells of Chelsea Tempranillo La Mancha (3 litre) 15 F

A bright, cherry/plum dry wine of really good fruit, balance and a really attractive finish.

Torres Sangredetoro Tres Torres 1989 14 C

SPANISH WINE WHITE

Corba Campo de Borja 1994 8 B

Jaume Serra Macabeo 1993 13 B

La Mora, Moscatel de Valencia 15 B

Great fun! Liquid raisins laced with nougat ice-cream.

Morrisons Spanish Dry 13 A

Great value for large groups.

Solana Torrontes Treixadera 1993 10 C

Interesting, brave, but hopeless. It has an intriguing lemon sherbet smell but the fruit is poor value and spineless to boot.

Torres Sangredetoro 1991 `15.5` `C`

Licorice!? Very dry, starts well. Drink it in an hour – it fades.

USA WINE   RED

Blossom Hill California `12.5` `C`

Sweet and almost flowery.

Glen Ellen Merlot 1992 `15` `C`

Has raspberry and strawberry overtones and yet maintains a solid serious dryness. Delicious.

Sutter Home California Zinfandel 1992 `14` `C`

Shadow-boxes rather than walloping you with big rich fruit but with pastas (olive-sauced) this is an attractive partner.

USA WINE   WHITE

Blossom Hill `12` `B`

Blossom Hill White Zinfandel `14` `C`

A rose which is a truly delicious aperitif – like a dilute Dubonnet.

Glen Ellen Chardonnay 1993 `12` `C`

Not as greatly enticing or as exciting as it once was.

Glen Ellen Proprietor's Reserve Chardonnay 1993 `13.5` `C`

Rather prim, severely fruity, schoolmarmish wine (sit up straight at the back there!) which somehow manages to stick in the throat.

FORTIFIED WINE

Cavendish Late Bottled 1979   13 D
Raisiny and ripe. Suits cheeses.

Inocente Extra Dry Fino   16 D
Sherry, yes, but so dry it puckers your cheeks. Fabulously satisfying when it's well chilled and taken with grilled prawns. The mineral, flinty fruit tiptoes on the tongue like a ballet dancer on shoes spun from cobwebs. Remarkable value.

Rozes Ruby   13 C
A rich ruby with lots of flavour. Good with currant cakes.

Rozes Special Reserve   11 D
Nothing special. Too reserved.

Rozes Tawny   12.5 C
Mild version of the breed, good for putting in gravies.

SPARKLING WINE/CHAMPAGNE

Asti Spumante Gianni (Italian)   11 C
Sweet and peachy. Pour it over ice-cream.

Brut de Channay   16 C
This is an outstanding dry wine for the money (£4.99). It offers good balanced fruit and acid, neither overblown nor

sharp, and drops down the throat as smoothly as many an Australian sparking wine. If it was repackaged and the store ditched the hypnotically horrendous black and gold label, which is the only tarty aspect of the wine, it would go like hot cakes – which, incidentally, the wine will cheerfully accompany. Rock cakes, unsweetened, warm from the oven for afternoon tea, may not be as fashionable as they once were, but this wine is priced handsomely enough to spark a revival.

Cava Cristalino Brut (Spanish) `15.5` `C`

A touch, only a touch, of cava earthiness and restrained fruit, but the acidity's fine and firmly controlled and the balance is excellent. Certain hairy-chested men will wear the gold round their necks.

Moscato Spumante `11` `B`

Shaving foam in a glass.

Nicole d'Aurigny Champagne `15` `E`

Still one of the most stylish, serious champagnes under £9 around.

Omar Khayyam, India `12` `D`

Paul Herard Brut Champagne `13` `F`

Paul Herard Demi Sec `14` `F`

Not at all sweet but delicious and maturely fruity.

Raimat Sparkling Chardonnay (Spain) `15` `D`

Brilliant flavour here. Real class at a bargain price.

Seaview Brut Morrisons `15` `D`

Stylish, refined, and quite delicious.

Seppelt Great Western Brut   `14` `C`
Light and breezy.

Sparkling Deinhard Yello (Germany)   `12` `D`
Expensive, not very classy.

SAFEWAY

The obscene surge this year in sales of Krug champagne when, according to *The Times* newspaper, 'it was flowing in the Savoy Grill as bankers and lawyers toasted ... the glorious £8.9 billion engagement between the two giants of world pharmaceuticals Glaxo and Wellcome', took place against a general background of falling champagne sales. In the three years prior to 1992, champagne in the UK lost 28 per cent of its market and sparkling wine generally receded 23 per cent. 'It seems,' commented the British wine trade magazine *Harpers Wine & Spirit Gazette*, 'that when the bottom fell out of the champagne market in the early 1990s, there were no real sparkling alternatives to take its celebratory place, and the overall sparkling market will have to wait for the full recovery of champagne before it gains new ground.'

How does this concern us here, with Safeway? Two reasons, both concerning a Safeway wine. First, Safeway's Cava is a much better bottle of bubbly for the money than any bottle of Krug, and if only those City slickers drank it to celebrate deals we would all know we were living in a saner world, and, second, this wine stands as eloquent refutation of *Harpers'* comment that there were no sparkling alternatives to champagne available. The reason that the people who gave up champagne didn't turn to sparkling wine is not because they couldn't find a substitute but because they didn't want to touch any form of bubbles – the fizz had gone out of their lives and they didn't feel like celebrating any more ... period. Incredibly, for a short while last spring that Cava was on special offer at £3.99 a bottle.

The torpidity in the housing market is a concrete fact and the fall in the popularity of pop goes hand in hand with this;

both will be very long-term. It is only through the efforts of wine retailers like Safeway, who continue to keep (in spite of piratical interventions by that esurient clod the Chancellor of the Exchequer) sparkling wines at £4.99, like Cava and Australian Sparkling, that the fizz market as a whole has any attraction for the everyday drinker. It is this conspiracy between the customer and the supermarket which lies at the heart of the reason why the latter establishments now dominate wine retailing in Britain so utterly.

Supermarketing is regarded as a collaborative affair, precisely mirroring the Marxist view of history. Individuals count for less than do corporate policy and its implementation. Underlying everything lie mass movements – echoing the Brechtian notion that Columbus didn't discover America, he was merely the leading member of the crew which did; he was just one wave in a historical current. This is an attractive (and fairly important) theory of unspeakable dullness. A.J.P. Taylor, the Oxford historian who brought history alive for so many people during the days of black and white TV, would have spat in the theoretician's eye. It's a theory which makes *Hello!* magazine irrelevant. Stuff the film star, the theory says – who typed the script? Arranged the lights? Painted the sets? The hero is relegated to being historical spokesperson; or at best a mere respondent to deep historical shifts. Retailing at the level expressed by a giant like Safeway is surely all about such responses. And where the wine department of such an enterprise is concerned surely there is no room for individual flair. Isn't it all about running with the prevailing wind?

This is true and not true. Let Elizabeth Robertson MW, who possesses a distinctive mind of her own, explain. Mrs Robertson runs Safeway's wine-buying department.

'There are drinking revolutions taking place and there are technology revolutions taking place,' she told me during a conversation at that bastion of intellectual rigour behind Park Lane in London, The University Women's Club. 'The first thing that's happened is the revolution of the Northern beer and spirits races taking to Mediterranean food and drink. We've taken to olive oil and wine instead of beer and spirits. Modern processing techniques have made wines which fit with our simple, fruit-juice palates. We don't have to be brought up as we are with beer. We don't have to like something we don't start off liking. Wine has been turned into a flavour that you can enjoy from day one. Wine is increasingly going in this direction so money gets put in to do it better. So there are more fermentation tanks and better processing and universities teaching courses and graduate wine-makers full of bright ideas about how to make wine, and it all rolls on. The whole world is making wine in the new manner and selling it to all cultures. And the supermarket wine buyer is part of this revolution because he or she is part of the new commerce created to handle it.'

This new commerce very largely revolves around super-markets. And although Mrs Robertson recognises that behind this is a response mechanism triggered by mass trends she is quick to point out that the most revolutionary firework in wine retailing was lit by a single individual. Have we found our Columbus?

'Who created the sea-changes? The late James Rogers of Cullens. James was the first retailer in the UK to bring in wine from Australia, America and Eastern Europe. Everybody followed on from James. He taught us all. That's where Alan Cheesman got brave enough to do it for Sainsbury's. And let's not forget Adrian Lane of Tesco and Julian Brind of Waitrose.'

But just as we glimpse in those words a refutation of the Marxist historical view, and the *Hello!* magazine printing presses can recommence rolling, the other end of the see-saw lands on our foot.

'Supermarketing is quite a new business, isn't it? Retailing is one of the oldest trades going of course, but retailing as it's done nowadays is quite a new . . . science? And it is done that way because it's consumer-led. We are led by our customers.

We run most of our marketing systems on the basis of what customer research tells us we ought to be doing. And every supermarket is the same.'

But it wasn't an arid piece of customer research which gave Mrs Robertson her next insight.

'It's a curiously British piece of behaviour to be minimalist about what you buy. We're not like the Latins who are great displayers of wealth. We think we're cleverer when we've bought something cheap. We enjoy finding bargains. I think that's one of the pleasures of discovering bottles in supermarkets. Drinkers say to themselves "Aren't I clever? I was able to beat the system. I found something at half the price simply because it doesn't have the right label."'

It is, without question, these wisely wrought considerations which most shape the attitude of Mrs Robertson and her team of wine buyers. Look at the store's list of top sellers:

1. Liebfraumilch.
2. Lambrusco Bianco.
3. Minervois red.
4. Muscadet.
5. Chianti.
6. Bulgarian Cabernet Sauvignon jointly with Hungarian Chardonnay.

In spite of the honey-dentured, dyed-in-the-wool image this presents of Safeway's wine buyers, this is not how Mrs Robertson exclusively sees her customers. 'A large group of our customers are young and experimental,' she reports. 'We're big in the twenty to thirty age group. But we are also popular with another very large group. These are the "fifty-somethings" whose children have grown up and who have time to make choices for themselves.'

What does she believe that these two distinctly different groups of wine buyers see as the special strengths of Safeway's wine range? 'I hope they appreciate our flexibility. We buy, in other words, what we believe to be good, rather than buy to fill a huge pre-selected range.' I am not entirely convinced that this is altogether true, otherwise why are these customers still buying so much poor-value muscadet? However, it may be that the Hungarian chardonnay will continue to creep up the top-sellers list and eventually replace its Loire competitor. 'I also think,' adds Mrs Robertson, 'that our commitment to freshness is starting to get across. This involves our drive to put a vintage on almost every bottle. It is a radical new commitment to delivering the youngest, freshest quality to all customers every day. The vintage is a legal declaration that the supplier must be able to prove.'

This is an important initiative to my mind. Many non-vintage wines suffer periods when they are simply not as fresh, brisk and flavoursome (particularly white wines) as they might be because they are too old and they have not sold fast enough to enable the new vintage which will replace them to come on stream. If Safeway's idea in its purest form is to make a real difference to this sector of the market then it will mean only the newest available vintage will be sold and any of the old vintage not yet bottled will not find its way into Safeway stores. As far as I know other retailers have not followed Safeway's lead in this.

Safeway itself is very conscious of its place in the market and the competitive activity of other supermarkets and wine retailers. When I asked Mrs Robertson what was the most significant change in Safeway's wine business in 1994, she replied, 'It was our continual gearing up to meet and win the battles of increased competition. This competition came from the discount stores, the re-built high street chains, a re-awakened and brighter Sainsbury's, a busier and bossier Tesco and an increasingly confident Asda. We have responded with bigger and better promotions, deeper price cuts, our Wine Fairs, our case discounts and our discounts for volume purchases.'

The store also provided a new twist to the wine-in-cardboard debate. Be it in the 3-litre box or the TetraPak (like Safeway's excellent Australian Red & White), wine in cardboard has had to weather scorn from professional critics, but Mrs Robertson's department has come up with a new cardboard container which no one can beef about. It is a wine carry-case which takes six bottles and, when home, can be put on its side and converted into a wine rack. Buy any six Safeway wines and the case walks out of the store with you, free.

The wine department also removed all its wire racking, on the grounds that 'it is simply not where wine was bought from, no matter what people's fantasies suggest'.

More significantly, Safeway closed its least successful stores – numbering seventeen – and opened twenty-five new ones. 'Twenty-five new and beautiful stores,' in Mrs Robertson's own words.

I must say I would never have applied the word beautiful to a supermarket – even the odd one which wins an architectural award. But I would apply the word beautiful to Mrs Robertson because of the condition of her mind. She thinks more elegantly than any other supermarket wine buyer. I cannot for the life of me understand how this came about but there it is. Enjoy her thinking as represented by the wines on the pages which follow.

Safeway plc
Safeway House
6 Millington Road
Hayes
UB3 4AY

Tel 0181 848 8744
Fax 0181 573 1865

SEE STOP PRESS SECTION AT END OF BOOK FOR LAST-MINUTE ADDITIONS TO THIS RETAILER'S RANGE.

ARGENTINIAN WINE   RED

Argentine Syrah, Mendoza 1994 (Safeway)   `15` `C`
Sweet finish to the hugely plummy fruit. Delicious, rich, ripe.

Carrascal 1985   `13` `D`

AUSTRALIAN WINE   RED

De Bortoli Shiraz/Cabernet 1994   `14` `C`
Tasty, dry, rounded. Good food wine.

Eileen Hardy Shiraz 1990, South Australia `15` `E`
Hugely elegant and stylish. Deeply disturbing fruit.

**Hardys Barossa Valley Cabernet Sauvignon
1992**   `15` `D`

Hardys Barossa Valley Shiraz 1993   `14.5` `D`
Impactful aroma, fruit and finish. Has a dank centre which
holds the palate's attention.

**Hardys Nottage Hill Cabernet Sauvignon/
Shiraz 1993**   `16` `C`
Controlled soft spice laid on smooth blackcurrant fruit. Deli-
cious, firm, well-styled.

Hardys Stamp Shiraz/Cabernet 1994   `14` `C`
Gently spicy, rather obvious fruit, but the flavour gets it
its rating.

Houghton Wildflower Ridge Shiraz 1993 [14] [D]

Flavour and depth.

Jacob's Creek Dry Red 1991 [12] [C]

Moondah Brook Cabernet Sauvignon 1991 [14] [D]

Orlando RF Cabernet Sauvignon 1991 [15] [D]

Aromatic, rich, balanced, classy, dry (good tannins) and altogether sweetly turned out.

Penfolds Koonunga Hill Shiraz Cabernet 1992 [14] [C]

Getting pricey at over a fiver, this wine. Has lush sweet finishing fruit but not a lot of complexity.

Penfolds Organic Cabernet/Merlot, Clare Valley 1993 [14] [D]

It is delicious and it is organic (not always one and the same thing). The fruit is rich, soft, gently tannic but the price is a little skew-whiff.

Penfolds Rawson's Retreat Bin 35 Cabernet Sauvignon/Ruby Cabernet/Shiraz 1993 [10] [C]

Soft and rather expressionless.

Peter Lehmann Barossa Cabernet Sauvignon 1992 [14] [D]

Lush, sweet finish on the dry fruit.

Ryecroft Flametree Cabernet/Shiraz, McLaren Vale 1993 [15] [C]

A potently berried, jammy wine of great flavour and style.

Safeway Australian Red · 14 · B

A lovely wine for picnics (scissors needed for the Tetrapak rather than a corkscrew) and the fruit is sound, correct and satisfying.

Stowells of Chelsea Shiraz Cabernet (3 litre) · 14 · G

Rich fruit with earthy undertones. Has a long, meaty finish with a firm, purposeful balance of fruit and acid.

Taltarni Cabernet Sauvignon 1988 · 13 · E

The Magill Estate 1988, South Australia · 13 · F

Wildflower Ridge Shiraz 1992, Western Australia · 16 · C

Windy Peak Victorian Cabernet/Merlot 1991 · 13 · D

Wolf Blass Yellow Label Cabernet Sauvignon 1993 · 13.5 · D

Is this deeply fruity wine worth seven quid? It's a fiver's worth of flavour here, no more.

Wynns Cabernet/Shiraz 1989, Coonawarra · 14 · D

Rich and saucy.

AUSTRALIAN WINE   WHITE

Australian Chardonnay 1993, Safeway · 14 · C

Evans & Tate Classic, W Australia 1994   12   E

Hardys Barossa Valley Chardonnay 1993   15   D

Has a lovely coarse fruit edge. Great with chicken dishes.

Hardys Nottage Hill Chardonnay 1993   15   C

Rich-edged, sunny fruit. Great with chicken dishes.

Hardys RR Medium White 1993   11   C

Quite why Hardys puts its name to this dull wine is one of life's exceedingly tedious mysteries I have no interest in solving.

Jacob's Creek Semillon/Chardonnay 1993   13   C

Kingston Estate Colombard, Riverland 1994   13   C

Lindemans Bin 65 Chardonnay 1993   16   C

Orlando RF Chardonnay 1994   15.5   D

The essence of Australian white wine-making: bold yet elegant, fruity yet never overblown, this is turbo-charged fruit cruising at a comfortable speed which easily, in second gear, outpaces Old World equivalents at two and three times this price.

Penfolds Organic Chardonnay/Sauvignon Blanc, Clare Valley 1994   13.5   D

Tasty, fresh, decent. Touch expensive.

Quagga Colombard/Chardonnay, Western Cape   14   B

Has a rich edge and is convincingly structured and fruity.

Rosemount Estates Chardonnay, Hunter Valley 1993 | 17 | C |

Huge fruit (rounded, ripe, brilliant), great balance, class, style and price. Utterly delicious – a wine to love!!

Rosemount Show Reserve Chardonnay, Hunter Valley 1991 | 13 | E |

Safeway Australian Chardonnay 1994 | 13 | C |

Safeway Australian Dry White 1994 | 13 | B |

Semillon Chardonnay SE Australia 1994, Safeway | 13.5 | C |

Bright and sunny – with a gently lemon hint.

Wakefield Chardonnay, Clare Valley 1992 | 16 | D |

Bargain, snooty wine. Lots of rich woody fruit beautifully pinned down by an elegant acidity.

AUSTRIAN WINE WHITE

Lenz Moser Pinot Blanc 1992 | 14 | C |

Seewinkler Impressionen Ausbruch 1991 (half bottle) | 13 | D |

A burnt honey edge to the fruit which is aromatically attractive. Has some botrytis character (i.e. the true noble rot fungus has set into the grapes thus dehydrating them and enriching the fruit) but this is not hugely concentrated and you pay through the nose for it.

BULGARIAN WINE RED

Cabernet Sauvignon Reserve, Sliven 1990

Has a green vegetable undertone to the soft, jammy fruit. Odd but oddly attractive.

Bulgarian Country Wine, Pinot/Merlot Sliven, Safeway

Firm and fruity – sound style.

Cabernet Sauvignon, Suhindol, Safeway (3 litre)

Cabernet Sauvignon Svischtov 1991, Safeway

Juicy and full with its affections, this is a forward red of charm.

Estate Selection Cabernet Sauvignon, Svischtov 1992

Mature damson and blackcurrant fruit. Fruity, full, a great food wine.

Gorchivka Estate Selection Cabernet Sauvignon 1993

Individual, serious, dry, gently soft (yet tannic hints) and good with cheese and rice dishes.

Lovico Suhindol Cabernet Sauvignon Reserve 1990

Has chewiness and flavour in equal amounts. Decant it an hour beforehand into a wellington boot if you like, and the fruit flows like a torrent of velvet.

Vinenka Merlot/Gamza Reserve, Suhindol 1991   `13.5` `B`

Great with cheese dishes.

Young Vatted Cabernet Sauvignon, Rousse 1994, Safeway   `13.5` `B`

Ripe edge on the fruit gives it some charm.

Young Vatted Merlot, Rousse 1994, Safeway   `15` `B`

Brilliant, richly endowed bargain.

BULGARIAN WINE   WHITE

Bulgarian Country Wine, Safeway   `11` `B`

Chardonnay/Sauvignon Preslav 1994   `13.5` `B`

I am strongly opposed to this marriage – usually. This one works.

Rikat, Rousse 1994   `13.5` `B`

Crisp and fruity.

CHILEAN WINE   RED

Caliterra Cabernet Sauvignon 1991   `16` `C`

Dry, lovely dry blackcurrant fruit. Very classically moulded and finished.

Chilean Cabernet Sauvignon, Lontue 1994, Safeway
14   B

Attractive edge to the fruit. Good with light cheeses.

Cono Sur Pinot Noir Chambarongo 1993
12   C

Santa Rita Medalla Real Cabernet Sauvignon, Maipo 1991
13.5   D

Tocornal Malbec 1993
13.5   B

Sweet and dusky.

Villa Montes Cabernet Sauvignon 1992
14   C

Rich and delicious. Not vividly complex but good.

Villa Montes Gran Reserva Merlot 1992
14   C

Curious digestive cream biscuit richness to the fruit. Only a limited volume available.

CHILEAN WINE   WHITE

Aurelio Montes Winemakers Reserve Sauvignon Blanc, Curico 1994
14   C

Shows some class, fruit, acid and balance.

Caliterra Chardonnay, Curico 1994
17   C

Must be the finest chardonnay under £4 in the world. Superb balance of acid and demure fruit, taste and refreshment.

Santa Carolina Special Reserve Chardonnay, Santa Rosa Vineyard 1993
15.5   D

A great standard-bearer for Chilean chardonnays.

Villa Montes Sauvignon Blanc, Curico 1994

CZECHOSLOVAKIAN WINE WHITE

Czech Pinot Gris 1994 `14` `B`

Real pinot gris varietal character here: subdued peach edge (never overripe) and a dry finish.

ENGLISH WINE WHITE

Elmham Park 1991 `10` `D`

Estate Selection Dry, Sharpham, 1990 `13` `C`

Reasonable delivery of fresh fruit, sane and balanced.

Lymington Medium Dry 1991 `10` `C`

Pilton Manor Dry Reserve 1991 `12` `D`

A bit muddy on the front and a bit short on the finish. Rather expensive for the fruit on offer.

Stanlake, Thames Valley Vineyards 1994 `12.5` `C`

For a limey bottle, it ain't bad. Should be £2.25 but blame the Exchequer for this gross distortion, not the wine-maker.

Sussex Reserve 1990 `12` `C`

Someone farts in the glass just as you take in the bouquet but this is a minor niggle. Probably excellent with shellfish.

Three Choirs Seyval/Reichensteiner 1990   `13` `C`

Apple-bright fruit, developed and attractive, wrapped in wet wool, i.e. that musty feral aroma given off by a sodden sweater drying in front of the fire.

Valley Vineyards Regatta 1991   `13` `C`

Keen, fresh, dry – a grilled sardine wine.

Valley Vineyards Fume 1992   `16` `E`

Beautiful, elegant, stylish and clean with lovely fruit and a good structure. Will age well too. Selected stores only.

FRENCH WINE   RED

Abbayes de Tholomies, Minervois 1991   `14` `C`

Rich with savoury fruit (blackcurrant/cherry) and a husky tannic quality which stops short of being full-throated. This wine has a degree of class.

Beaujolais Villages 1994, Safeway   `11` `C`

Beaune, Luc Javelot 1992, Safeway   `10` `E`

Bergerac 1994, Safeway   `12.5` `B`

Gently tannic and savoury.

Bourgogne Grand Ordinaire, Bouchard 1994   `10` `C`

Bourgogne Pinot Noir 1994, Safeway   `10` `C`

Bourgogne Rouge 1991, aged in oak, Safeway   `11` `C`

Brouilly, Duboeuf 1992 `11` `D`

Chambole Musigny C. Masy-Perier, 1991 `11` `F`

Chateau Andron Blanquet 1990 `13.5` `F`

Dry and stalky, great tannins evolving.

**Chateau Canteloup, Cru Bourgeois Medoc
1992, Safeway** `13` `D`

Somewhat pricey compared to New World peers and somewhat
less full of fruit.

Chateau Castera, Bordeaux 1993 `15` `C`

**Chateau de Caraguilhes, Corbieres 1992
(Organic)** `13` `C`

**Chateau de Chorey, Chorey-les-Beaune
1992** `10` `E`

Chateau de Fieuzal 1992 `15` `F`

Superb rich wine. Great classic stuff.

Chateau Joanny, Cotes du Rhone 1993 `12` `C`

**Chateau la Tour de Beraud, Costieres de
Nimes 1993** `14` `C`

If you like grilled sausages and mash with onion gravy you will
like this wine.

Chateau Leoville Barton 1992 `11` `G`

**Chateau. Les Ormes de Pez, St Estephe
1991** `12` `E`

Lay down.

Chateau Lynch Moussas 1988   `12` `G`

Chateau Montner 1993   `16.5` `C`

It has a lovely earthy touch to delicious sweet fruit. Wonderful accommodating fruit.

Chateau Peymartin 1992   `13` `E`

Chateauneuf-du-Pape, La Source Aux Nymphes 1993   `13.5` `E`

Flavourful, expensive, rich.

Claret, Safeway   `12` `B`

Approaches a reasonable depth of dry, tannic fruit.

Corbieres, Safeway   `14.5` `B`

What a little cracker! Real tasty, soft-centred fruit shrouded in good, friendly, dry tannins. A very attractive package for the money.

Cotes de Duras Oak Aged 1992   `13` `B`

Cotes de Nuits Villages 'Le Prieure' 1992   `10` `D`

Cotes de Roussillon Villages, Safeway   `13.5` `B`

Earthy and boldly finished, this is an excellent bangers 'n' mash bottle.

Cotes de Ventoux 1994, Safeway   `13` `B`

Cotes du Rhone 1994, Safeway   `12` `B`

Cotes du Rhone Villages, Meffre 1994   `13.5` `C`

Domaine Anthea, Merlot, Vin de Pays d'Oc 1993, Safeway   `14` `B`

Startling depth of flavour to this organic merlot.

Domaine La Tuque Bel-Air, Cotes de Castillon 1993 `12.5` `D`

Not so lush and lively a vintage as previously. This has an austerity I am not convinced will soften in bottle over time.

Domaine Marbrieres, Faugeres 1992 `15.5` `C`

Lovely chocolate-edged tannins which briskly control the blackberry fruit. Excellent.

Domaine Richeaume Cabernet Sauvignon, Cotes de Provence 1991 `17` `E`

Powerful, forward, dry and complex. Blackcurrants brushed with dry tannins yet smooth and full. This is a lovely bottle of wine.

Domaine Roche Vue, Minervois 1993 `14` `C`

Solid fruit here. Tasty, rich, savoury, reasonable, deep. Excellent casserole partner.

Fortant de France Cabernet Sauvignon, Vin de Pays d'Oc 1993 `14` `C`

Like a bargain-basement claret of minor growth but startlingly major style.

French Organic Vin de Table, Safeway `13` `B`

Fruity, gently earthy.

French Red Wine, Safeway (1.5 litre) `13.5` `C`

This is the way to package wine! No corks – just a plastic screwcap. The wine is a good soft rustic red.

Gabriel Corcol St Emilion 1993 `12` `C`

Gevrey Chambertin Premier Cru 1990   `11` `F`

La Cuvee Mythique Vin de Pays d'Oc 1993   `14` `D`

Expensive but expansively fruity – and very dry.

Laperouse Val d'Orbieu & Penfolds, VdP d'Oc 1994   `13.5` `C`

The fruit has a somewhat namby-pamby attitude to the tannins. Needs time to develop in bottle (6 months or more).

Les Trois Moulins de Cantemerle Haut Medoc, 1990   `13` `E`

Margaux, Barton & Guestier 1989   `11` `E`

Merlot Domaine des Salices, VdP d'Oc 1994   `12` `C`

Merlot, Vin de Pays des Coteaux de l'Ardeche 1994   `12.5` `B`

Minervois, Safeway   `14` `B`

This is a juicier edition of the Corbieres, less earthy, more eager.

Moulin a Vent Mommessin 1994   `10` `D`

Nuits St Georges, Javelot 1992, Safeway   `10` `E`

Oak Aged Medoc 1993   `13` `C`

Impressive in a quiet way.

Oak-aged Claret 1993, Safeway   `13` `C`

Regnie Duboeuf 1994   `11` `D`

Sarget du Chateau Gruaud Larose 1992   13 E

St-Julien 1990   15 E

A special bottle of highly polished fruit for Christmas.

Stowells of Chelsea Vin de Pays du Gard (3 litre)   14 F

Delightful smooth fruit with flavour and balance. A lovely touch – a distant echo, really – of earth.

Syrah Galet Vineyards 1994   14.5 C

A handsome, rugged beast softened by rich tannins of some gentility and a warm, savoury finish. A delicious soupy wine for all sorts of lamb dishes.

Vegetarian Red Wine, Oak Aged Claret, Bordeaux Superieur 1992   13 C

Some herby, earthy flavour here but not very sweet-natured or quite as fruity as it might be. Needs another year to soften?

Vieux Manoir de Maransan, Cotes du Rhone 1994   14.5 C

Tasty fruit with a delicious hint of sweetness which does not dominate the essentially dry, earthy style.

Vin de Pays de l'Ardeche 1994, Safeway   14 B

Seriously drinkable, light and dry, cherryish and agreeable if chilled and drunk with grilled salmon.

Vin de Pays de Vaucluse 1994, Safeway   12.5 B

Modern peach/pear fruit of juvenile weight.

Vin Rouge, Vin de Pays Catalan, Safeway   10 B

FRENCH WINE WHITE

Bergerac Sauvignon 1994, Safeway `13` `B`

Blanc de Bordeaux Oak-aged, 1994, Safeway `13` `C`

Blaye Blanc 1994 `13.5` `B`
Dry shellfish wine. Good value.

Bordeaux Blanc Demi-Sec, Safeway `11` `B`

Bourgogne Blanc Oak-aged 1993, Safeway `9` `D`

Bourgogne Chardonnay 1994, Safeway `12.5` `C`
Grasps at flavour and just about makes it but the grip is loose.

Cabernet d'Anjou, Rose `11` `B`

Cavalier du Roi, Vin de Pays des Cotes de Gascogne, Safeway `13` `C`

Chablis Cuvee Dom. Yvon Pautre 1994, Safeway `11` `D`

Chablis Cuvee Domaine Yvon Pautre 1993 `10` `E`

Chablis Premier Cru Fourchaume, L. Javelot 1990, Safeway `11` `E`

Chablis Premier Cru Mont de Milieu 1993 `12.5` `E`

Chardonnay Aged in Oak, VdP des Coteaux de l'Ardeche 1992, Safeway `14` `C`
A solid structure of well-mannered fruit.

Chardonnay VdP du Jardin de la France 1994
14.5 B

Drink this in preference to Safeway's Sancerre. An altogether fruitier, more together, better balanced wine at less than half the price.

Chardonnay Vin de Pays des Coteaux de l'Ardeche 1993, Safeway
13 C

Chateau de Berbec 1989, Premieres Cotes de Bordeaux (half bottle)
13 B

Chateau de la Botiniere, Muscadet Sur Lie 1991
13 C

Chateau de Plantier Entre Deux Mers 1993
13 C

Chateau Haut Bonfils, Bordeaux 1994
12.5 C

Corbieres Blanc de Blancs 1993, Safeway
11 B

Cotes de Beaune C. Masy-Perier 1992
10 D

Cotes du Luberon 1994, Safeway
12 B

Rustic.

Cotes du Luberon Rose 1994
13 B

Pear-drops and cherries.

Domaine Bergerie Rose, VdP d'Oc 1994
13.5 B

Very good flavour to be found here. Good with salmon.

Domaine Brial Muscat de Rivesaltes 1994 (half bottle)
14 C

Waxy and honeyed and soft with fruit. Good with raisin cake.

Domaine de l'Ecu Muscadet de Sevres et Maine Sur Lie (Guy Bossard) 1993 | 10 | D |

Cauliflower overtones to an extremely overpriced wine.

Domaine de Malardeau, Cotes de Duras H. Ryman 1993 | 15 | C |

Delicious, undercutting, subtle grassiness to rich-edged freshness. Great shellfish wine or for solo drinking pleasure. Selected stores.

Domaine de Petits Perriers Sancerre 1994 | 10 | E |

Ludicrously overpriced.

Domaine de Rivoyre Chardonnay Vin de Pays d'Oc (Ryman) 1993 | 16 | C |

For the full description of this wine, see the entry under Somerfield.

Domaine du Rey Vegetarian White Wine, VdP des Cotes de Gascogne 1993 | 13 | C |

Layers of fruit.

Fortant de France, Syrah Rose, Vin de Pays d'Oc 1994 | 13.5 | C |

Flavour, style and bite! Good solid, pretty rose.

Gewurztraminer d'Alsace, Turckheim 1994 | 15 | D |

The unique taste of rose-rich gewurztraminer from Alsace. Powerful, rich finish of compressed rose blossoms. Great with Chinese food.

Hugh Ryman Chardonnay aged in oak, VdP d'Oc 1994 | 14.5 | C |

Delicious firm style with a serious edge.

J&F Lurton Chardonnay/Terret VdP d'Oc Sur Lie 1994 13 B

Jacques Lurton Rose d'Anjou 1994 13.5 B

Some real classy bite here.

La Coume de Peyre Vin de Pays des Cotes de Gascogne 1994 14 B

Zip with serious style. Drinkable, fruity, fun.

Laperouse Blanc Val d'Orbieu & Penfolds, VdP d'Oc 1994 14 C

Rich rolling elegance. Very attractive wine for grilled sole.

Macon Villages 1994, Safeway 12.5 C

Mercurey 'Les Mauvarennes', Faiveley 1993 13.5 E

Rather tasty. And you can't say that about many burgundies these days.

Meursault 'Les Grands Charrons' 1993 10 F

Montagny Premier Cru 1994 12.5 D

Muscadet de Sevre et Maine, Safeway 10 B

Muscat, Cuvee Jose Sala 16 C

Honeyed nougat on sweet raisin toast. Offensively fruity.

Philippe de Baudin Sauvignon, VdP d'Oc 1994 14.5 C

Good depth of fruit here. Has style and structure. Selected stores only.

Pinot Blanc d'Alsace, Turckheim 1993 `14` `C`
Soft apricot touches to the fruit. Delightful drinking.

Pouilly Fuisse, Luc Javelot 1992, Safeway `10` `E`

Pouilly Fuisse, Luc Javelot 1992. Safeway `11` `E`

Premieres Cotes de Bordeaux, Safeway `11` `C`
Tough to rate. It's too light for puds, too sweet for pre- and prandial tippling, and not acidic enough to go with other foods. Quandary.

Puligny Montrachet 1988 `10` `F`

Sauvignon Blanc, VdP d'Oc 1994 `13.5` `B`
Quietly tasty.

St Romain 1994 `10` `D`

Stowells of Chelsea Vin de Pays du Tarn (3 litre) `12` `F`
Sound but dullish – not a lot of fruit.

Touraine Sauvignon 'Les Silleries' 1993 `14` `B`

Vieux Manoir de Maransan, Cotes du Rhone 1994 `16` `C`
Complex, delicious, firm – this has character, flavour and style. Rich edge of baked fruit, subtle nutty background, brilliant with all sorts of fish dishes.

Vin Blanc (Domaines Virginie) VdP de l'Herault, Safeway `12` `C`

Vin Blanc Safeway (1 litre) `10` `B`

Vouvray Demi-Sec, Safeway `10` `C`

GERMAN WINE   RED

**Dornfelder Trocken, Rheinhessen 1992,
Safeway** `15` `C`

GERMAN WINE   WHITE

Auslese 1993, Pfalz, Safeway `12` `C`

**Bereich Bernkastel, Mosel-Saar-Ruwer,
Safeway** `12` `B`

Bereich Nierstein 1993/4, Safeway `12.5` `B`
Has some nutty qualities.

**Dienheimer Tafelstein Kabinett 1993,
Rheinhessen Organic** `13` `C`
Try it as a different aperitif. Yes, it is off-dry but it's wonderfully
mellow and orchard-ripe.

Gewurztraminer Rheinpfalz, Safeway `13` `C`
A model and inexpensive introduction to the grape but experienced gewurzophiles may find it too undemanding.

Goldener Oktober Red Orange `15` `A`
Great but not wine. Really vivid fruit fun for near-teetotallers.

Hock, Deutscher Tafelwein, Safeway
`10` **A**

Kabinett 1993, Pfalz, Safeway
`13` **B**

Summery and pleasing as an aperitif. It has a sweet finish.

Liebfraumilch 1994, Safeway
`11` **A**

Morio-Muskat 1993, St Ursula
`11` **B**

Mosel 1994, Safeway
`12` **B**

Has some slight charm.

Piesporter Michelsberg, Mosel-Saar-Ruwer 1994, Safeway
`12.5` **B**

Good aperitif.

Rudesheimer Rosengarten 1993, Nahe, Safeway
`11` **B**

Ruppertsberger Nussbein Riesling Kabinett 1992
`13` **C**

Chilled with smoked eels.

Spatlese 1990, Safeway
`12` **B**

St Ursula Pinot Blanc 1991
`10` **D**

St Ursula/Ryman Riesling 1993, Pfalz
`15` **B**

A very interesting German riesling. It has a lot of approachable fruit yet it's dry. Excellent – great oriental food plonk.

St Ursula/Ryman Scheurebe/Rivaner, Pfalz 1993 (Organic)
`13` **B**

GREEK WINE RED

Xinomavro Naoussis 1990 `14` `C`

HUNGARIAN WINE RED

Cabernet Sauvignon, Villany 1993, Safeway `12` `B`

Great Plain Kekfrancos 1993 `15` `B`

Freshness of fruit yet depth of flavour which is rather special and very endearing.

**Hungarian Country Wine Kiskoros
Region 1993** `16` `B`

All the gorgeous, savoury-edged fruit of the Kekfrancos grape – better than Gamay at freshness and yummy fruit flavour. A layered cake of a wine with a bitter cherry and almond fruit combo underpinned by the bite of balancing acidity.

Merlot, Villany Region 1993, Safeway `12` `A`

**Private Reserve Cabernet Sauvignon,
Villany 1993** `16` `B`

A great bargain! Stunning dry tannic shroud to the classy blackcurrant fruit.

HUNGARIAN WINE WHITE

Badger Hill Chardonnay 1993 `14` `C`
Fruit and freshness equally balanced.

Cabernet Sauvignon Rose 1993   14 B

Cabernet Sauvignon Rose, Nagyrede 1994, Safeway   13 B

Not as rich as previous vintages but still an attractive wine.

Chapel Hill Barrique-fermented Chardonnay, Balaton 1994   13 C

Flavour and style. Not bad.

Dry Muscat, Nagyrede 1994, Safeway   13 B

Amusing aperitif.

Gyongyos Chardonnay 1994   12 B

Not as lively as previous vintages.

Gyongyos Sauvignon Blanc 1993   14 B

Some attractive herbaceous fruit. More characteristic of the grape than the '92.

Hungarian Chardonnay 1993, Safeway   14 B

Fresh and young, a touch of apple or pear-drop fruit and acid-drop fruit. Sounds like a kid's sweet but it isn't. It's dry with a streak of seriousness that makes it a bargain.

Hungarian Country Wine 1993, Safeway   15 B

Lemons, pears and melons and a touch of zesty slightly orange acidity. What a brilliant little fruit salad of a wine for a silly price.

Matra Mountains Chardonnay, Nagyrede 1994   13.5 B

Some interesting fruit here.

Nagyrede Sauvignon Blanc 1994 `13` `C`

Curious soapy quality to the finish.

River Duna Pinot Gris 1993 `15` `B`

Typical soft-centred pinot gris. Lovely touch of fruit.

**River Duna Sauvignon Blanc, Szekszard
Region 1993** `12` `B`

ISRAELI WINE   RED

Carmel Cabernet Sauvignon `12` `C`

An interesting curiosity; dry and respectably clothed in fruit.

ISRAELI WINE   WHITE

Carmel Dry Muscat 1993 `9` `B`

Yarden Chardonnay, Golan Heights 1992 `11` `E`

ITALIAN WINE   RED

Bardolino, Safeway `13` `B`

Barolo 1990 `14.5` `D`

Gentle style. Expensive but has a gorgeous, subtle, licorice-fruit
finish. Lovely to drink just for the pleasure of individuality
and flavour.

Casa di Giovanni VdT di Sicilia 1992, Safeway   16 C

Hammy, smoky overtones to the new vintage (which is much better than the previous one). A really tasty, deep wine of style, flavour and wonderfully savoury fruit.

Chianti 1993, Safeway   13 B

Lost a little of its earthy grip, this vintage.

Chianti Classico Rocca delle Macie 1993, Safeway   14.5 C

A classy specimen. Controlled, but persistent, tannins shaping firm blackcurrant fruit.

Country Cellars Puglian Red, Le Trulle   14 B

Cheeky and flavourful though possibly too light for food.

Lambrusco Secco, Tenuta Generale Cialdini 1993   10 B

Merlot/Cabernet Sauvignon, Vino da Tavola delle Tre Venezia   13.5 C

Montepulciano d'Abruzzo Miglianico 1993   15 C

Lovely soft fruit at heart, cherries and plums, but there's a brisk dry edge giving it true complexity and depth. Bargain.

Montepulciano d'Abruzzo 1992   13 B

Rosso di Verona, Vino da Tavola 1994   13 B

Soft, squelchy and great with pizza and pasta.

Safeway Sicilian   14 B

Terrific little plonk at a terrific little price.

Salice Salentino Riserva 1990   `16` `C`

Sweet, cough-linctus texture – thick, ripe, delicious and brashly fine. Terrific with the Christmas bird.

'Salvanza' Sangiovese di Toscana 1990   `14` `C`

Delicious soft fruit.

Tenuta San Vito Chianti 1991 (Organic)   `13` `C`

Valpolicella 1993, Safeway   `12` `B`

Villa Pagello Merlot, Braganza 1993   `13` `C`

ITALIAN WINE   WHITE

Bianco di Verona 1994   `13` `B`

Gentle little thing. Might suit shellfish.

Chardonnay del Salento, 'Le Trulle' 1993   `13.5` `C`

Not as highly rated as once it was, this vintage, because the fruit is beginning to crumble – it's getting too old.

Chardonnay del Triveneto 1993, Safeway   `14` `B`

Excellent balance and varietal character.

Frascati Superiore 1994, Safeway   `13.5` `C`

Not a bad frascati as these things go. And this example should go very nicely with a fish stew.

Frascati Superiore Secco 1994, Safeway   `12` `C`

Good flavour here.

Grave del Friuli Pinot Grigio 1994 `13.5` `C`

Nice creamy almond undertones.

Grave del Fruili Pinot Grigio 1993 `15` `C`

'I Frari' Bianca di Custoza Santi 1992 `13` `C`

Lambrusco Rose, Safeway `10` `B`

Lambrusco Rosso, Safeway `11` `B`

With the Christmas turkey, the sensorily infirm and the sweet-toothed will find this red most agreeable.

Lambrusco, Safeway `10` `B`

Sweet and peachy for total beginners.

**'Le Monferrine' Chardonnay del Piemonte
1993** `12` `C`

Le Monferrine, Moscato d'Asti 1994 `13` `B`

Semi-sparkling, sweet, apricoty. Lovely aperitif in the torrid summer months.

Lugana Santi, 1994 `14` `C`

Classy, clean fruit. Great with poached fish dishes.

Orvieto Classico Secco 1994, Safeway `13` `C`

Nutty, attractive finish to the fruit.

Pinot Grigio del Triveneto 1994, Safeway `12` `C`

Riva Trebbiano di Romagna 1993 `13` `B`

Sicilian Dry, Safeway `11` `B`

Soave 1993, Safeway `11` `B`

MOLDOVAN WINE WHITE

Hincesti Feteasca 1993 `14` `B`

Hincesti Premium Chardonnay 1993 `14` `B`

Kirkwood Chardonnay, Moldova 1994 `14` `B`
Drink chilled with fish.

MORAVIAN WINE WHITE

Czech Country Wine, Moravia 1994 `13.5` `B`
Some nutty undertoned flavour here.

MOROCCAN WINE RED

Domaine Sapt Inour `11` `B`

NEW ZEALAND WINE WHITE

**Millton Vineyard Barrel-fermented
Chardonnay, Gisborne 1994** `13.5` `E`
Expensive but rich-edged. Not as crisp as previous vintages.

Millton Vineyard, Chardonnay 1992   14.5 E
Deep rich fruit and flavour.

**Millton Vineyard Chardonnay/Semillon
1993 (Organic)**   14 C

Montana Chardonnay 1992   13 C

**Montana Sauvignon Blanc, Marlborough
1993**   15 C
Outstanding herbaceousness on the nose, great fruit on the palate.

**Stowells of Chelsea New Zealand
Sauvignon Blanc (3 litre)**   13.5 G
Keen, grassy aromas, good fruit, rather a quiet finish.

Timara Dry White 1994   14 C
Grassy and keenly fruited. Lovely shellfish wine.

PORTUGUESE WINE   RED

Alentejo Vinho do Monte 1992   13.5 D

Bairrada 1991, Safeway   12 C
Dry, brusque, rather crusty.

Duque de Viseu, Dao 1991   14 C
Ripe, stylish, full of flavour.

Falua Ribatejo 1993, Safeway   14.5 B
Straightforward fruit, fresh and fruity with an underlying earthy elegance reminiscent of soft chianti. Excellent drinking wine for the occasions which simply celebrate living.

210

SAFEWAY

Joao Pires Tinto da Anfora, Alentejo 1990 `13` `D`
Soft and very juicy.

**Quinta da Pancas Cabernet Sauvignon
1991** `13.5` `D`

PORTUGUESE WINE   WHITE

**Bright Brothers Fernao Pires/Chardonnay,
Ribatejo 1994** `13` `C`

Falcoaria Almeirim VQPRD 1991 `15` `C`

**Joao Pires Dry Muscat Terras do
Sado 1991** `14` `C`

Sogrape Bairrada Reserva 1991 `15` `C`

**Terre de Lobos Vinho Regionale Ribatejo
1992** `14` `B`

ROMANIAN WINE   RED

Romanian Pinot Noir 1989, Safeway `16` `B`
Brilliant, just brilliant.

**Special Reserve Cabernet Sauvignon,
Suhindol 1986, Safeway** `14` `C`
Curiously the bright, jammy edge of this wine does not detract
from its serious fruitiness.

SOUTH AFRICAN WINE   RED

Kanonkop Kadette, Stellenbosch 1993   `14` `D`

Has a prim side which belies the ability of this wine to throw
itself at food and dance wildly with it.

Kleindal Pinotage, Robertson 1993   `16.5` `C`

Quagga Cinsault/Cabernet Sauvignon, Breede River Valley 1995   `15` `F`

By a touch, not as vibrant or rounded as previous vintages but
this is still a brilliantly fruity bargain.

Simonsvlei Pinotage Reserve, Paarl 1993   `12` `C`

Aromatic, leathery and even a touch boot-polishy. Odd beast.

Simonsvlei Shiraz Reserve, Paarl 1993   `15` `C`

Wobbles with fruit like a blackberry blancmange – but much
drier and fiercer. Superb wine for roast and grilled meats.

Stellenzicht Merlot, Stellenbosch 1992   `13` `C`
Sweet and simple.

SOUTH AFRICAN WINE   WHITE

Boschendal Chardonnay, Franschoek 1994   `15.5` `D`

Very elegant, finely cut, mature yet youthful. A strikingly quiet
yet delicious, authoritative wine.

Colombard 1994, Robertson, Safeway   `14` `B`

Fruity (pears and peaches) and keen.

Danie de Wet Chardonnay Sur Lie, Robertson 1993
`15` `D`

Excellent style, elegance and restrained power. Citrus bitter fruit. Well-structured.

Namaqua Dry (Wine in a Box) (3 litre)
`15` `F`

Modern style, full of ripe fruit. Terrific freshness, too, so it's good for thirsts as well as being good for fish.

Roodevallei Dry NV
`15.5` `B`

Fleshy yet fresh. Lots of fruit yet stylish. Hugely drinkable. Great stuff.

Sauvignon Blanc Vredendal 1994
`14` `B`

Not as brilliant as last year's superb wine, but still a very attractive tipple.

Van Loveren Colombar/Chardonnay, Robertson 1994
`13` `C`

Selected stores only.

SPANISH WINE   RED

Agramont Tempranillo/Cabernet, Navarra 1990
`14.5` `C`

Glorious lingering finish. Lots of flavour to the fruit, which hangs on for grimly delicious death.

Carinena 1988 Safeway
`12` `B`

Castilla de Sierra Rioja Crianza 1992, Safeway
`15` `C`

Lovely, creamy, vanilla edge to the fruit. Sinfully gluggable.

Cosme Palacio y Hermanos, Rioja 1991 | 14.5 | C

Little of the old wood or overwrought vanilla edging to the fruit of this plummy, smooth, delicious wine.

Don Darias | 15 | B

The Old Don seems a bit thinner than when I last encountered him but he's still hale and hearty and full of vanilla-ey fruit.

Faustino V, Rioja Reserva 1989 | 15 | D

Big, brassy, bold – bruisingly fruity, full, yet not overdone.

Stowells of Chelsea Tempranillo (3 litre) | 15 | F

A bright, cherry/plum dry wine of really good fruit, balance and a really attractive finish.

Valdepenas Aged in Oak Reserva 1987, Safeway | 13 | B

Vilamar Jumilla 1994 | 13 | B

Earthy intensity. Good bruising fruit.

Vina Albali Cabernet Sauvignon, Valdepenas 1991 | 13.5 | D

Very good but £2.50 more than it should be.

Vina Albali Tempranillo, Valdepenas 1994 | 16 | B

Bargain by a long chalk – the delicious dusky edge of which (tannins) cloaks the fruit most impressively. Superb food wine.

Vino de Valencia, Safeway | 13 | B

Good, sound, dry, fruity stuff.

Young Vatted Tempranillo 1993, La Mancha `17` `B`

Out-beaujolais's beaujolais raspberry-soft aromatic fruit of massive quaffability. Makes the tastebuds hum with pleasure.

SPANISH WINE WHITE

Agramont Viura Chardonnay, Navarra 1994 `14.5` `C`

Lashings of flavour, gently buttered.

La Mancha 1993, Safeway `13` `B`

Moscatel de Valencia, Safeway `16` `B`

Still brilliant value. Glorious, subtly marmalade and honey fruit.

Valencia, Aged in Oak 1993, Safeway `15` `B`

Vina Ardanza Rioja Reserva 1989 `10` `D`

Amazing old-fashioned woody rioja.

Vinas del Vero Chardonnay Barrel fermented, Somontano 1991 `13` `D`

Vino de Valencia Dry, Safeway `14` `A`

USA WINE RED

Brook Hollow Californian Red `14` `B`

Perfectly formed and fruity. Stylish, not overrich or brutal.

Fetzer Zinfandel 1993

Big, bouncy, blissful – soft, sweet (in the most delightfully fruity way) yet dry to finish, with controlled spiciness. Gently exotic and lithe, this is a delicious wine.

USA WINE   WHITE

Californian White, Safeway

Brilliant sunny fruit and biting acid. Full of flavour yet refreshing.

Stoneybrook Chardonnay 1992

A bargain under a fiver. Has weight and class, oily fruit and acidic balance. Delicious.

WELSH WINE   WHITE

Cariad Gwin da o Gymru 1991

FORTIFIED WINE

10 Year Old Tawny Port, Safeway

Rather sweet and one-dimensional.

Bowmans Reserve Tawny Port

Nothing like real tawny from Portugal but helps to make a good sauce for roast game birds.

Cream of Cream Sherry, Pedro Ximenez   15 E

This is as thick as engine oil and as rich as figs and custard with demerara sugar on top.

Cream Sherry, Safeway   13 C

Fruity and thick.

Fino Sherry, Safeway   14 C

An oily, nervously fruity fino not of such austere dryness that it comes across as mean. Good with grilled prawns and ham.

Fonseca Guimaraens 1978   12 G

Gonzales Byass Matusalem Muy Viejo Oloroso   15 G

Like boot polish and brandy.

Graham's Crusted, bottled 1987   14.5 G

Graham's LBV 1986   13 F

Delicious blue-cheese port.

LBV 1987, Safeway   12 D

Lustau Manzanilla Sherry (half bottle)   14 B

Very dry and camomile-tinged. Aperitif (of course) – for lovers of the stuff.

Lustau Mature Cream Sherry (half bottle)   15 B

A wonderfully rich, treacly tipple to set alight family reunions.

Lustau Old Amontillado Sherry (half bottle)   14 B

Goes with unlit pipes, Hush Puppies and unreadable Greek love poetry. If you can supply these props, this wine is delicious.

Lustau Old Dry Oloroso Sherry (half bottle) `14` `B`

To be drunk with nuts.

Ruby Port, Safeway `12` `D`

Sound, very sound.

Safeway LBV 1988 `12` `D`

Not as complex as some examples at the same price.

Taylors LBV 1989 `13` `F`

Flavour, yes – but not as fulsome as it has been.

Vintage Character Port, Safeway `12.5` `D`

Dry, rich.

Warres Warrior Vintage Character Port `16` `E`

Rich ripe fruit with a lovely rounded flavour. Very attractive depth with vinosity. Delicious.

SPARKLING WINE/CHAMPAGNE

Albert Etienne Brut, Safeway `12` `G`

Albert Etienne Rose, Safeway `13` `F`

Albert Etienne, Safeway `13` `F`

Albert Etienne Vintage Brut, 1989, Safeway `12` `G`

Asti Spumante, Safeway `11` `C`

Sweet and unadventurous – but then some women marry men like that.

Australian Sparkling, Safeway `15` `D`
Firmly fruity and keen. Excellent value.

Blanquette de Limoux, Bernard Delmas (Organic) `13` `D`
An organic sparkler full of delicious peachy/nutty fruit.

Bollinger Special Cuvee Brut `12` `H`
Over twenty quid is it worth it? I wish I could provide a whole-hearted yes in spite of Bollinger's very particular dry charms.

Cava, Safeway `17` `C`
Delicious fruit and fine acidity. Has flavour and yet refreshes. One of the most delicate, least earthy, most satisfyingly delicious cavas on sale.

Cava Brut, Safeway `13` `F`
Buy it for the style and the big fat magnum.

Chardonnay Spumante Brut, Safeway `12` `D`
Not exciting. Sound, but not exciting.

Chartogne-Taillet Champagne Brut `13` `G`

Cremant d'Alsace Brut (J. Keller) `13` `D`

Cremant de Bourgogne Brut, Safeway `13` `D`

Cuvee Napa, USA `13.5` `E`

Freixenet Cordon Negro Brut Cava `13` `D`

Heritage English Sparkling Brut `14` `E`
Thoroughly well-made, decent, subtly citric bubbly. Shock the Frogs with it.

'Le Baron de Monceny' Chardonnay Brut, Blanc de Blancs

`12` `D`

Lindauer Brut, New Zealand

`13.5` `D`

Lionel Derens Champagne Brut

`15` `E`

A dry but fruity champagne, without the intimidating acidity of the classic brut examples, this is a very satisfying tipple and under £9 a good price.

Maison la Motte Chardonnay 1992

`14` `E`

Lovely peachy touch to acids.

Moscato Spumante, Safeway

`12` `C`

Very fruity and sweet-edged.

Saumur Brut, Safeway

`14` `D`

Has a depth of flavour of some class.

SAINSBURY'S

This is the only supermarket upon whose wine department the good Lord looks down benignly – and often. Lord Sainsbury retired a little while back but his love of wine keeps him in touch with his old boys and girls and he takes a keen interest in what they get up to. 'He's as obsessed,' a Sainsbury wine buyer told me earlier this year, reducing her voice to a whisper as if she was about to impart a significant indiscretion, 'as you are when it comes to value for money.' Ennobling grocers and sticking them in the House of Lords is patently a worthwhile pursuit. Indeed, it would make great sense to disqualify all other categories of businessmen and women; and while we're at it let's also disbar politicians, civil servants, diplomats and all the other fart catchers. Membership of the House of Lords should be restricted by edict to retailers (Arise Lord Kwik Save!), entertainers (Lady Dawn French – don't you love the sound of it?), chefs and restaurateurs (Lord Ladenis – has a ring), pavement artists and poets (Lady Wendy Cope!), teachers (Good morning, miss – I mean your ladyship) and sports persons (and in lane one it's Lord Linford going like a steam train!). The musty anachronism presently mouldering by the Thames might begin to make a positive contribution to the lifeblood of this country were it to be so reconstituted.

It cannot be doubted that Sainsbury's makes a positive contribution to the lifeblood of this country, for several million people a week shop there and one in seven of the bottles of wine bought annually in this country has crossed a Sainsbury's check-out. (You don't actually need to visit the store to buy the wine. This year, Sainsbury's became the first of the big girls to offer wines

221

for sale on the Internet. Forty wines are available and Sainsbury's home page access ID is http://www.j-sainsbury.co.uk.)

Is Sainsbury's now the world's number one wine retailer? Or has Tesco, now ahead of Sainsbury's as the nation's number one grocer as reckoned on value of turnover, pipped it? Neither outfit will give me the figures which would decide the matter either way. However, there is certainly justification for considering Sainsbury's as one of the world's top handful of wine retailers not only on the grounds of the number of bottles sold but also taking into consideration the quality, variety and innovativeness of many of these bottles and the way its wine department has been traditionally staffed and managed.

The store has come a long way since 1962 when its Weybridge branch was the only one with an alcohol licence (and had had one since 1920). Now there are 355 Sainsbury's supermarkets and a dozen Savacentre hypermarkets with an off-licence and the range runs to 650 wines, 270 beers, and 200 different sorts of spirits. Its Calais store, the first one in a ferryport by a UK supermarketeer, flogged a million bottles of booze in its first year of business which ended last April (with Bergerac Blanc going there for 83 pence a bottle I'm surprised that sales figure isn't higher). The company also will have opened twelve new branches plus two hypermarkets by the end of the year.

Precise sales statistics for the United Kingdom are guarded jealously (for some reason) and Sainsbury's competitors are, Asda excepted, just as protective when you ask them (nicely). However, Sainsbury's does admit to a market share of the off-trade wine market of around 18 per cent. I estimate that the company gets through around an average of more than 2.5 million bottles of non-beer booze (wines and spirits) *each week*. Of ordinary red and white table wine, I reckon Sainsbury's probably sells around 90 million bottles a year. Even if my figures are only half right, it is easy to appreciate why the store's buyers need to be such canny negotiators; a fraction of a penny on a bottle here, a tiny percentage of a franc off a case there, and it adds up to mountains of moolah.

Just who buys wine at Sainsbury's is a philosophical question; that is, the question may be put but the answer may not arrive. Claire Gordon-Brown MW, who used to be Sainsbury's champagne buyer but now concentrates on marketing and product development, says that 'Our customers vary from the completely novice, unfamiliar wine drinker to the confident and the knowledgeable – the latter two characteristics not necessarily to be found in the same people.'

For a long while other retailers regarded Sainsbury's as the university of wine (certainly this was how a generous member of the wine department of a rival retailer so described it to me) on the grounds that if there were vacancies in their own departments which could not be internally filled, then the immediate thought was how someone from Sainsbury's could be poached for the job. I doubt this is as true as it once was. Other retailers, Tesco and Safeway in particular, are neck and neck with Sainsbury's in many respects and have some first-rate wine-buying personnel. With six active buyers (plus two marketing people) under a manager, and above him a hands-on director, no retailer has a department with more depth and width.

The store's top six bestsellers are:

1. Own-label Liebfraumilch.
2. Own-label Lambrusco Bianco.
3. Own-label Muscadet.
4. Own-label Vin de France rouge (1.5 litre bottle).
5. Own-label Navarra.
6. Bulgarian Cabernet Sauvignon 1990.

Hard on the heels of these wines are Rosso and Bianco di Verona, the own-label Hock and the Niersteiner Gutes Domtal. On the basis of that list you might think Sainsbury's is a boring place to buy wine, but nothing could be further from the truth. True, over 70 per cent of what the store sells in wine is own-label, but many of these wines are the buying department's own initiatives and the projects they are involved with include several bold moves with Australian wine-makers Peter Bright and Geoff Merrill who pop up all over the world and will, I am quite sure, increase their activities on behalf of Sainsbury's for several years to come. Indeed, at one point Peter Bright had more wines under his own name at the store than the total number of German wines in the Sainsbury's range.

The store has always gone where interesting fruit and value are to be found. This year, Spain, Eastern Europe, Australia, the Pacific coast of North America, Argentina and Chile, and South Africa were regions where most of this value was to be found – much of it not at £3 level but at the £4–£6 mark. But classic areas are not forgotten, hence a bold range of 1990s clarets. The new Tarrawingee range of Australian wines (named after the edible nocturnal flying insect, said to taste of asparagus, which swarms in New South Wales – hence the reason so many Aussie men stand around after dark with their mouths open) is a bold move, so are the Uruguayan wines, and the new blend of Blancs de Noirs champagne is superb. The areas where further bold wines are expected to originate at Sainsbury's include the south of France, South Africa, Spain, Chile and Romania.

What don't I like about Sainsbury's? The orange corporate colour sucks. I don't warm to the stiff, civil service ethos which pervades many of their attitudes. I'm cold to the idea of the Selected Vintage range, stuck-up and separated from 'humbler' bottles, and I'm most unconvinced by the blue flash disfiguring some of their wines which announces 'Specially selected by Sainsbury's buyers to offer exceptional quality and value'. Surely, if a wine doesn't offer exceptional value and quality what's it doing in store? What wisdom guided the decision to incorporate the blue flash in the first place?

My opinion, for what it's worth, is simple. It's the old St Michael syndrome. In other words, brand every product you sell with your own name, or a name to which you have sole and exclusive use, and if you can't get away with that or you can't carry off the next best thing which is labels saying Sainsbury's This or Sainsbury's That, then stick on a slogan with your name in it. It has to be said that this idea is very seductive and it's certainly more reassuring for customers than the sight of the odd gruesomely labelled bottle I've seen on sale at other retailers which is totally the vineyard's own and which seems to have strayed in, unchecked, off the street, so remote is the label from the rest of the wines and the general image of the store.

These are, of course, somewhat minor quibbles. But then I have an incurable medical condition, I should confess, which induces sickness if I am consistently pleasant about anyone or anything. I am forced to quibble; result of a horrific genetic quirk (my father was a critical misanthrope nearly his entire life until he repented at eighty-four years of age after being finally persuaded by an increasingly hysterical doctor to renounce cheap cigars). It is a difficult condition to bring under control but where this supermarket is concerned I have developed some sophisticated techniques. I have bullied my two children straight from school when they are tired and listless and irritable and dragged them round my local Sainsbury's to do the shopping, and though I scream and shout at their swinish behaviour and swear I'll never set foot inside the hell of a Sainsbury's ever again, I get home and open a bottle of Sainsbury's Chilean Red and the quibbling dies under a torrent of rich fruit (cheap rich fruit). I have also queued for Sainsbury's petrol with a car full of screaming babies in steamy mid-summer without being put off ever doing it again. As the father of an asthmatic child I do try to buy the new Sainsbury's gasoline, introduced earlier this year, which promises to emit less poisonous exhaust gases. On a lighter note, I once asked the rookie at the fish counter if he wouldn't mind filleting my pound of whitebait. He turned paler than tempura batter.

'What? All of them?'

'Thanks very much. Shall I drop back when I've filled my trolley?'

'But ... but ... but ...'

'Oh ... and keep the heads on, would you?'

I just hope that young man, following the usual incredible Sainsbury's career route, doesn't one day end up in the wine department buying the stuff. He might be tempted to doctor a sample bottle sent out to yours truly and ... bye bye *Superplonk*.

Sainsbury's career routes cause much amusement and bafflement amongst my contemporaries (I use the term in its vocational rather than chronological sense – many writers on wine are so out of touch with contemporary mores that if they do indeed live in the same time zone as the one I inhabit then so does Kaiser Wilhelm). When the store's long-serving Head of Wine Buying, Mr Allan Cheesman, was suddenly yanked out of buying booze and bunged into buying beetroots etcetera five years ago there was widespread disbelief and astonishment. But Mr Cheesman is now back! George Foreman – eat your heart out. After nearly five years of boring all his friends to death about how he bought sufficient potatoes in a week to fill the Houston Astrodome five times over and purchased more lettuce in a day than would be needed to block the Ganges delta, Mr Cheesman has returned as the wine department's supremo and Mr Mike Conolly, a delightfully urbane chap who received all my quips with unflinching good grace, has returned to the marketing department, whence he came.

What has prompted the return of the prodigal? Answers on a postcard please to *Superplonk*, c/o Hodder & Stoughton, Euston Road, London NW1, and everybody is eligible to enter – even employees of J Sainsbury who are no more likely to know the correct answer than the rest of us. Your guess is as good as anybody's and the prize is a lifetime's free supply of turnips.

J Sainsbury plc
Stamford House
Stamford Street
London
SE1 9LL

Tel 0171 921 6000
Fax 0171 921 7608
Internet order http://www.j-sainsbury.co.uk

**SEE STOP PRESS SECTION AT END OF BOOK FOR
LAST-MINUTE ADDITIONS TO THIS RETAILER'S
RANGE.**

ARGENTINIAN WINE RED

Bright Brothers Malbec, Las Palmas 1992 `16` `D`

A big, rich, soupy wine with lots of berried fruit flavour.
Out-Cahors Cahors. Very impressive and broad-shouldered.

Mendoza Cabernet Sauvignon/Malbec
Peter Bright, Sainsbury's `15` `B`

Bargain. Great big soft fruity bargain, with an edge of serious
dryness and haute couture styling.

Mendoza Country Red, Sainsbury's `15.5` `B`

Delicious fruit with a lovely bright touch on the finish – like
shine on an apple. But this wine is no hard fruit. It is all plums.
Lovely throat-charming liquid.

ARGENTINIAN WINE WHITE

Mendoza Country White Wine, Sainsbury's `15` `B`

Lots of rich fruit, comfortingly well-packaged and smooth.

Tupungato Chenin Chardonnay Peter
Bright, Sainsbury's `14.5` `C`

Lovely refreshing wine with balanced fruit. Delicious with rich
fish dishes.

AUSTRALIAN WINE   RED

Arrowfield Cabernet Merlot 1992   13   D

Sweet, uncomplex, expensive for the style.

Australian Red Wine, Sainsbury's   16   B

Nice touch of dusty drawers on the aroma of the fruit, which is
full and plummy, sunny and ripe. Lovely rich fruit with gentle
tannins. Good with roasts and cheeses.

Baileys Shiraz 1992   15   D

This leathery, furry fruited wine may well be descended from
the one which sozzled Ned Kelly, for it was in the Victorian
hamlet of Glenrowan, where Baileys built their winery in 1870,
that the law finally caught up with the drunken bandit. Baileys
Shiraz grabs the drinker by the throat every bit as effectively,
though somewhat more affectionately, as the noose from which
the rogue finally swung. Linctus-like texture offering layered
fruits, blackcurrants to plums, wild touches of tobacco and
coffee. Superb, if available in only 7 Sainsbury's stores.

Cockatoo Ridge Cabernet Sauvignon/ Merlot, Yalumba 1993   14   C

Savoury fruit well matched by the excellent acid balance. Not
huge but very tasty.

Eileen Hardy Shiraz 1990

Expensive toy for jaded executives who enjoy keeping a picture
of an old lady locked in their cellars while the tannins develop.
Big wine to see in the year AD 2000.

Hardy's Stamp Series Shiraz/Cabernet Sauvignon 1994

14 C

Interesting chocolate biscuit undertones to the fruit.

Hardys Nottage Hill Cabernet Sauvignon/ Shiraz 1993

16 C

Controlled soft spice laid on smooth blackcurrant fruit. Delicious, firm, well-styled.

Jacob's Creek Shiraz Cabernet 1993

15 C

Flavour and richness here with terrific balance and fruity exuberance. Great stuff!

Lindemans Bin 45 Cabernet Sauvignon 1992

13.5 C

Good flavour and balance – good cheese wine.

Mildara Cabernet/Shiraz/Merlot 1992

16.5 C

Such effrontery! It makes St Emilion at twice the price look a pretty poor bargain. It's soft, ripe, gorgeously fruity and classic – with a subtle streak of Aussie iconoclasm.

Mount Hurtle Grenache Shiraz 1993

14.5 C

Soft fruit, hard fruit – plus a touch of almond cream. Delicious. Unusual. Highly entertaining.

Orlando RF Cabernet Sauvignon 1992

14.5 C

Touch of beefiness here and velvet tannins. Too soft? For claret die-hards yes. Not for me.

Penfolds Coonawarra Cabernet Sauvignon 1991

16 E

Subtle, minty, composed, authoritative, very soft and delightfully lengthy and rich.

Penfolds Koonunga Hill Shiraz Cabernet 1993
`13.5` `D`

Peter Lehmann, Vine Vale Shiraz 1992
`15` `C`

Delightful fruit with hints of plum and blackberry. Has some soft spice. Good with fried sausages.

Rosemount Estate Cabernet/Shiraz 1994
`15.5` `D`

Almost totally brilliant. It's a lovely wine from the start (smell) through the middle layers of soft rich fruit and only fails by a whisker to produce a grandstand finish.

Rosemount Estate Shiraz 1993
`16` `C`

Wonderful beefy brew. Aromatic, rich and deep – a lake of flavour for the tastebuds to luxuriate in. It is possible that this wine is the smoothest Aussie since Richie Benaud.

St Hallett Cabernet Sauvignon/Cabernet Franc/Merlot 1992
`16` `D`

Echoes of mint and licorice to the rich edge of the fruit, which is seductively soft.

Tarrawingee Shiraz Cabernet, Sainsbury's
`13` `B`

Sweet, soft fruit.

Tim Knappstein Cabernet Merlot 1991, Clare Valley
`16` `D`

Lovely chocolatey finish on this soft, rich, fruity wine. Has complexity, flavour and forceful style.

Wynns John Riddoch Cabernet Sauvignon, Penfolds Coonawarra 1988
`16` `E`

Such great flavour and smoothness it's actually a £10 wine.

Yarra Ridge Cabernet Sauvignon 1993

Very soft. Some easy elegance, but that of a £4 wine at twice the price. Only available in the top 36 stores.

AUSTRALIAN WINE WHITE

Australian Chardonnay, Sainsbury's

Only a suggestion of the bruising Aussie fruit of yesteryear. Has elegance and refined bite.

Australian White Wine, Sainsbury's

Mean on the fruit a bit.

Barramundi SE Australian Semillon/ Chardonnay

Rich, fruit-salad nose. Lots of pineapple acidity and great, swinging melon/mango fruit. Smashing wine to let the heart soar.

Dalfarras Marsanne Tahbilk 1993

Interesting. Fresher than the usual marsanne.

Geoff Merrill Chardonnay McLaren Vale, 1990

Lovely aroma, and it aims at elegance, but a subtle coarseness with the wood/fruit integration very slightly mars the finish. Fine with grilled fish dishes, though.

Hunter Valley Chardonnay Denman Estate 1994

Balanced, flavourful, classy. The fruit has depth without drowning the tastebuds.

Jacob's Creek Dry Riesling 1994   `13` `C`

Pleasant fish 'n' chips wine.

Jacob's Creek Semillon/Chardonnay 1994   `13` `C`

Jacobs Creek Chardonnay 1994   `14` `C`

A reliable performer. No tricks. No gimmicks. Good fruit.

Lindemans Bin 65 Chardonnay 1994   `15` `C`

Good as ever it was. Oily, ripe, balanced, very fruity. Lovely with grilled chicken.

Penfolds Koonunga Hill Chardonnay 1994   `14.5` `C`

Still one of the best branded Aussie chardonnays in spite of the fearsome fiver staring it in the face.

Peter Lehmann Barossa Valley Semillon 1994   `12` `C`

Rosemount Estate Chardonnay/Semillon 1994   `15.5` `D`

Wonderful accompaniment to smoked salmon.

Rosemount Estate Diamond Label Chardonnay, Hunter Valley 1994   `16.5` `D`

Tastes deliciously on the edge of overrichness and then, in a bound, it is free and flowing with flavour and depth. Lovely wine for rich food. Top 150 stores only.

Tarrawingee Semillon/Chardonnay, Sainsbury's   `15` `C`

Lots of deep, rich, peach, pawpaw and melon fruit.

Tyrrell's VAT 47 Pinot Chardonnay, Hunter Valley 1993　12　F

Like a meursault with a fresher finish. The lovely aroma makes the wine. But it doesn't make it a bargain.

Wynns Coonawarra Riesling 1993　14　C

Try it and dare say 'I don't like riesling' afterwards. Only a faint mineral tinge on the finish of rich fruit hints at its grape variety.

Yarra Ridge Chardonnay 1994　15.5　E

Aromatic, melony, balanced, with a creamy edge and citric undertones. Expensive but expansive – yet not blowsy. Delicious, delicate, decisive.

Yarra Ridge Sauvignon Blanc 1994　15　D

Rings with gently citric flavour and is keenly fruity, but is not keenly priced. The cost of the oak is not evident in the wine.

BULGARIAN WINE　RED

Bulgarian Cabernet Sauvignon 1993, Oak Aged, Russe Region, Sainsbury's　15　B

Oodles of tastebud-lashing soft fruit. A pasta wine and a huge bargain.

Bulgarian Cabernet Sauvignon, Sainsbury's (3 litre)　15.5　F

Young fruit with lots of vim and gusto allied to polished, smooth, flavour-filled depth of fruit which is both intense, gluggable, and very good with food. A delicious clean red.

Bulgarian Merlot 1993, Oak Aged, Liubimetz Region, Sainsbury's

`16` B

Seriously dry-finishing fruit (plummy and soft). Terrific flavour and class for the money.

Bulgarian Reserve Cabernet Sauvignon, Lovico Suhindol 1989

`16.5` B

Quite brilliant. Lovely brisk fruit with a deep serious side matched by lovely balancing acidity. Excellent with grilled vegetables and cheese. Fantastic style for the money.

Bulgarian Reserve Gamza, Lovico Suhindol Region 1990

`15` B

Soft plums, rich and drily edged.

Bulgarian Reserve Merlot, Lovico Suhindol 1991

`14` B

Dry and outstanding with rich, savoury foods.

Country Red Russe Cabernet Sauvignon/ Cinsault, Sainsbury's (1.5 litre)

`15.5` D

Brilliant: dry, textured, chewy, savoury, firm, fruity.

Country Wine, Suhindol Merlot/Gamza Sainsbury's

`12` B

Svischtov Special Reserve Cabernet Sauvignon 1988

`16` C

Gentle mintiness on the nose, rich fruit with dark, swirling cherry and blackcurrant flavours and a soft finish. An elegant, flavourful wine of restrained class and no little style.

Vintage Blend Oriachovitza Merlot and Cabernet Sauvignon Reserve 1990

`16.5` B

Vibrantly rich fruit mingling soft blackcurrants and dried raspberry with firm-edged acids. Terrific bargain.

Zlatovrach Reserve Mavrud, Assenovgrad Region 1990

Superb fruit, multi-layered and rich. Has flavour, style and satisfactory depth for relative peanuts.

BULGARIAN WINE WHITE

Bulgarian Chardonnay, Lyaskovets, Sainsbury's

Terrific value. Lots of rich fruit and style. Superb fish wine which is classier than many a feeble chablis.

Bulgarian Country Wine Muskat and Ugni Blanc, Sainsbury's

Very attractive, powder-compact soft fruit undercut by a tingling freshness. Good value.

Bulgarian Misket, Slaviantzi 1993

Vintage Blend Khan Krum Chardonnay and Sauvignon Blanc Reserve 1992

Bargain richness and flavour. Versatile with food – from fish to fowl. Not at all stores.

CHILEAN WINE RED

Chilean Cabernet Sauvignon, Sainsbury's

Serious hints of class here, with its vegetal, minty undertones. These are very subtle but they do give the soft fruit complexity and style.

Chilean Cabernet Sauvignon/Merlot, Sainsbury's

Bargain. Elegant, soft, fruitily benign and satisfying.

Chilean Merlot San Fernando 1994, Sainsbury's

Has a hint of mint to go with your grilled lamb chops.

Chilean Red, Sainsbury's

Ripe plums, fresh and yielding. Lots of flavour here with a shroud of characterful dryness. Delicious food wine.

Santa Carolina Merlot Reserva, Maipo Valley 1993

Humdinging fruitiness of the quietly impactful sort. Top 70 stores only.

Villa Montes Oak-Aged Cabernet Sauvignon Gran Reserva, Curico 1992

Impressively soft, finely woven and classy. Complex deliciousness.

CHILEAN WINE   WHITE

Chilean Chardonnay 1993, Sainsbury's

Brilliant potency of woody rich fruit and acidity. Polished, cheap, complex, flavourful, striking – this is a great chardonnay for under £4.

Chilean Sauvignon Blanc, Maipo Valley, Sainsbury's

Creamy, nutty quality to the fruit here. Very attractive.

Chilean Sauvignon Semillon, Sainsbury's

Chilean White, Sainsbury's

So simple! Take rich fruit and elegant acidity and weld them firmly together. Here you have this bargain bottle of elegant wine.

Santa Carolina Sauvignon Blanc Reserva 1994

Clean, with a lovely rich oily texture on the fruit. Lovely wine. Impressive balance. Top 10 stores only.

Santa Rita Chardonnay, Estate Reserve 1994

Demurely rich and fine with an aristocratic feel. Easy to drink, extremely elegant and fruity.

ENGLISH WINE WHITE

Hastings, Carr Taylor Medium Dry 1993

Lamberhurst Sovereign Medium Dry

ENGLISH WINE RED

Denbies Surrey Red 1992

Surprisingly fruity for an English red wine, but poor value. If it was £1.99 it might be acceptable but even at this price it would only score 13. Sentiment has bought it, and sentiment will move it off the shelf. To compare it, say, with the store's

1991 Copertino Riserva at 5p less is to compare Kiri Te Kanawa with a bookie shouting the odds.

Denbies Estate English Table Wine, 1992   13 C

Lamberhurst Sovereign Medium Dry   13 B

Some good fruit here at a good price.

Three Choirs 1992, English Table Wine   14 C

Has a fat touch of off-dryness that I'm less convinced about than I was.

Wootton Trinity, English Wine, Somerset   14 C

Nothing wrong with this: flavour, balance, style. Delicious.

FRENCH WINE   RED

Beaujolais, Sainsbury's   11 B

**Beaujolais-Villages, Les Roches Grillees
1994**   12 C

Bergerac Rouge, Sainsbury's   12 B

**Bergerie de l'Arbous, Coteaux du
Languedoc 1991**   15 C

Extremely well-mannered and almost silky. Delicious classy drinking under a fiver – and so much better value than the same store's more highly priced burgundies.

Bordeaux Rouge, Sainsbury's   13.5 B

Light, cheap, decent.

Bourgueil 1992, Sainsbury's

14   C

Wild, delicious raspberry fruit.

Cabernet Sauvignon Syrah VdP d'Oc, Sainsbury's

15.5   B

Real syrah class, subtle earthiness, flavour and style. Has a hint of Northern Rhone luxury without the Northern Rhone price tag.

Cabernet Sauvignon VdP d'Oc 1984, Sainsbury's

14.5   C

A soft, friendly, eminently quaffable cabernet of flavour and charm. Selected stores.

Cahors, Sainsbury's

14   B

Bargain price for a rich dark wine which is brilliant with grilled food. Chewy like coal, but a lot softer to swallow. Excellent.

Chais Baumiere Cabernet Sauvignon Vin de Pays d'Oc 1993

12   C

Again, not as rich as compelling as the previous vintage. What's going on? Are the yields too high?

Chais Baumiere Merlot 1993

13   C

Not as rich or compelling as the previous vintage.

Chais Baumiere Syrah, VdP d'Oc 1993

14.5   C

Some soft, rich, spicy fruit. This new introduction is much better than the two other Chais Baumieres at the store.

Chassagne Montrachet Cote de Beaune 1991

12   E

Dryness and flavour. Pricey.

Chassagne Montrachet, Picard Pere et Fils 1991

`12.5` `E`

Top 100 stores. Smooth but not especially gamy or exciting.

Chateau Blaignan Medoc, Cru Bourgeois 1989 (1.5 litre)

`14` `G`

A real dark chewy claret of depth and power. Great roast beef wine!

Chateau Bois de la Clide, Bordeaux 1994

`13` `C`

Chateau Carsin, Premieres Cotes de Bordeaux 1993

`13.5` `D`

Has evolving tannins yet to ripen fully and make this a more exciting wine. I do not know why the back label should say drink this wine within 2 years as I would think it better in 3.

Chateau Chasse-Spleen, Moulis en Medoc 1990

`14` `G`

At only 6 stores, this wine will be superb in 5/7 years. It is impressive, with its herby, cherry-plum fruit, but very expensive.

Chateau d'Aigueville, Cotes du Rhone 1994

Soft, rich, deep yet lively and characterful.

Chateau de Gourgazaud, Minervois 1992

`14` `C`

Chateau de Roquetaillade la Grange, Graves 1988

`16` `D`

Serious stuff – leathery, rich, concentrated. Dry, textured, perfect with a steak au poivre.

Chateau des Capitans, Julienas 1994

241

Chateau Fournas Bernadotte, Haut-Medoc 1990   16   D

A very smooth package with enough personality from the wood and the tannins to provide complexity and flavour. Classy.

Chateau Grand Bourdieu, Bordeaux Superieur 1992   12   C

Pleasant soft, savoury tannins to the fruit.

Chateau Haut Faugeres, Grand Cru St Emilion 1990   14   E

Fancy fruit – soft, smooth, polite. Decant for one and a half hours before drinking.

Chateau Hauterive le Haut, Corbieres 1992   15   C

A wine to keep for 5 years and also to drink now with roast foods. It has great acid/fruit balance. Not at all stores.

Chateau la Gurgue, Margaux 1990   12   E

Chateau La Rose Coulon, Bordeaux 1990   14   D

Excellent, dry, soundly constructed fruit. Has spiciness, style and some depth.

Chateau La Vieille Cure, Fronsac 1992   15.5   E

Rich, savoury, lovely soft tannins.

Chateau la Voulte Gasparets, Corbieres 1991, Sainsbury's   14   C

Aromatically wonderful (like an aged, hammy beaujolais), soft fruit, rather a flattish finish.

Chateau Lalande d'Auvion, Medoc 1990   14.5   D

A mature claret, perfectly full and fruity, with the serious dryness of the Medoc.

Chateau le Boscq Les Vieilles Vignes, Medoc Cru Bourgeois 1990   `14` `E`

Dry, deep, flavourful and expressive. Top 100 stores only.

Chateau Marsau, Bordeaux Cotes de Francs 1994   `15` `C`

Rich, charcoal-edged fruit with the potential to develop and soften in bottle for some years. A classy merlot. Top 70 stores only.

Chateau Maucaillou, Moulis 1989   `13` `F`

Chateau Poujeaux, Moulis-en-Medoc 1990   `17` `G`

Chateau Rolland, Bordeaux 1992   `14` `C`

Has fruit and flavour and real bordeaux style for not a lot of money. Superb roast food wine.

Chateau Salvanhiac, St Chinan 1993, Sainsbury's   `13.5` `C`

Savoury-finished fruit which suits grilled meat and veg dishes. Not at all stores.

Chateau Segonzac, Premieres Cotes de Blaye, Cuvee Barrique 1991   `15` `C`

Structured, tannic (yet soft), lots of purposeful fruit. Excellent fruit wine (and cheese). Lush yet savoury edge. Good value from Bordeaux!

Chateau Suduiraut, Premier Cru Classe 1990 (half bottle)   `13` `F`

Chateauneuf-du-Pape, Les Galets Blancs 1993   `13` `E`

Chinon, Domaine du Colombier 1993 $\boxed{13.5}$ $\boxed{D}$

A sleeper. It will wake up and rate more highly in the spring of '96.

Claret Cuvee Prestige, Sainsbury's $\boxed{13.5}$ $\boxed{C}$

Good tannins and fruit. Good with roast meats.

Claret, Sainsbury's $\boxed{13.5}$ $\boxed{C}$

Some richness, some smoothness. Some.

Comte de Signargues, Cotes du Rhone Villages 1993 $\boxed{15}$ $\boxed{C}$

Rich, rounded, polished, soft – lush and firm at the same time in that unique Rhone way, with just an echo of earthiness.

Corbieres, Sainsbury's (3 litre box) $\boxed{13.5}$ $\boxed{F}$

Young, fresh, fruity.

Cotes du Luberon Rouge, Sainsbury's $\boxed{12.5}$ $\boxed{B}$

Better than a lot of beaujolais.

Cotes du Rhone, Sainsbury's $\boxed{14}$ $\boxed{B}$

Outstanding value for a soft, earthy, fruity wine of some character.

Cotes du Rhone Villages, Beaumes de Venise $\boxed{13}$ $\boxed{C}$

Cotes du Rhone Villages Saint Gervais, Laurent Charles Brotte 1990 $\boxed{14}$ $\boxed{C}$

Fruity, soft, simple.

Cotes du Roussillon Villages, Saint Vincent 1990, Sainsbury's $\boxed{14}$ $\boxed{B}$

Very dark rich fruit on display here with an admirably balanced overall style. Dry, full, very good with roasts and grills. Almost vies with Australia for softness and depth of colour. Not a drink for the faint-hearted, needs food, etc.

Crozes Hermitage, Sainsbury's 13 C

Dry and slaty – like slurping blackcurrant off a roof tile.

Domaine de la Grangerie Mercurey 1991 13 D

Some rich-edged fruit, meaty and fulfilled – helped by soft tannins. Expensive idea but keep till the end of the century.

Domaine Dury Millot, Paul Dugenais Meursault 1992 10 F

Too much! Too much! Too much! (And not enough fruit or complexity in return.)

Domaine le Cazal Minervois 1992 15.5 B

Really deliciously polished, plummy fruit of great smoothness.

Domaine Saint Apollinaire Cotes du Rhone 1991, Sainsbury's 13 D

Depth and class – touch pricey.

Domaine Sainte Anne, St Chinian 1992 11 B

Domaine St Marc, Syrah VdP d'Oc 1994 15 C

A wine to keep and a wine to drink now with savoury food. Dry tannic touches to the brambly fruit.

Faugeres 14 B

A healthily fruity red wine from southern France, perfect with sausage and mash. Some excellent on-form fruit here.

Fitou Chateau de Segure 1991 14.5 D

Interesting tannins here, a touch austere for the tender-palated. Lay it down for 2 years at least. Or drink it with rare beef.

Fitou, Les Gueches 1992

A big softie with a hard edge. Don't persist with it unless you're going into battle armed with a rich casserole.

Fleurie, La Madone, 1994

Difficult for me to find it in my heart, not to mention my intestines, but this is a rich savoury wine of typically La Madone sweetness.

Gevrey Chambertin, Maurice Chenu 1990

Some attractive sweet fruit but not worth the money.

Gigondas Tour du Queyron, 1990

Expensive but expansive. Big, hearty, huge, smoky fruit. Concentrated soft centre. Lovely wine.

Graves Selection Sainsbury's, Louis Vialard

Good, soft fruit.

Grenache/Syrah, Cave de la Cessane VdP d'Oc 1993

Big, serious, rich complex. Tremendous tannins. Top 30 stores only.

Hauts Cotes de Nuits, Les Dames Huguettes 1990

Les Forts de Latour, Pauillac 1987

Madiran, Chateau de Crouseilles 1989

OK, nature lovers, get your laughing gear round this brambly, earthy, soft-fruited (with a hard-edge) beauty. Great with roasts and stews. Has character and drinkability – and claret lovers should be able to quaff it for breakfast.

Minervois, Sainsbury's `13` `B`

Soft fruit with a good smack of acidic freshness on the finish.

Moulin a Vent, Cave Kuhnel 1994 `10` `E`

Nuits St Georges, Paul Dugenais 1993 `12.5` `E`

Hints of class – will they develop over the next couple of years? Can't say for sure.

Peter Sichel Selection, Oak Aged Bordeaux 1990 `14.5` `C`

Truly deep structure and weight of fruit. Dry, rich tannins and blackcurrant edginess. Solidly built and well-priced.

Red Burgundy Pinot Noir, Sainsbury's `11` `C`

Vacqueyras, Paul Jaboulet-Isnard 1990 `13` `E`

Has delicious texture but it's somewhat expensive.

Vin de Pays de l'Ardeche, Sainsbury's `13.5` `B`

Simple, dry, cherry-edged. Good chilled.

Vin de Pays de la Cite de Carcassonne Merlot 1994 Sainsbury's `13.5` `B`

Good depth of fruit.

Vin de Pays du Gard Red, Sainsbury's 25 cl `13` `A`

A quarter-litre can. Good fruit for picnics (and excellent chilled).

Vin Rouge de France, Sainsbury's (1.5 litre) `13` `C`

Plastic-bottled but far from plastic-fruited – good, simple, rustic glugging.

Vosne Romanee, Georges Noellat 1989 11 F

Greatly wrinkled but amusing – especially in the arrogance of its price.

FRENCH WINE   WHITE

Alsace Gewurztraminer, Sainsbury's 12 D

Alsace Pinot Blanc, Sainsbury's 14 C

Not a bad price for the real thing: rich-edged, peach/apricot fruit, good acidic background, sound structure.

Bergerac Blanc, Sainsbury's 13 B

Blanc Anjou Medium Dry, Sainsbury's 12 B

Blanc de Mer Loire 1994, Sainsbury's 12 B

Tasty. Good with fresh winkles.

Bordeaux Blanc Cuvee Prestige, Sainsbury's 13 C

Sound rather than sock-it-to-me thrilling.

Bordeaux Sauvignon Blanc, Sainsbury's 13 B

Solid.

**Chablis Domaine Sainte Celine, Brocard
1993, Sainsbury's** 10 D

**Chablis Grand Cru, Preuses, Jeanne Paule
Filippi 1990** 15 G

More in the mersault style than pure chablis.

Chablis Premier Cru, Montmains, Brocard 1992 `16.5` `E`

Expensive but very satisfying: complex, finely balanced, stylish.

Chais Baumiere Chardonnay Vin de Pays d'Oc 1993 `16` `C`

Delicious – a really delightful fruity chardonnay without being an overrich or overripe one. Has balance and style.

Chais Baumiere Sauvignon Blanc Vin de Pays d'Oc 1994 `15.5` `C`

Elegant, firm, poised – a balanced s.b. of decisively modern wine-making techniques but with a touch of good old-fashioned softness and French 'country' character.

Chardonnay VdP d'Oc, Cave de la Cessane 1994 `14.5` `C`

Rich rounded finish to dry, gooseberry-edged fruit which is softly intentioned. Delicious. Hints of nuts, too. Not at all stores.

Chardonnay VdP d'Oc, Sainsbury's (3 litre) `12.5` `G`

Winebox – not at all stores.

Chardonnay Vin de Pays d'Oc, Ryman 1994 `15.5` `C`

A roast fowl chardonnay. By which I mean there is a lovely gamy edge to the fruit which chimes with chicken.

Chateau Bastor-Lamontagne Sauternes 1990 (half bottle) `14` `E`

Zippy marmalade edge to the burnt honeyed fruit.

Chateau Carsin, Bordeaux Blanc 1993 `16` `D`

Waltzing Matilda meets Gerard Depardieu and they cut a splendidly elegant and fruity couple on the dance floor. A decisive wine of style, flavour and presence.

Chateau de Davenay, Montagny Premier Cru 1993

`12.5` `D`

Chateau de Rully Blanc, 1990

`10` `E`

Chateau l'Ortolan, Bordeaux Blanc 1994

`14` `C`

Solid and distinctive by virtue of what it is not rather than what it is. If that sounds a rather backhanded compliment I can only add it is a wine of quiet class, decent fruit and good balance. Also, the price is good.

Chateau Les Bouhets, Bordeaux Blanc Sec 1993

`15` `C`

A fruity, well-balanced wine in the white Graves mould. Classy and not expensive.

Chateauneuf-du-Pape, Andre Brunel 1992

`14` `E`

If you like wine this soft, seductive and purring like a pussy-cat, your money's well spent.

Clos St Georges Graves Superieures 1990/91

`15` `E`

Try this as an aperitif. It's wonderful even though it's honeyed and toffeed.

Corbieres Blanc, Sainsbury's

`12` `B`

Domaine d'Aubian Chardonnay, Fortant de France 1994

`15.5` `C`

Superb polished richness to the fruit which never overplays its hand and smothers the acidity. Not at all stores.

Domaine de Grandchamp Sauvignon Blanc, Bergerac 1994

`16` `D`

Classy, vivid, cool. Hints of rich fruit but the freshness

is controlled and impressive. Lovely stuff. Top 100 stores
only.

Domaine de la Tuilerie Merlot Rose, Hugh Ryman 1993
 15 | C

Firm and delicious. Depth of fruit and flavour surprising
in a rose.

Domaine St Marc Sauvignon Blanc, VdP d'Oc 1994
17 | C

Enclos des Lilas Blanc VdP de l'Aude 1994
15.5 | B

Style, balance, flavour – gifted at the price.

Four Terroirs Chardonnay VdP d'Oc 1993
14.5 | D

Selected branches. Expensive but very good fruit in this bottle:
warm, expressive (of grape, region, and a sunny disposition),
soft and classy.

Gentil 'Hugel', Alsace 1992
14 | C

Typical: quiet, reserved. A TV wine.

Gustave Lorentz Riesling Reserve, Alsace 1992
 13 | D

Only at 10 stores but there are probably only 10 people who
will appreciate this petrol-scented young riesling – needs 5 years
more development in bottle to be really great.

Le Lizet Colombard Chardonnay, VdP des Comtes de Tolosan 1994
14 | C

An excellent clean fish wine. Pert, fresh, demurely fruity.

Macon Blanc Villages, Domaine les Chenevieres 1993
 13 | C

Some depth of flavour here.

Macon Chardonnay, Domaines les Ecuyers 1993

13.5 D

A modest white burgundy of not totally inoffensive price or flavour.

Menetou Salon, Domaine Henri Pelle 1993

13 D

Moulin des Groyes, Cotes de Duras Blanc 1994

15 C

Top 100 stores. What a terrific fish-stew wine we have here. Ripples with melony flavour which is never overdone or too adolescent in feel.

Mouton Cadet 1993

12 C

OK but dull – and at this price why pay for such dullness?

Muscadet de Sevre et Maine, Sainsbury's (3 litre)

13 B

A decent muscadet! In a cardboard box! Shiver my timbers – a double miracle.

Muscadet de Sevres et Maine sur Lie, Premiere Jean Drouillard, 1993

11 D

Muscadet Sur Lie la Goelette 1994

11 C

Really, compared with the other wines that are currently available, these people should pack up and grow carrots.

Muscat de Beaumes de Venise 1994, Sainsbury's (half bottle)

14 C

Light style of pud wine which is better as an aperitif or with hard fruit and cheese. Top 100 stores only.

**Muscat de Saint Jean de Minervois
(half bottle)** 14 B

Sweet satin.

**Oak Aged Chablis, Madeleine Matthieu
1993, Sainsbury's** 15 D

Lots of flavoursome woody fruit. Class act.

Pouilly Fume Figeat 1993 10 D

Premieres Cotes de Bordeaux NV 11 C

**Puligny Montrachet, Domaine Gerard
Chavy 1992** 14 F

Difficult to rate. It is fine, solid, well made, even a touch
classy, but at three times the price of other French chardonnays
at Sainsbury's is it even twice as good? It is only 50 per
cent better.

Rose d'Anjou, Sainsbury's 10 B

Sancerre 1993, Sainsbury's 13.5 D

Expensive but not at all bad considering the silly price of so
many underfruited sancerres nowadays. This isn't a bad wine
by any means.

Sancerre, Les Celliers de Ceres 1993 16 C

A miracle! Sound sancerre under a fiver! Indeed, it's better than
sound, it's terrific.

**Saumur Blanc, Domaine des Hauts de
Sanziers 1991** 12 C

Lip-puckering curiosity of interest to live shellfish eaters.

Sauvignon de St Bris, Bersan 1993 14 C

Tokay Pinot Gris, Cave de Ribeauville 1989

Brilliant apricot aroma. Captivating fruit of great concentration of flavour and complexity and firmness of finish. A superb bottle of wine.

Touraine Sauvignon Blanc, Sainsbury's

Rather fleshless fruit here.

Vin Blanc Dry, Sainsbury's

Old-fashioned in feel but modern in fruit. Tasty, fresh, simple, good to glug or with fish dishes.

Vin Blanc Medium Dry, Sainsbury's

Excellent step-on-the-way-up to drier styles for the Liebfrau-milch fresher.

Vin de Pays d'Oc, Sainsbury's

Good-value clean wine.

Vin de Pays de Gascogne, Domaine Bordes 1993

Vin de Pays des Cotes de Gascogne, Sainsbury's

One of the most attractive white Gascons on sale: lush fruit, fresh and flint-edged. Lovely style for the money.

Vin de Pays du Gard Blanc, Sainsbury's 25 cl

Picnic can with a rounded finish – both can and fruit.

Vin de Pays du Gers, Sainsbury's

A lovely refreshing mouthful. Terrific price for this quality of fruit and structure.

Viognier, VdP d'Oc 1993

Superb peach and apricot softness cut with balancing acidity. Fresh, individual, excellent varietal character.

Vouvray, Sainsbury's

Yes, it's sweet but it is delicious and an interesting aperitif. Lovely controlled, waxy, honeyed fruit.

White Burgundy, Sainsbury's

Touch dull – especially compared with other JS chardonnays at the same price.

GERMAN WINE WHITE

Baden Dry, Sainsbury's

This has a curious woolly aroma but the fruit is delightful and delicious with poached fish.

Bereich Bernkastel, Sainsbury's

Binger St Rochuskapelle Spatlese 1993

Erdener Treppchen, Riesling Spatlese, Moselland 1983

Peaches with an almond echo. Lovely fruit and lovely acidic balance. A delicious, exciting summer aperitif.

Hock, Sainsbury's

Musty fruit, sharp edge. Also available in a quarter-litre can.

Kabinett Sainsbury's, Dalsheimer Berg Rodenstein 1992

Kim Milne Riesling 1993, Sainsbury's `14.5` `C`

Has a hint of the steeliness that this grape in its Moselle guise offers but this counterpoints the fruit which, whilst never full, is restrained and most becoming as an aperitif.

Liebfraumilch, Sainsbury's `10` `B`

Also available in litre bottles.

Morio-Muskat St Georg, Pfalz `11` `B`

Mosel, Sainsbury's `12` `B`

Do try it as a summer aperitif or in a spritzer.

Niersteiner Gutes Domtal, Sainsbury's `11` `B`

Reasonable aperitif. Also available in 1.5-litre bottles.

Oppenheimer Krotenbrunnen Kabinett `12` `B`

Good with smoked fish.

Peter Nicolay Bernkasteler Johannis-brunnchen Rivaner 1992 `11` `C`

Piesporter Michelsberg, Sainsbury's `12` `B`

Aperitif.

Spatlese Mosel-Saar-Ruwer, Bernkasteler Kurfurstlay 1992, Sainsbury's `11` `C`

Trocken Rheinhessen, Sainsbury's `11` `B`

Wiltinger Scharzberg Riesling Kabinett, Moselle 1993 `14` `B`

Light, summer aperitif – good, rich yet subtle. Just undercut by firm, balancing acidity. Has a good peasant elegance about it.

GREEK WINE WHITE

Retsina 13 B

Resinated and fruity, but also clean to finish, and under £3 I find this wine both a bargain and excellent with grilled fish as well, of course, as with Greek starters.

Kourtaki VdP de Crete Red 13 B

A very bright and eager wine. Good with pastas.

Kourtaki VdP de Crete White 12.5 B

HUNGARIAN WINE WHITE

Chapel Hill Chardonnay, Balaton Boglar 1994 14 B

Flavour, style, richness. Excellent price.

Chapel Hill Irsai Oliver, Balaton Boglar 1994 13.5 B

Delicious aperitif. Not at all stores.

Gyongyos Estate Chardonnay 1994 12 B

Not as lively as previous vintages.

Hungarian Cabernet Sauvignon Rose, Nagyrede Region, Sainsbury's 16 B

The best rose for the money I've tasted in ages. Apple-cheeked, raspberry/cherry fruit, soft yet fresh – it's brilliant.

**Hungarian Pinot Gris, Nagyrede Region,
Sainsbury's** `13` `B`

ITALIAN WINE   RED

Bardolino Classico, Sainsbury's `13` `B`

Cherries and white chocolate.

Barolo, Giordano 1988 `14` `E`

Expensive but possessing great length of flavour (which is fruit of a soft berried nature enhanced by a faint licorice echo).

**Barrique Aged Cabernet Sauvignon,
Atesino 1993** `16` `C`

Brilliant, soft, warm fruit with hints of eucalyptus. Superb roast food wine. Brilliant.

**Cabernet Sauvignon delle Tre Venezie
Geoff Merrill, Sainsbury's** `13` `C`

Castelgreve Chianti Classico Riserva 1990 `16.5` `D`

Has perfect age and maturity and fires on all cylinders. Controlled earthy overtones to the rich, soft-berried fruit give this wine commanding style and flavour. Superb.

Chianti Classico, Briante 1990 `16` `C`

Full, dry, savoury, gently earthy. A wonderful chianti for posh roast food.

Chianti Classico, Villa Antinori 1990 `12` `D`

Fleshy but not as fulsome as it might be.

Chianti, Sainsbury's `14` `B`

Copertino Riserva 1992, Sainsbury's `16` `C`

Brilliant coffee-edged fruit, fully ripe and mature. Lovely texture and fruit.

Lambrusco Rosso, Sainsbury's `12` `B`

Sweet fruity fun with bubbles. For wakes.

Merlot Corvina Vino da Tavola del Veneto, Sainsbury's `10` `B`

Well, wine is fruit juice and this wine's surely that.

Montepulciano d'Abruzzo, Sainsbury's `15` `B`

Wonderful soft, zippy, cherry/plum fruit of lush style and drinkability.

Rosso di Verona, Sainsbury's `11` `B`

Sangiovese di Romagna, Sainsbury's (1.5 litre) `13.5` `D`

Excellent dry party wine for food and glugging.

Sangiovese di Toscana, Cecchi 1994 `15` `B`

Dirt-cheap earth – with a touch of youthful fruit. Bargain.

Sicilian Nero d'Avola & Merlot, Sainsbury's `15` `C`

Incredibly polished savouriness and smooth, well-turned-out depth here. Lovely.

Sicilian Red, Sainsbury's `14` `B`

Brilliant pasta-eaters' bargain. Soft, touch of sunny earth – good finish. Excellent stuff for the money.

Teroldego Rotaliano Geoff Merrill, Sainsbury's

12 C

Top 115 stores only.

Valpolicella Classico Amarone, Sartori 1989

13.5 D

Valpolicella Classico Negarine 1993, Sainsbury's

14 C

Dry yet soft, with yielding plummy fruit.

Valpolicella Classico, Sartori 1994

13 B

Vino Nobile di Montepulciano, Cecchi 1991

14 D

A dry one, this. Top 30 stores only.

ITALIAN WINE WHITE

Barrique Aged Chardonnay Atesino Geoff Merrill, 1994

15 C

Delicious underlying richness and flavour to the freshness.

Bianco di Custoza, Geoff Merrill 1994

13.5 B

Okay.

Bianco di Verona, Sainsbury's

13 B

Some profundity to the flavour – not a lot but enough to tickle the palate.

Chardonnay delle Tre Venezie Geoff Merrill, Sainsbury's

14 C

Some flavour and style here.

Frascati Superiore 1994, Sainsbury's   `13.5` `C`

An attractive specimen.

**Frascati Superiore, Cantine San Marco
1994**   `16` `C`

Stupendously tasty frascati. Complex fruit, fine balance. Quite
delicious.

Gavi Bersano 1993   `13` `D`

Expensive curiosity – with a nod, fruit-wise, to Chateauneuf-
du-Pape Blanc.

Grechetto dell'Umbria, Sainsbury's   `13.5` `C`

Reasonable.

Inzolia & Chardonnay (Sicily), Sainsbury's   `14` `C`

Tasty, very tasty. Bright and breezy.

Lambrusco Rosato, Sainsbury's   `10` `B`

Lugana San Benedetto, Zenato 1992   `14` `C`

**Orvieto Classico Secco Geoff Merrill,
Sainsbury's**   `13` `C`

Fair enough.

Pinot Grigio Atesino 1994, Sainsbury's   `13.5` `B`

All right.

Sicilian White, Sainsbury's   `12` `B`

Some echoes of richness to the fruit.

**Soave Classico Costalunga Pasqua 1994,
Sainsbury's**   `11` `C`

Soave, Sainsbury's `11` `B`

Soave Superiore, Sartori 1994 `12` `B`
Some evidence of fruit here.

Tocai del Veneto (3 litre) `11` `E`

**Trebbiano di Romagna, Sainsbury's
(1.5 litre)** `10` `D`

**Trebbiano Garganega Vino da Tavola del
Veneto, Sainsbury's** `12` `B`

LEBANESE WINE   RED

Chateau Musar 1988 `13` `E`
Not the great wine it once was. Getting too juicy and one-dimensional (and expensive).

MOROCCAN WINE   RED

Moroccan Red, Sainsbury's `14` `B`
Very classy dry edge to the fruit which has depth and richness.
Great with casseroles.

MOROCCAN WINE   WHITE

Moroccan White, Sainsbury's `14` `B`
Plenty of flavour and a fair degree of depth here.

NEW ZEALAND WINE   WHITE

Grove Mill Sauvignon Blanc, Marlborough 1994   `14` `D`

Asparagus blossoms gently in the background. Excellent with mussels.

Matua Chardonnay, Hawkes Bay 1994   `15` `D`

Top 25 stores. Impressively deep and rich but not as impudent as its sauvignon blanc partner.

Matua Sauvignon Blanc, Hawkes Bay 1994   `16.5` `D`

An oleaginous beauty available, sadly, at only 25 stores. Has a delicate grassy aroma then whacks it to your tastebuds with lush rolling fruit as textured as corduroy. A lingering, gently citric, mellow finish completes the job. A stunning glug. A stupendous fish wine.

Montana Sauvignon Blanc, Marlborough 1994   `15` `C`

Fresh-mown wet grass and aroma (good with shrimps and oysters), rich fruit with muted honey edge cut with pineapple (great with grilled chicken), and a finish reminiscent of asparagus and cauliflower (good with Thai mussels). In short, therefore, we have a gently exotic wine for exotic food.

Nobilo Chardonnay, Poverty Bay 1994   `13` `C`

Fresh and striking. Top 50 stores only.

Nobilo White Cloud, 1994   `13.5` `C`

Not as exciting as the 1993 but still among the cheapest NZ wines on the market and sound, fruity drinking.

Timara Dry White 1994 `14` `C`

Grassy and keenly fruited. Lovely shellfish wine.

Villa Maria Private Bin Sauvignon Blanc, Marlborough 1994 `15.5` `D`

Delicious, elegant, very New Zealand. Superb with smoked fish, poached salmon or merely to lift the blues.

PORTUGUESE WINE RED

Arruda, Sainsbury's `14` `B`

Burly fruit yet balanced and dry. One of this book's long-term favourite reds which is now beginning to be a little overshadowed by the rest of the JS Portuguese red range.

Do Campo Tinto Peter Bright, Sainsbury's `14.5` `B`

Bargain ripeness of fruit, structure and smoothness. Has a saucy, rumbunctious edge.

Quinta da Bacalhoa Cabernet Sauvignon 1992 `14` `D`

Classy and rich.

Santa Marta 1992 `14` `C`

Ripe, rounded yet dry. Deliciously full of itself and warm.

PORTUGUESE WINE WHITE

Do Campo Branco Peter Bright, Sainsbury's `14` `B`

Pleasant freshness and lilting fruitiness. Agreeably priced and flavoured.

Portuguese Rose, Sainsbury's `8` `B`

Santa Sara 1993 `15` `C`

Fresh and nutty. Lovely style of balanced fruit.

Vinho Verde, Sainsbury's `12` `B`

ROMANIAN WINE RED

Romanian Pinot Noir Dealul Mare, Sainsbury's `14.5` `B`

Lighter, more youthful than previous batches, this new style is still a fruity bargain.

SOUTH AFRICAN WINE RED

Kanonkop, Paul Sauer, Stellenbosch 1990 `14` `E`

A rich and very potently berried wine.

Pinotage, Coastal Region, Sainsbury's `15` `B`

A brilliant alternative to overpriced beaujolais. Just as soft and fruity but with a lovely dry edge.

South African Cabernet Sauvignon, Sainsbury's `16` `C`

A wonderfully soft, sweet-finishing yet tannic, fruity wine – not hugely complex but superbly drinkable.

SOUTH AFRICAN WINE WHITE

Chardonnay Vergelegen 1993 `15` C

Chardonnay, Western Cape, Sainsbury's `15` B

Elegance and concentration. Superb! No vintage on the label
but it's a '92 all right and it's remarkable stuff for the money,
with a delicious touch of exotic fruit to the subtle butteriness
and fresh, lemony finish. It cries out to be drunk with rich
crustaceous dishes. Smashing wine for just over £3.

Chenin Blanc, Sainsbury's `15` B

Gets to be a fruitier bargain every vintage. Pear-drops and sticky
toffee to finish – oodles of fruit and great with fish and chips.

Danie de Wet Grey Label Chardonnay 1994 `16` C

I'm a sucker for the extreme elegance, restrained fruitiness and
delicate moodiness of this wine.

Fairview Estate Semillon/Chardonnay, Paarl 1994 `17` C

Almost a medicinal malt whisky edge to the lovely rounded
fruit. But it finishes beautifully.

Neil Ellis Sauvignon Blanc, Groenekloof 1994   C

One for the sancerre lover disillusioned with poor fruit and
wicked prices. Neil's wine is aromatic, gently nutty, restrained
and whistle-clean. Very good value for the sheer class on
offer here.

South African Colombard, Sainsbury's   B

Starts fruity and full, finishes fresh and wild. Very African.

266

South African Sauvignon Blanc, Sainsbury's   13   B

**Vergelegen Sauvignon Blanc, Stellenbosch
1994**   15   C

Nuts under the deep fruit which is not laid on thick but
still has a lovely rich, rolling feel in the mouth. A wine to
unwind with.

SPANISH WINE   RED

Rioja Reserva, Vina Ardanza 1987   12   E

Old, crotchety, bad-tempered – good for octogenarians who
need winter warmth.

**El Conde Oak-Aged Vino da Mesa,
Sainsbury's**

Still a dry, fruity bargain.

**La Mancha Castillo de Alhambra 1994,
Sainsbury's**

Bargain, and the best vintage yet. Full, rich, ripe, soft,
flavoursome.

**Marques de Caceres Rioja, 1990
(1.5 litre)**

A modern fruity example of sound wine-making. Doesn't sound
exciting? Maybe not. But the big bottle helps glamorise the
presentation.

**Mont Marcal Cabernet Sauvignon Reserva,
Penedes 1990**

Surprisingly vigorous for half a decade old. Lovely mature fruit with solid ripe edge of flavour and depth. Great food wine. Top 65 stores.

Navarra, Sainsbury's

Navarra Tempranillo/Cabernet Sauvignon 1991, Sainsbury's

Quieter than before but still has soft yet chewy fruit.

Ribera del Duero Crianza, Conde de Siruela 1989

A reluctant 14, I must admit. It is expensive, though the fruit is polished, deep and attractive, but it lacks acidity to give real balance, which a wine at nearly £7 must have to partner food.

Rioja Crianza Bodegas Olarra 1990, Sainsbury's

Smooth, controlled, not one whit over-wooded or coarse.

Rioja, Sainsbury's

Bargain fruit and flavour. Light, unwoody, very fresh and delicious yet with hints of depth.

Stowells of Chelsea Tempranillo La Mancha (3 litre)

A bright, cherry/plum dry wine of really good fruit, balance and a really attractive finish.

Valencia Red, Sainsbury's

Excellent value for pizzas.

Vina Herminia, Reserva Rioja, 1985, Bodegas Lagunilla

Lush, raunchy stuff – delicious cheese wine.

Vino de la Tierra Tinto Peter Bright, Sainsbury's　15　B

Lovely sunshine-filled, fruity wine of softness and flavour.

SPANISH WINE　　　　WHITE

Moscatel de Valencia, Sainsbury's　16　B

Brilliant honeyed wine with a finish like marmalade. Superb pudding wine for a song.

Navarra Barrel Fermented Viura Chardonnay 1994, Sainsbury's　14　C

Clash of vibrancy and calmness. The acid is vibrant, the fruit is solid and unruffled. Top 50 stores only.

Navarra Blanco, Sainsbury's　14　B

Bargain nuttiness and subtle depth and flavour.

Rioja Blanco, Sainsbury's　13　B

Milky, coconutty, but also fresh and light. Good salad wine.

Santara Conca de Barbera Hugh Ryman 1994　14.5　B

Dry but soft edged with always a hint of crispness about it. A most agreeable aperitif or first-course soup and salad wine.

Vino de la Tierra Blanco Peter Bright, Sainsbury's　15　B

Simple good value here – for fish and chips parties.

Vino de la Tierra Medium, Extremadura, Sainsbury's　13　B

Vino de la Tierra Sweet, Extremadura, Sainsbury's   `13` `B`

Do try it! It's tastier than any amount of Liebfraumilch.

URUGUAYAN WINE   WHITE

Canelones Chardonnay Semillon, Sainsbury's   `12` `C`

USA WINE   RED

Californian Red, Sainsbury's   `13` `B`

South Bay Vineyards California Pinot Noir   `13.5` `C`

Sweet fruit maturity. Expensive for the complexity on offer.

South Bay Vineyards Zinfandel   `17` `C`

Delicious soft, riotous fruit with leathery richness, soft spices and a lovely black cherry and spice finish. Lingering and lovely.

USA WINE   WHITE

Californian White, Sainsbury's   `12` `B`

If you like fruit juice you'll like this.

Gallo White Grenache 1993   `5` `C`

Sheer rhubarb crumble. It seems absurd to go to the trouble of growing grapes to make wine so gauche – if wine gums could be persuaded to ferment into alcohol this is the wine they would make.

Sauvignon Blanc, Firestone 1993, Sainsbury's 15 C

Curiously delicious and idiosyncratic. Fat fruit with a mellow finish but vibrant acidity stops it cloying. Rather impressive. Top 110 stores only.

South Bay Vineyards California Chardonnay 13.5 C

Washington Hills Chardonnay, Columbia Hills 1992 13 C

FORTIFIED WINE

10 Year Old Tawny Port, Sainsbury's 16 F

Magnificent, raisiny fruit which starts basso profundo and finishes mezzo soprano. Great cheese wine and also worth trying with fruit cake.

Aged Amontillado, Sainsbury's (half bottle) 14 B

Aperitif. Top 90 stores only.

Calem Quinta da Foz 1980 15 F

Incredibly smooth and round.

Cockburns Anno 1988 LBV 17 E

Resoundingly rich fruit with a chocolate and cherry liqueur ripeness to its edge. Lovely stuff for blue cheese.

Cream Montilla, Sainsbury's 14 B

Drink it with creme caramel and ice cream.

Fonseca Guimaraens Vintage Port 1978 `17` `G`

Rich spiced plums plus a cassis-like concentration and ripeness of fruit which is always, magically, dry.

Manzanilla, Sainsbury's `12` `C`

Medium Dry Amontillado, Sainsbury's `12` `C`

Medium Dry Montilla, Sainsbury's `14` `B`

A cheap alternative to sherry – not sweet exactly but great with hard cheese and hard fruit.

Medium Sweet Oloroso, Sainsbury's `13.5` `C`

Excellent with fruit cake.

Moscatel Pale Cream, Sainsbury's `15` `C`

The ultimate ice-cream wine.

Old Oloroso, Sainsbury's (half bottle) `14` `B`

Very dry and stuffy. Drink with a volume of odes (Greek). Top 100 stores only.

Pale Cream Montilla, Sainsbury's `13` `B`

Sweet aperitif, well chilled.

Pale Cream Sherry, Sainsbury's `14` `C`

Superb sweet aperitif.

Pale Dry Amontillado, Sainsbury's `15` `C`

Brilliant. Drink it well chilled.

Pale Dry Fino Sherry, Sainsbury's `16.5` `C`

Sherry to bring people back to sherry. Lovely aroma (hay-like), beautiful oily structure with a hint of an echo of fruit and a great dry, nutty finish. A wonderful aperitif. Great with grilled prawns.

Pale Dry Montilla, Sainsbury's `13.5` `B`

Drink chilled with ham dishes. A dry, sherry-like wine of excellent value.

Palo Cortado, Sainsbury's (half bottle) `14` `B`

Aperitif. Top 80 stores only.

Rich Cream Sherry, Sainsbury's `14.5` `C`

Have it with a helping of flaming Christmas pudding.

Sainsbury's 5 Year Old Sercial (half bottle) `14.5` `E`

A curious dry yet raisiny rich wine. Good with fruit cake, nuts and old woman novelists. Top 60 stores only.

Sainsbury's LBV 1988 `13.5` `D`

Sainsbury's Madeira (half bottle) `14` `C`

Great to add to gravies (5 minutes' cooking minimum). Not at all stores.

Sainsbury's Ruby `13.5` `D`

Good basic stuff.

Sainsbury's Tawny `14` `D`

Rich yet not too rich for cheese.

Taylor's Vintage Character, Sainsbury's `14.5` `D`

Finishes dry yet it is complex, potent and richly figgy and ripe. Lovely stuff.

Warres Warrior Vintage Character Port `16` `E`

Rich ripe fruit with a lovely rounded flavour. Very attractive depth with vinosity. Delicious.

SPARKLING WINE/CHAMPAGNE

Asti, Sainsbury's `11` `C`

Australian Sparkling Wine, Sainsbury's `14` `C`
Excellent stuff for cheap wedding givers.

Blanc de Noirs Champagne, Sainsbury's `16` `F`
Elegant, so very elegant.

Cava, Sainsbury's `15` `C`
Delicious as ever. And very good value.

Champagne Extra Dry, Sainsbury's `15.5` `G`
Subtle richness. Available in half bottles as well.

Champagne Rose, Sainsbury's `13` `F`

Cockatoo Ridge Sparkling Wine `13` `D`

Cuvee Napa, Mumm California `13.5` `E`
Quiet, not explosive, and rather like a reasonably made
champagne.

Gallo Brut NV `10` `D`
Good for dinners when no one has any reason to celebrate.

**Green Point Vineyard Domaine Chandon
1991 Australia** `12` `F`

**Lambrusco Bianco Medium Sweet,
Sainsbury's** `10` `B`

274

Lambrusco Secco, Sainsbury's `8` `B`

Louis Kremer Champagne Brut `16` `E`

Creamy Kremer! Lovely rich champagne (but not too rich) with good balance.

Madeba Brut, Robertson (South Africa) `12.5` `D`

Mercier Brut `11` `G`

Mercier Demi Sec `12` `G`

Saumur, Sainsbury's `14` `D`

Bargain. Pleasant dry fruit of some distinction for the price.

Sekt, Sainsbury's `11` `C`

Veuve Clicquot Vintage Champagne 1988 `12` `H`

Not worth five times the price of a £4.99 bottle of JS Cava.

Vin Mousseux Brut, Sainsbury's `12` `C`

Vintage Cava, Mont Marcal 1991 `15` `D`

Deep, richly attractive aroma of compelling quality. The fruit tends towards fatness but is not blowsy. Good with smoked fish.

Vintage Champagne Blanc de Blancs 1989 Sainsbury's `13` `G`

Yalumba Pinot Noir/Chardonnay, Australia `16` `E`

Absolutely stunner for the money: rich and biscuity, great balancing acidity and an overall style hinting refinement and class. Rheims quakes in its Gucci boots!

SOMERFIELD/ GATEWAY

Welcome to the thrilling world of supermarket arithmetic. The sums may come in handy should you ever decide to become a wine buyer or wine marketeer with a big retailer, and I must pay tribute to Somerfield for selling wine at prices which make the following fractional calculations and attendant minutiae worthy of interest. What my exertions reveal is that if you want to pick up a bargain, someone, somewhere, has to pay for it.

You have, then, five seconds to answer the following question: what does 17,142 times 175 divided by 600 equal? When you have worked this out we can go into the more difficult equation of how anyone, in fact, makes such figures add up – or at least make commercial sense.

The answer to the question is A Very Merry Christmas. That is the answer. A Very Merry Christmas.

For what those figures mean, in commercial terms, is that during November and December last year the German suppliers of Somerfield's own-label hock shipped 175 containers of wine to the store for sale over Christmas; a single container, one truckload of wine, is around 1,428 cases or 17,142 bottles. This adds up to three million bottles in all and during the Christmas season Somerfield and Gateway customers swallowed the lot. The wine was distributed to 600 stores, so we can readily extrapolate from this that each store, on average, got through 5,000 bottles. (In practice, of course, the large branches got through 50,000 bottles, the smaller ones a few hundred.)

Now at this point the most important set of figures of all must be introduced into the equation. Each one of those bottles cost the customer £1.55 to buy, VAT included and duty paid.

This is one of the few sobering thoughts in this whole book – £1.55. (An even more sobering thought comes soon after.)

The largest slice of this £1.55 which the hock fancier hands over to Somerfield goes to Kenneth Clarke – he of the Hush Puppies and the 'honest, guv, I didn't do it' smile. The Exchequer takes £1.01 in duty, for a start, and then a further slice in VAT. On a wine costing the final purchaser £1.55 the VAT content is 23p. The difference between £1.24 and £1.55 amounts to 31p.

It is out of this statuesque figure that the cost of the bottle, its filling with wine (bottling), the cork and foil capsule, the labels (front and back), the cartons, the transportation, the retailer's distribution costs, and, oh yes, I nearly forgot, the production cost of the actual wine itself, must come. Oh yes! Shouldn't there be an allowance in there for the retailer's profit? We shall see. These costs, by my approximate calculations (based on current French franc prices in Bordeaux adjusted for a large-scale run), add up thus:

One 75cl glass bottle – 11p.
One cork – 5p.
Two labels (plus adhesion cost) – 1.25p
Capsule – 0.5p
Carton – 10p
Bottling – 0.125p
Transport – 0.15p
Wine: 2.975p

This adds up to exactly 31 pence. In addition, or should I say in subtraction, there is the retailer's cost of distribution and the margin for profit. Something doesn't add up here.

Well, it isn't supposed to. The retailer is swallowing the distribution cost and making not a penny profit. Indeed, Somerfield must make a small loss on the wine – not only by virtue of making no margin to cover the cost of the distribution of all those bottles to 600 stores but also no margin to cover other administration costs involved in marketing a wine.

Why, you might reasonably ask yourself, would anyone sell a £1.55 bottle of wine at a loss?

Let me, talmudically, answer this question with another question – for if you think £1.55 is ridiculous how does £1.39 grab you?

As I live and breathe, £1.39.

Somerfield, having enraged its competitors ('retail scum of the earth' a rival head of supermarket wine-buying threw at it when I asked him what he thought of the store) with a £1.55 bottle of hock, went one better: a bottle of red Vin de Pays de l'Herault at £1.39. It is hardly necessary to go through the figures again – though apparently certain members of the wine trade, furious that they cannot compete, did, and accused the store of somehow dodging VAT. A £1.39 bottle of wine in the United Kingdom in 1995, it was claimed, was impossible.

Several wine writers weighed in, too. The wine was rubbish, they said. But it was not. It was an utterly drinkable, fruity bottle of simple rustic red and the only thing it did to get up so-called professional people's noses was break all the rules.

No wonder it's a wine I admire. Vin de Pays de l'Herault sold 720,000 bottles in five days. 'It's about what we would normally sell in six years,' wine buyer Lewis Morton told me.

But the ultimate question is still begging for an answer. Why is Somerfield selling certain wines at a loss?

The answer is to be found in the official retail trading statistics which are published on a regular basis and which show how the supermarket sector as a whole is performing and how individual store groups within it are doing. For the period during which Somerfield has been flogging its cheapies, volume sales through supermarkets as a whole rose 9 per cent.

At Somerfield, sales rose 35 per cent.

It is now that another set of figures parade themselves. The additional custom represented by that handsome statistic is more than one million extra customers a week. Fifty-two million customers a year – customers who would not normally be doing their shopping at Somerfield.

Now, I am not permitted to see any figures beyond this point but it seems reasonable to my mind that if we assume that half those customers simply bought the cheap wines and rushed home and made nothing but merry we are still left with some 26 million people who more than likely did their weekly, or even their monthly, shop at the store. A good few of them probably felt sufficiently enthused to become regular customers.

Thus, if those 26 million people spent what people seem to spend on a low average weekly shop, say between £20 and £30, we are left with the possibility of an increase in annual turnover by Somerfield of around half a billion pounds.

There is, then, a fortune to be made out of a £1.55 bottle of hock. And I have no doubt the shareholders, the board of directors, the banks and the employees of Somerfield are delighted that Lewis Morton and his colleague Angela Mount have loads of other bargains up their sleeves which will get up even more people's noses.

This leaves only one small matter to clear up which I touched on above. Who is really paying for all this increased Somerfield turnover?

The answer is, the other retailers in this book – some of them more than others. But pay they have to since the customers flocking to Somerfield's stores are not patronising theirs. Unless, of course, these retailers get some under-two-quid wines themselves, and this is, I am delighted to report, happening more and more. This is all to the canny drinker's advantage.

When I published the first of these *Superplonk* books, in 1991, I felt fairly convinced that the then abundance of £1.99 bottles of wine would shortly end and the under-two-quid market would die. I was wrong and I have had my lack of faith thrown in my face every time the Chancellor has yet again put up alcohol duty, when yet again the sterling exchange rate has moved to the wine buyer's disadvantage, and when inflation and rising production costs overseas have surely increased wine prices beyond which the £1.99 bottle would never return.

But return it has time and time again and Messrs Mount & Morton deserve the thanks of a thirsty nation. They provide as much amusement and as good value as French and Saunders.

Somerfield
Gateway House
Hawkfield Business Park
Whitchurch Lane
Bristol
BS14 0TJ

Tel 0117 9359359
Fax 0117 9780629

AUSTRALIAN WINE

RED

Australian Dry Red, Somerfield `13` `B`
Fruity, honest.

Cabernet Sauvignon, Somerfield `13.5` `C`
Dry and most agreeable.

Chateau Reynella Cabernet Sauvignon 1988 `13` `D`

Hardys Nottage Hill Cabernet Sauvignon 1992 `15.5` `C`
Still sporting a day-old growth of beard to the smooth fruit (courtesy of the tannins). Lovely performer – one of the best-made cabernets sauvignons around for the money. Not stocked in the majority of Somerfield stores.

Hardys Nottage Hill Cabernet Sauvignon/ Shiraz 1993 `16` `C`
Controlled soft spice laid on smooth blackcurrant fruit. Delicious, firm, well-styled.

Montana Cabernet Sauvignon 1992 `14` `C`
Must be drunk with beef stew or ham dishes. Not available in all stores.

Mount Hurtle Cabernet Sauvignon/Merlot `11` `D`

Penfolds Bin 35 Shiraz Cabernet 1992 · 15 · C

Ripe, soft fruit with some development ahead of it. Attractive berry flavours, well-structured and balanced. Very drinkable now but a 17/18-pointer in 3/4 years.

Penfolds Bin 389 Cabernet/Shiraz · 13 · E

Excellent stuff.

Penfolds Koonunga Hill Shiraz Cabernet 1992 · 14 · D

Shouldn't be over a fiver.

Penfolds Shiraz, Somerfield · 12.5 · C

Preece Cabernet Sauvignon, Mitchelton 1992 · 15 · D

Lovely fruit, quite delicious and seductive. Complex, flavoursome, rich without being overripe. Not available in all stores.

Somerfield Cabernet Shiraz · 13.5 · C

Extra zing here.

Stowells of Chelsea Shiraz Cabernet (3 litre) · 14 · G

Rich fruit with earthy undertones. Has a long, meaty finish with a firm, purposeful balance of fruit and acid.

AUSTRALIAN WINE · WHITE

Berri Estates Unwooded Chardonnay 1994 · 14 · C

Nice whack of flavour here.

283

Chardonnay, Somerfield · 13 · C

Church Hill Chardonnay, Mildara 1994 · 14.5 · C

Woody, with some oil on the surface of the fruit which is subtly rich and has a pleasant trimming of silken acidity. Very good for white burgundy lovers. Not in all stores.

Coopers Creek Chardonnay, Gisborne 1992 · 13.5 · D

Stylish, but should be under a fiver. Not available in all stores.

Hardys Nottage Hill Chardonnay 1993 · 15 · C

Bargain oily fruit with a serious undercurrent of well-structured acid. Tasty. Good value.

Hardys Nottage Hill Chardonnay 1994 · 17 · C

Best vintage yet. Lovely textured, oily fruit, never overdone or blowsy and a buttery, melony finish of surefooted delivery. Terrific value for such classy drinking.

Jacob's Creek Chardonnay 1994 · 14.5 · C

Lots of the usual rich fruity attack underpinned by a delicious freshness. Good, balanced, good with food.

Jacob's Creek Dry White · 12 · C

Lindemans Bin 65 Chardonnay 1994 · 15 · C

Aromatic, stylish, fruity, with depth and style. Not as gripping as previous vintages? Maybe.

Moondah Brook 1993 · 16 · D

A melange of fruit: full, ripe, quirky, oddly delicious. A luxuriously exotic wine with lots of personality.

Penfolds Australian Chardonnay, Somerfield · 13.5 C

Good rich echo here.

Penfolds Australian Dry White, Somerfield · 13.5 B

Fails to make 14 only because the finish is not as gripping as the opening paragraph.

Penfolds Bin 21 Semillon Chardonnay 1993 · 15 C

Fresh and lively yet a dollop of pineappley melon keeps intruding. Delicious refreshing wine.

Penfolds Koonunga Hill Chardonnay 1994 · 14 C

Good old standby getting perilously close to a fiver but not losing its fruit/acid balance and grip.

Penfolds Organic Chardonnay/Sauvignon Blanc, Clare Valley 1994 · 13.5 D

Tasty, fresh, decent. Touch expensive.

Penfolds Padthaway Chardonnay 1992 · 16 D

Decidedly classy and striking. Compared with white burgundies at £15 this is a steal. Impressive weight.

Penfolds Rawson's Retreat Bin 21 Semillon Chardonnay 1994 · 15 C

Great clash of soft mango/melony fruit and pineapple acidity. Slightly exotic, generous, bold, delicious. Good with Thai chicken dishes.

Stowells of Chelsea Semillon Chardonnay (3 litre) · 14 G

Presence and lift, style and purpose – this fruit knows where it's going. Good with food and mood.

BULGARIAN WINE RED

Cabernet Sauvignon, Melnik 1989 `13` `C`

Dusty, old blackcurrant fruit, a bit reheated – not fresh. Good with yesterday's leftovers.

Sliven Country Red Merlot/Pinot Noir, Somerfield `12` `B`

Austere echo.

Stambolovo Merlot Reserve 1989 `13` `C`

Mature, very dry-edged. Good with cheese dishes.

BULGARIAN WINE WHITE

Sliven Chardonnay 1994, Somerfield `11` `B`

Somerfield Bulgarian Country White, Russe Region `14` `B`

Fun, fruity, tasty, expressive. Great value.

CHILEAN WINE RED

Cabernet Sauvignon Segu Olle, Somerfield `13.5` `C`

Easy to like. Too easy? Maybe for difficult food. Probably best with pasta.

Santa Rita Cabernet Sauvignon Reserva, 1991   `13.5` D

This specimen of a wine I usually rate highly seems lacking a little something.

CHILEAN WINE   WHITE

Caliterra Sauvignon Blanc 1994   `13` C

Losing the brilliance of its finish now it's ageing.

Chilean Sauvignon Blanc Sograda Furnilla, Somerfield   `15` C

Delicious, classy, fresh, ripe, zingy. Works on all fronts as a superb fish wine, grilled chicken wine, oriental food wine (not overspiced dishes) and as a lovely tipple to slurp at the end of the day. Has surprising elegance for the money.

Estorila, Benfica Co-op, Ribatejo NV   `14.5` B

Cosmetic fruit, powdery and soft, but finishing fresh. Interesting aperitif for both dry and medium-dry white wine lovers. Not in all stores.

ENGLISH WINE   WHITE

Denbies Engilsh   `12` C

Lamberhurst Sovereign   `13` B

Apply and sweet melon fruit. Some freshness. Good aperitif and garden party wine.

Lamberhurst Sovereign Medium Dry   13   B

Some good fruit here at a good price.

FRENCH WINE   RED

Beaujolais-Villages, Duboeuf   12   C

Beaune 1989   11   E

Brouilly, Duboeuf 1994   10   D

Cabernet Sauvignon VdP d'Oc, Val d'Orbieu 1994, Somerfield   14   B

Brilliant accompaniment to savoury substances. Not as exciting as the '93 but a really good cabernet for the money.

Chateau Carbonel Cotes du Rhone 1994   15   C

One of the best C-d-R around for under £4. Soft, ripe, very smooth, with just a hint of Rhone earth – a light smack of the soil which is most delicious.

Chateau de Caraguilhes, Corbieres 1990   15.5   C

Earthy yet impressively fruity without being too giving or overcooked. Lots of dry flavour and style.

Chateau de la Liquiere, Faugeres 1991   13   C

Very individual wine: chewy with dry-edged fruit, it will come alive with roast meat and vegetables.

Chateau de la Valoussiere, Coteaux du Languedoc Jeanjean, 1992   14.5   C

Character and colour, that is, earthy but soft tannins with a proper multi-edged fruit finish. Lovely.

Chateau de Montmal Fitou, Jeanjean 1993 `14` `C`

Soft, spicy, dry, plummy. An excellent casserole bottle.

Chateau La Chapelle Baradis, Cotes de Castillon 1989 `13` `C`

Some nice fruit, and creeping tannins at the rear of the fruit, but not overly rich or thrilling enough at this price.

Chateau la Chappelle Baradis, Cotes de Castillon 1990 `10` `C`

Chateau la Rocheraie, Bordeaux Superieur 1993 `13` `C`

Simple, fruity claret with few aggressive tannins.

Chateau le Clariot, Bordeaux 1992 `15` `C`

A superb introduction to the classic Bordeaux blend of cabernet sauvignon, cabernet franc and merlot. It is soft and friendly with just a faint bristle of the punk haircut of the tannic franc showing through the smoothly berried fruit (some lovely touches here) and though a dry wine, it is rounded to finish. If Bordeaux could turn out more wines like this unpretentiously drinkable bottle for these sorts of prices then the Australians would have nightmares.

Chateau Les Confreries, Bordeaux 1992 `13.5` `C`

Bargain claret: soft and fruity.

Chateau Monfaucon Red `12.5` `C`

Dry.

Chateau Montmal Fitou, Jeanjean 1993 `14` `C`

Very attractive, earthy, soft fruit.

Chateau Saint Robert, Graves 1992 `14` `D`

A tiny bargain. Put it away for 2/3 years to develop really well.

Chateau Talence, Premieres Cotes de Bordeaux 1989 `13.5` `D`

Elegant fruit.

Chateauneuf-du-Pape La Solitude, 1990 `14` `E`

The real thing at a real price. Now, if we could only divorce these two stable mates where C-du-P is concerned, many of us would be much happier.

Claret NV, Eschenauer, Somerfield `12` `B`

Corbieres, Val d'Orbieu 1994, Somerfield `13.5` `B`

Bright and fruity. Lighter than some.

Coteaux de Tricastin, Somerfield `13` `B`

Very pleasant. Not a rough edge in sight.

Cotes de Duras 1994 `13.5` `B`

Ah! Tannins! (Good, gravy-like fruit.)

Cotes de Gascogne Red 1994, Somerfield `12` `B`

Cotes de Provence, La Cave des Seigneurs de Saint Tropez 1993 `13.5` `C`

Fun and fruity.

Cotes du Rhone, Celliers de l'Enclave des Papes, Somerfield `13` `B`

Very soft and likeable – a teddy bear of a wine. Very sweet to finish. A beginner's Cotes du Rhone.

Cotes de Roussillon, Jeanjean 1994, Somerfield — 13.5 B

Cotes de Roussillon Villages — 12 B

Cotes de Ventoux, Somerfield — 12 B

Cotes du Marmandais 1993 — 12.5 B

Croix du Marquis 1990 — 13 E
Excellent classic-style dry fruit. Keep for another 4/5 years? Not available in all stores.

Crozes Hermitage, Celliers de Nobleus 1991 — 14 C
100 per cent syrah as soft and juicy as you like. Good pure fruit – no oak. Touch pricey? Not for syrah fans.

Domaine d'Abrens Minervois, Jeanjean 1992 — 15 B
Aromatic, rich, swirling fruit. Deep, well-structured, striking. Perfectly balanced and a touch classy. Terrific fruit.

Domaine d'Abrens Minervois, Jeanjean 1993 — 12.5 B
Very soft. Almost a whisper compared to some raucous minervois. Touch young.

Domaine de Bonserine, Cote Rotie 1989 — 11 F

Domaine de la Solitude, Cotes du Rhone 1992 — 10 C

Domaine de Rivoyre Cabernet Sauvignon, VdP d'Oc 1993 — 14 C
Good-looking beast. Almost too good-looking. Wouldn't mind

a cauliflower ear or a bent nose here to give it some character. But smooth? Yes. Limited distribution.

Domaine de Saint Julien VdP l'Herault, les Chais Beaucairois `13.5` `B`

Domaine des Salaises 1992, Saumur Remy Pannier `13` `C`

Domaine des Salaises, Saumur Remy Pannier 1993 `15` `C`

Terrific Loire red which oozes dry, raspberry fruit yet has that touch of slaty tannicity which distinguishes it. Balanced and stylish, this is a great price. Not available in all stores.

Fitou Caves de Mont Tauch, Somerfield `14` `B`

Dry, but the plummy fruit shines through.

Fitou Cuvee Rocher-d'Embree 1992, Somerfield `13` `B`

Sound, likeable fruit.

La Pelissiere, Cahors 1992 `11` `C`

Macon Rouge 1993, Somerfield `12` `C`

Hint of dark, savoury fruit. A hint – no more.

Macon Rouge, G. Desire 1991 `12` `C`

Margaux, Peter Sichel 1990 `12` `D`

A declassified Chateau Palmer? Could be, could be.

Mas Segala Cotes de Roussillon Villages 1993 `16` `C`

Rich, dry, almost imperiously fruity with its stylish blackberry fruit and subtle tannic shroud. Lovely food wine – cheeses especially.

Medoc 10 C

Merlot, Domaine de la Magdelaine 1993 12 B

Merlot VdP d'Oc Jeanjean 1994, Somerfield 14 B

Bargain. Dry coating to the rich, rolling fruit but this only makes the wine all the better with food. Gripping finish.

Merlot/Syrah, VdP de l'Ardeche 1993 13 B

Stalky, evolving tannins and fruit. Needs time – not soft or smooth enough yet. Not available in all stores.

Minervois Jeanjean 1994, Somerfield 14 B

Lovely, impactful rusticity. Great with sausage and mash.

Nuits St Georges, Cottin Freres 1991 11 E

Not available in all stores.

Red Burgundy 1994, Somerfield 10 D

Saint Chinian 1992 12 B

Saint Joseph, Cuvee Medaille d'Or, Caves de Saint Desiderat 1990 15 E

Pricey but sheer chocolate-coated delight. Lovely fruit.

Saint Tropez Cotes de Provence 1993, Les Caves de Provence 14 C

Chewy, brambly fruit. Very attractive flavours – fun for picnics and barbecues. Not stocked in the majority of Somerfield stores.

Somerfield Beaujolais 1994 `12.5` `C`

Pleasant, earthy, but hugely overpriced.

Somerfield Bergerac Rouge 1993 `11` `B`

Somerfield Claret, Eschenauer `12` `B`

Soft and approachable.

Somerfield Oak Aged Claret, Eschenauer `13` `C`

Very attractive proposition for steak and chips.

St Chinian 1991, Caves de Cucumont `12` `B`

St Joseph Cuvee Medaille d'Or, Cave de St Desiderat 1990 `14` `E`

Can't fault the fruit on this syrah-based beauty – but the price is a touch prohibitive.

Stowells of Chelsea Claret Bordeaux Rouge (3 litre) `13` `G`

A good simple quaffing claret with an agreeable echo of the dry, tannic heritage of the region.

Stowells of Chelsea Vin de Pays du Gard (3 litre) `14` `F`

Delightful smooth fruit with flavour and balance. A lovely touch – a distant echo, really – of earth.

Syrah VdP d'Oc Jeanjean 1994, Somerfield `12.5` `B`

Soft and jammy with an earthy edge.

Vacqueyras Vieux Clocher, Arnoux 1993 `14` `C`

A resounding tinkle of good firm fruit from this old bell.

VdP des Coteaux de l'Ardeche Rouge, Somerfield

Dry and good for well-attended pizza parties.

FRENCH WINE WHITE

Bordeaux Blanc Sec 1992, Somerfield

Can't complain at this with oysters. Good-style fruit/acid balance.

Buzet, Caves Co-operatives de Buzet 1993, Somerfield

Has flavour – can't deny that.

Chablis Premier Cru, Grande Cuvee, La Chablisienne 1990

The best-selling wine in the store's fine wine range. Doesn't excite me hugely.

Chardonnay VdP d'Oc, Somerfield

Touch of earth to the fruit which is ripe-edged and impressively balanced. Has style, flavour and great food compatibility.

Chardonnay, Vin de Pays de l'Herault 1993

Chateau Bastor-Lamontagne 1989 (half bottle)

Chateau de Brizay Sauvignon Blanc, Haut Poitou 1993

Musky, grassy, weird. Delicious with shellfish.

Chateau de la Bouletiere, VdP des Coteaux de Cabrerisse 1994

`13` `C`

Fresher and brisker than the '93. Limited distribution.

Chateau Monfaucon White 1993

`13` `C`

Chateau Tour de Montredon Corbieres Blanc, Val d'Orbieu 1994

`13.5` `B`

Nutty and dry.

Domaine de Bordeneuve VdP des Cotes de Gascogne Blanc, Yves Grassa 1994

`14.5` `B`

Fifty pence more than the basic Somerfield Gascogne blend but half a point more exciting.

Domaine de la Bouletiere Rose 1993

`13` `C`

Domaine de la Tuilerie Chardonnay, Hugh Ryman 1994

`14.5` `C`

Rich fruit of melon and camomile with flowery undertones. Bit frilly for a chardonnay? Possibly. But highly drinkable.

Domaine de Montjoui, Cotes de Thau 1993

`12` `B`

Domaine de Rivoyre Chardonnay, VdP d'Oc 1993

`16` `C`

Full ripeness of melons in the mouth. Quite superb and polished with tongue-tingling acidity. Stylish, explicit, fine. Limited distribution.

Domaine Fontanelles Sauvignon Blanc, VdP d'Oc 1993

`16` `B`

A complete wine brilliantly put together – such elegant assertiveness. Fruity, fresh, foodworthy, yet a great solo glug. This is a terrific bottle for the money. Not available in all stores.

Domaines Grassa 1993, Somerfield `12` `B`

Entre Deux Mers, Yvon Mau 1994, Somerfield `13` `B`

Was a brilliant big-rating bargain at £2.39 but at a quid more it struggles. Good clean fruit, however.

Gewurztraminer d'Alsace, Cave de Turckheim 1994 `13` `C`

Three years' time and lovely lush fruit will emerge.

Hautes Cotes de Beaune Blanc 1992 `12` `D`

James Herrick Chardonnay VdP d'Oc 1994 `14` `C`

Pleasantly flavoured and comforting but somehow not as exciting as it pretends. Rates well, can't deny it that.

Macon Blanc Villages 1993, Somerfield `12.5` `C`

Touch pricey.

Meursault, Cottin Freres 1990 `12` `E`

Not in all stores.

Muscat a Petits Grains, VdP des Collines de la Moure 1993 (half bottle) `14` `B`

Treat for days when you're all alone and all you want to do is tackle the newest Loretta Lawson mystery with fresh fruit and cheese for company.

Oak Aged Bordeaux Blanc, Eschenauer `12` `C`

Pinot Blanc d'Alsace, Cave de Turckheim 1994 `13.5` `C`

Let it age 2 years. It'll emerge a 15/16 pointer wine with more concentrated peach/apricot fruit.

Sancerre, Domaine Brock 1993   `13` `D`

Better, the '93 vintage, than before. Sancerre is stirring, but still has to fully awake to the under-£5 New World wines which compete with it and offer better value.

Somerfield Bordeaux Sauvignon Blanc   `12` `B`

Somerfield Chablis 1993   `12` `D`

Stowells of Chelsea Muscadet (3 litre)   `10` `G`

Rather spineless – not much fruit here.

Stowells of Chelsea Vin de Pays du Tarn (3 litre)   `12` `F`

Sound but dullish – not a lot of fruit.

Syrah Rose Val d'Orbieu, VdP d'Oc 1994   `13` `B`

Limited distribution.

Terret, Jacques Lurton VdP d'Oc 1993   `13` `B`

Terret Vin de Pays Lurton 1994   `12` `B`

VdP de Cotes des Gascogne Blanc, Yves Grassa 1994, Somerfield   `14` `B`

Zip and flavour. The usual medley of fruit, muted rather than fluorescent, but a good white at a good price.

VdP des Cotes de Gascogne Blanc 1993   `16` `B`

Brilliant zip to the pineapple acid coating the almost mango ripe fruit. A lovely modern glug. Stupendous value.

Vin de Pays des Coteaux de l'Ardeche, Somerfield   `13` `B`

Cheap soft fruit with a crisp undertone.

White Burgundy 1994, Somerfield   `12` `C`

Some hints of interesting fruit. Pricey hints.

GERMAN WINE   RED

Dornfelder Trocken, St Ursula   `13` `C`

GERMAN WINE   WHITE

Baden Dry NV, Somerfield   `12.5` `B`

**Bodenheimer Burgweg Juwel Beerenaus-
lese 1989 (half bottle)**   `14` `D`

With a slice of fruit tart or an apple and a hunk of cheese this
wine is a jewel indeed. Alas, it's over a fiver for the half bottle
which is an angelic size for such a wine but a devilish price
tag and though it is beautifully stratified sipping, with layers
of herby honey-tinged fruit wound around subtle orange and
lime peel flavouring.

**Gewurztraminer Halbtrocken Rietburg
Co-op, Pfalz NV, Somerfield**   `12` `C`

**Grauer Burgunder Trocken, Rietburg
Co-op 1990**   `10` `C`

Not in all stores.

Morio Muskat St Ursula 1994   `12` `B`

**Mosel Riesling Halbtrocken, Rheinberg
Kellerei, Somerfield**   `13` `B`

Very attractive, some lemonic cut but not a lot, and a soft fruit.

Mosel Rudolf Muller, Somerfield `12.5` `B`

Very pleasant, well-priced summer evening aperitif.

**Niersteiner Spiegelberg Kabinett, Rudolf
Muller 1993, Somerfield** `14.5` `B`

Delicious wine for gatherings of smoked salmon sandwich eaters.

Oberemmeler Rosenberg Riesling 1989 `10` `E`

**Oestricher Doosberg Riesling Kabinett,
Schloss Schonborn, Rheingau 1983** `14.5` `D`

Aperitif – light, refreshing, gently lemony/petrolly fruit. Also good with grilled prawns.

Pinot Blanc Gallerei `11` `B`

**Pinot Blanc Trocken, St Ursula 1993,
Somerfield** `12` `C`

**Rheingau Riesling, St Ursula 1993,
Somerfield** `13` `C`

Real riesling. Good conversation oiler.

**Rheinhessen Auslese, Rheinberg Kellerei
1993, Somerfield** `12` `C`

**Rheinhessen Spatlese, Rheinberg Kellerei
1992, Somerfield** `12.5` `B`

Rudesheimer Rosengarten, Somerfield `12` `B`

**Scharzhofberger Riesling Kabinett, Rudolf
Muller 1990** `13.5` `C`

Expensive a little, but a pretty aperitif all the same.

Somerfield Hock, Rudolf Muller

13 A

A bargain aperitif. Not unpleasant in its lightness.

Somerfield Pfalz Riesling Trocken, Rietburg 1989

12.5 C

I suspect many readers will find this dry riesling, with its curious kerosene aroma and austere fruit, nigh undrinkable. But with Chinese food it might be a revelation.

St Johanner Abtei Kabinett, Rudolf Muller 1993, Somerfield

13 B

Bright and fruity.

St Ursula Weinkellerei Bingen Morio Muskat

10 B

Trocken G. Breuer, Somerfield

14 B

Excellent fruit style to this Baden Dry-type wine. Very aromatic and attractive.

HUNGARIAN WINE RED

Bulls Blood, St Ursula 1993

10 B

I suppose with a goulash this German-bottled Magyar might work but it is not a hugely exciting wine in other respects.

HUNGARIAN WINE WHITE

Chardonnay, Somerfield

13 B

Good fruit up front but not hugely effectively round right to the finish. But for all that very attractive and excellent value.

Chardonnay Villany 1992 `11` `B`

Gyongyos Estate Sauvignon Blanc, Hugh Ryman 1994 `12` `C`

Getting cabbagey.

Gyongyos Estate Dry Muscat 1992 `13` `A`

Pleasant aperitif, and less expensive than last year.

ITALIAN WINE   RED

Bardolino Fratelli Pasqua, Somerfield `11` `B`

Barolo, Castiglione Faletto 1988 `11` `D`

Barolo Gordana 1990 `12` `D`

Austere edge which is only just turning licorice and typical. I'd keep this wine for a couple more years yet.

Cabernet Sauvignon del Veneto 1993 `12.5` `B`

Dry, very dry.

Chianti Classico Conti Serristori 1992 `13.5` `C`

Cleaner than the non-Classico from Serristori and less characterful.

Chianti Classico Montecchio 1991 `13.5` `C`

Sweet finish to the baked, earthy fruit. Must be drunk with food. Not stocked in the majority of Somerfield stores.

Chianti Conti Serristori 1994, Somerfield `14` `B`

Apples, plums and a touch of earth. A supreme food wine.

Copertino, VdT Rosso di Puglia `14` `C`
Deep rich fruit with mild soft curranty flavours well baked.

Cortenova Grande Friuli Merlot 1992 `14` `B`
Squashy fruit, very black cherry-like and plummy. Excellent style, very drinkable.

I Grilli di Villa Thalia, Calatrasi (Sicily) 1990 `13` `C`

Lazio Red, Casale San Giglio 1993 `11` `B`

Librandi Ciro Antonia Cataldo 1990 `14` `C`
Serious but not too serious. Fun with a mushroom and red pepper stew.

**Merlot del Veneto Fratelli Pasqua,
Somerfield** `12.5` `B`
Some plumpness of flavour in the fruit.

Montereale `13` `B`

Montereale Sicilian Red, Calatrasi `13` `B`
Dry and fruity. Good with pasta.

Riserva di Fizzano, Chianti Classico `13` `E`

Rosso de Braganza 1991 `13` `C`

Salice Salentino 1986 `13` `C`
Rich, mature, figgy fruit.

Sangiovese di Romagna 1992, Fabbiano `14` `B`

Sangiovese di Romagna 1993, Fabbiano `16` `B`
Wonderful fruity wine for the money. Has sangiovese typicity (earthy yet polished plums) and great balance. Satisfying drunk by itself or with roasts.

Sangiovese di Romagna, Somerfield   `15` `B`

Black cherry fruit with a lovely brisk, dry edge. Brilliant chilled with fish, room temperature with meat, cool as a simple fruit glug.

Taurino Salice Salento 1988   `14` `D`

The usual medicine from Dottore Taurino. Take it, in large doses, with a beef stew. The overripeness of this wine, with its raisiny edge, demands food.

Valpolicella Fratelli Pasqua, Somerfield   `11` `B`

Vignetti Casterna Valpolicella Classico 1990   `13` `B`

ITALIAN WINE   WHITE

Bianco del Monferrato, Araldica 1994   `11` `B`

Casato delle Macie, Vino da Tavola di Toscana 1993   `13` `C`

Chardonnay del Piemonte Araldica 1994, Somerfield   `15` `C`

Quiet but most impactful. Low note chardonnay fruit, well-integrated acidity, a lovely finish making it a classy bargain.

Colli Lanuvini Vino da Tavola 1992, Somerfield   `11` `B`

Frascati Principe Pallavicini 1994, Somerfield   `12` `C`

Lazio Bianco Pallavicini 1994   `12` `B`

Fresh and bone-dry but not a lot of flesh on those bones. Good with shellfish stew, though.

Orvieto Classico, GIV 1994   `13` `C`

Some agreeable fruit here.

**Pinot Bianco del Veneto Fratelli Pasqua
1994, Somerfield**   `10` `B`

**Pinot Grigio Fratelli Pasqua 1994,
Somerfield**   `11` `C`

Soave Fratelli Pasqua 1994, Somerfield   `12` `B`

Some flavour here.

**Soave Classico Vignetti Montegrande,
Fratelli Pasqua 1993**   `13` `C`

Clean, fresh, very pleasant.

**Somerfield Montereale Sicilian White,
Calatrasi**   `15` `B`

Lots of astonishingly well-integrated flavour here. Has an almond touch on the finish.

Verdicchio Classico Bianchi 1994   `12` `C`

LEBANESE WINE   RED

Chateau Musar 1985   `15` `E`

This wine is in the luxury class as a mouthful of volatile, spicy, velvety fruit, quite superb with a richly stuffed festival fowl, and, alas, it is now touching the luxury class in price.

MOLDOVAN WINE — WHITE

Hincesti Moldovan Chardonnay 1993, Hugh Ryman — 12 B

Getting a touch creaky in the joints.

NEW ZEALAND WINE — WHITE

Montana Sauvignon Blanc 1994 — 14.5 C

Rich fruit in the middle, grassy acids surrounding. Excellent fish-stew bottle.

Nobilo White Cloud 1993 — 15 C

Best year yet for this muller thurgau/sauvignon blanc blend. Lots of balanced fruit, fresh and flavoursome. Not stocked in the majority of Somerfield stores.

Stoneleigh Sauvignon Blanc 1993 — 13 D

Delicious but pricey. Not in all stores.

Stowells of Chelsea New Zealand Sauvignon Blanc (3 litre) — 13.5 G

Keen, grassy aromas, good fruit, rather a quiet finish.

PORTUGUESE WINE — RED

Alta Mesa Estremadura 1994 — 14 B

Simple, soft, ripe, very fruity, delicious chilled and poured over parched tongues.

Caves Velhas Garrafeira 1990 `13` `D`

Dao Reserva, Caves Alianca 1990 `14` `B`

Rich, dry fruit. Husky voices but sweet notes intrude and with rich food it's a wonderful bargain.

Douro Foral, Caves Alianca 1991 `14.5` `B`

Delicious – there is no other word for it. It's dry to finish but fruity to kick off and it's thoroughly attractive and soft.

Estorila, Alentejo `14` `B`

Perfectly innocuous, refreshing drop of fruit – unforgivably soft, monstrously inexpensive.

Leziria Tinto, Co-Op da Almeirim 1993 `15` `B`

Raspberry flavours turning dry. Terrific value for a terrific chunk of fruit.

Quinta da Pancas 1990 `14` `C`

This wine has long been a favourite of mine. This vintage is jammy, perhaps too jammy for cabernet fans, but its sweetness of fruit brings a smile to my chops (grilled or roasted).

Terras d'El Rei, Alentejo 1992 `14` `B`

Terras del Rei, Co-Op da Reguengos 1993 `14` `B`

Herbs, baked earth and plum fruit. Good with food. Not stocked in the majority of Somerfield stores.

PORTUGUESE WINE WHITE

Bairrada Branco 1994, Somerfield `14.5` `B`

Delicious fish wine with enough mineralised fruit to make it a superbly refreshing glug.

Bairrada Rose 1992 `13` `B`

A pleasant summery rose with an aroma of particular appeal, appropriately, to rose growers. Excellent price.

Estorila Vinho Branco `15` `B`

Delicious. Has crispness, yet there on the finish lurks an undertone of creamy nuttiness. Great with smoked fish.

SOUTH AFRICAN WINE RED

Cape Selection Pinotage 1992 `12` `B`

Kumala Cinsault Pinotage `16` `C`

Brilliant flavour and texture. Polished, savoury, deep, massively drinkable yet balanced and complex enough to tackle food, this is delicious and decisive.

SOUTH AFRICAN WINE WHITE

Clearsprings Cape White `15` `B`

Wonderful medium sweet, pear-drop fruit of great interest as a chilled aperitif and for people who don't like bone-dry wine.

Simonsvlei Chenin Blanc 1994, Somerfield `15` `B`

Full, rich, ripe pear and melon fruit. Satisfyingly gluggable by itself or with fish and chips.

Vredenburg South African Chardonnay/ Sauvignon Blanc 1992 `13` `C`

SPANISH WINE RED

Berberana Tempranillo, Rioja 1992 15.5 C
Soft, sweet vanilla and dry coconut (echoes only) adding a lovely lilt to the rich plumminess of the fruit.

Campo Viejo Rioja Gran Reserva 1982 15 D
Perfect weight of supple-limbed, ripe yet not heavy fruit.

Don Hugo Tinto, Bodegas Vitorianas, Somerfield 14 B
Don Darias blended for Somerfield. And it's a good, fruity wine. Not a hair out of place.

Navarra Tinto 15 B
Grown in Spain and bottled in France, this is brilliant value, full of ripe, sunny fruit, plummy and fresh.

Rioja Bodegas Alemenar 1992 13 C
Light cherries on the finish.

Santara Conca de Barbera, H. Ryman 1994 14.5 B
Such smoothness, flavour, style and quiet richness that the price tag is a very pleasant surprise.

Senorio de Agos, Rioja Reserva 1989 13 D

Senorio de Val, Casa de la Vina 1989 14 B
Striking tannins on the finish. They deliciously turn the gums into saddle leather.

Valencia Red Vincente Gandia, Somerfield 14 B
Nice juicy finish on the fruit which is firm and well structured. Bargain pasta bottle.

309

Vina Albali Gran Riserva 1984

Lacks the weight to score more at nigh on a fiver.

Vina Ardanza Rioja Reserva 1985

SPANISH WINE WHITE

Somerfield Valencia Dry White, Vincente Gandia

Gentle musty edge.

Castillo Imperial, Vino da la Tierra Valle de Monterey

Cheap and cheerful. Bit mute on the finish but has clean, fresh fruit.

Don Hugo Blanco NV, Bodegas Vitorianas

Banana, vanilla, coconut – terrific breezy fruit just packed with flavour. Great with fish curries!

Moscatel de Valencia V. Gandia, Somerfield

Great stuff for the money. Honeyed with soft marmalade undertones.

Rioja Blanco Bodegas Mariscol 1991, Somerfield

Touch too balsa-woody for me to rate it higher.

Sangredetoro 1991

Licorice!? Very dry, starts well. Drink it in an hour – it fades.

Santara Conca de Barbera Hugh Ryman 1994   `14.5`   B

Dry but soft-edged with always a hint of crispness about it. A most agreeable aperitif or first-course soup and salad wine.

USA WINE   RED

Glen Ellen Cabernet Sauvignon 1988   `13`   C

Glen Ellen Merlot 1991   `13`   C

Not yet in the class of '90 which rated 16.

Sebastiani Californian Cabernet Franc 1994   `14`   C

Delicious smooth vanilla-ed fruitiness.

Sebastiani Californian Dry Red, Somerfield   `13.5`   B

Tasty. Very tasty.

Sebastiani Zinfandel 1988   `13`   D

Astonishingly anodine and well-mannered for a zin of this age when what we like in this wine is its brusqueness.

Somerfield Californian Red   `13`   B

Very good value.

USA WINE   WHITE

August Sebastiani's White Zinfandel 1994   `12.5`   C

Sweetish fruit but fair flavour. Rated at £2.99 only. Not worth £3.99.

311

Sebastiani Chardonnay

Absolutely nothing wrong with this – except it's a quid more than it should be.

YUGOSLAVIAN WINE RED

Pinot Noir 1989, Slovenijavino

Very pleasant, dry, chewy wine of no complex fruit or varietal character but it's cheering and cherryish and smooth.

FORTIFIED WINE

Luis Caballero Fino Sherry, Somerfield

A fino with fruit (dry) but not as bone-dry or as saline as aficionados demand – a good first step for oloroso fans looking to develop their palates, though.

Manzanilla Gonzales Byass, Somerfield

Chilled with grilled prawns or slices of mountain ham, this wine is the business – the business.

SPARKLING WINE/CHAMPAGNE

Cava Cordoniu NV, Somerfield

Great stuff. Elegant, controlled, very attractively put together – a real bargain.

Chardonnay Brut, Varichon (France) `15` `C`
A cool, elegant alternative to champagne. Not stocked in the majority of Somerfield stores.

Cremant de Bourgogne, Cave de Lugny `14.5` `D`
Excellent. Gentle lemony fruit, drily conceived but fruitily underpinned.

Lindauer Brut `13` `E`
What a pity it's a touch over £7! Still, it's a delicious lemon sparkler for all that.

Louis Domcourt Champagne NV `14` `E`
If you must have champagne, this is well priced, well blended and good value for money. It is blended from one third each of chardonnay, pinot noir and pinot meunier from the 1991 and 1992 vintages.

Moscato Fizz `13` `A`

Prince William Blanc de Blancs Champagne NV `12.5` `G`

Prince William Brut Reserve Champagne `13` `F`

Prince William Champagne NV `13` `F`

Prince William Rose Champagne, Henri Mandois NV `12` `G`

Seppelt Great Western Brut Reserve, Australia `15` `C`
Wonderful value. Gentle lemonic fruit with finesse and style.

Somerfield Cava, Conde de Caralt `15` `C`
One of the best-value sparklers for under a fiver in Britain. Terrific wine and knocks many a witless champagne speechless.

Touraine Rose 15 D

A richly aromatic wine, with a mature, elegantly fruity feel balanced by an assertive acidity (as a good sparkler must be to be refreshing and second-glass inviting), and it is a serious champagne sub: classy, distinguished and extremely good value for money.

Touraine Rose Brut, Caves de Viticulteurs de Vouvray 13 D

TESCO

Tesco sent me a lovely bunch of flowers a little while back. It was a £19.99 spray called, according to the glossy pamphlet entitled *Floral Express* which accompanied it, White Bouquet. It included 'fragrant longiflorum lilies' and 'white gerbera' which are 'perfect to enhance any decor'. The table supporting my word processor was suitably enhanced and my words emerged suitably fragrant.

But was this an out-and-out bribe? A shameless attempt to win my affection? Some wine writers can be suborned by a mere smile from a pretty PR woman thirty yards across a room, so a twenty-quid bunch of gerbera is big-league stuff. And I must admit this is not the first time I have been so treated. I have, in my time, been sent gifts of no relevance whatsoever to my job as a wine reviewer. I received a delightful morale-boosting floral bouquet from Oddbins' PR person Katie MacAuley when I told her I was bed-bound with food poisoning and unable to come to her wine tasting, and M & S have over the past five years sent me assorted confectionery, a side of smoked salmon, two pairs of St Michael socks, a sweater, and two shirts – one of which was silk.

I must say I feel so much better having got this enormous burden off my chest. It's been niggling away at me for years. What if the *Sun* got to hear of it? Or, worse, if Mr Jim Budd, the hound-dog editor of the Circle of Wine Writers' monthly newsletter, got wind?

Of course, I could be wrong. Tesco may have had no base motive whatsoever in sending me a bunch of flowers. They may merely have hit upon an obvious way to let me know about a new service (telephone FREEPHONE 0800 403 403, by the way, and each bunch is 'delivered by courier in a beautiful presentation box').

Is Interflora trembling in its boots? I doubt it. Wine merchants didn't turn a hair when Tesco got into wine retailing. Merchants believed that no one would ever buy a bottle of wine from a retailer who also sold soap flakes and baked beans, and no doubt Interflora feels exactly the same, *mutatis mutandis*. Tesco, of course, is now one of the biggest wine merchants in the UK (indeed, with its absorption of the Scottish supermarket chain William Low putting it ahead of Sainsbury's in total grocery turnover, Tesco may well now be the biggest wine retailer in the country) and those wine merchants still left in business after trying to compete with Tesco *et al.* during the worst British recession since the thirties don't have much hair left to turn.

No doubt Tesco is already considering a mail-order hair transplant service, or even one in store, for it seems to be quick to answer all the needs of its customers. And it isn't only Interflora which feels the chill wind of change. Sketchley's would also be wise not to rest on its laurels. The purchase by Tesco of the William Low chain bequeathed the new owners, in a single branch in Loughborough, a considerable dry-cleaning set-up, and who is to doubt that if this is a roaring success, and the idea expanded, I won't be receiving, from the same PR department which sent me flowers, an invitation to have my wine-stained shirts cleaned free for a trial period? I wait with bated breath and dirty shirts. MotherCare and Boots must also be wondering where they went wrong. *Mother & Baby* magazine named Tesco retailer of the year in 1994, ahead of such committed mother-lovers as the nation's favourite chemists and baby products chain, and one branch, Reading, picked up a Child Friendly award from its local borough council. And it is not only with the mothers among its customers that Tesco scores but also with mothers on its staff. One of its stores in Eastbourne has two personnel managers, working mothers both, who share responsibilities and work part-time in what has always traditionally been a job for one person only. But a modern superstore is now a seven-day-a-week operation, so how can one person do it anyway (with the need to have a personnel manager on call at all times)? Job sharing is surely one of the biggest challenges facing the job market in this country, indeed it may be the only way certain areas can solve the problem of endemic non-employment, and so it is heartening to find it working and working well. Tesco also stole a march on its superstore-committed rivals by expanding its city centre Metro store concept. On the evidence of my own eyes, Metro stores offer stiff competition even to Marks & Spencer on the take-away food front.

Following the purchase of William Low I don't doubt that the Scots are congratulating themselves on finding cheaper wines – even though, personally, I think it a pity that William Low lacked the acumen and drive to be a supermarket force in its own right, in its own country. But then I might say the same about Tesco's other foreign purchases, Catteau in France and Global in Hungary. The first Tesco store in the land of the gay hussar opened in 1994 but I have yet to visit it.

France has a place in the store's list of top-selling wines but not near the top. The list is:

1. Liebfraumilch.
2. Hock.
3. Lambrusco.
4. Australian Red.
5. Vin de Pays de l'Herault rouge.
6. Muscadet.

All of these wines are Tesco own-label bottles. When I asked wine buyer Janet Lee what sort of people bought wine at Tesco she said, 'All sorts, but the largest sector would be twenty-five- to forty-year-olds with young families.'

Tesco has a sharp eye for any opportunity to profit not just from trade but from publicity. They are a major seller of National Lottery tickets and during the launch razzmatazz there were live TV broadcasts from Tesco stores. Tesco also got into bed with Richard Branson. The launch of Virgin Cola, a splendid brand name bearing in mind Britain's *fin de siecle* sexual ethics and new-found celibate fashionability, was one in the eye for Coke which responded with an emotional TV campaign attempting to prove the claim that only Coke is It. It isn't, of course, and I've seen it proved in a blind tasting, in which I participated. Self-confessed American addicts of the 'real thing' discovered to their surprise that they preferred the new super-market colas (Sainsbury's also has one). Cost was never a factor, purely taste preference. I have to say I find all colas revolting, and have done since childhood, so I feel utterly impartial in reporting these amusing facts which were hardly scientifically arrived at and are barely meaningful statistically since less than a dozen people were involved. However, more than a dozen people did visit the Tesco stand at the Liberal Democrats party conference in 1994, which was another innovation for the company. Retail stands, at which PR people and corporate affairs executives demonstrate to otherwise ignorant MPs and their husbands and wives what life is like outside Parliament, are a feature of party conferences but Tesco was the only supermarket who bothered to turn up for the Lib Dem's shindig. Tesco likes to cover everyone (further exemplified by their being the only one of the majors to exhibit at the NEC's Good Food Show last year, but then Tesco does sell superb Highland beef and the store's cheese display is reckoned, by certain food commentators, to be the nattiest of any supermarket chain). Tesco also stole a feathery notion from the Co-op's cap (which introduced the idea of the dividend for loyal customers some time in the last century) and introduced a plastic card which enabled shoppers to receive money-saving offers on regular purchases.

The store also spent a fortune on TV commercials promising customers that they will never have to stand behind more than one customer at any checkout if there are checkouts not yet operational. A trifling thing? Not to any shopper with a bouncy bunch of kids who's forced to stand and wait in a queue of six people when there are only three tills operating out of a row of eight. Customers whose patience is tried, try elsewhere. And Tesco knows it. Somewhere within the sepulchral depths of Tesco's advertising agency there has to be a copywriter who's been unable to resist scribbling on a pad 'The store where shopping's less of a chore'.

However, the lengths Tesco will go to in order to soothe its customers' tempers is nothing compared to the heights it can reach massaging certain wine writers' egos. I am sure I was not the only wine hack to receive a floral tribute (they had to tell *someone* about the service in the absence of such creatures as Flower Correspondents) but surely I must be the only hack to have been sent – eat your hearts out, Goolden and Clarke – a bottle of Tesco wine with a label carrying a picture of a dead relative.

Well, I say relative. These things are, of course, relative. What I mean is a person my Aunt Millie has always sworn is a relative. My great-great-great-great-grandfather, to be exact. Alas, I hate everything about the wine. The shallow pompousness of the label, little relieved by Christoph Wilibald Gluck's (1714–87) grinning noodle, would sit better on an indigestible biography of the composer rather than on a £4.99 bottle of white rioja. True, Tesco had no say in the design of the label, so we can excuse them, but they did have a say in the blend, and the result is an inexcusably indecisive bottle of white rioja, Faustino V 1989. My laughing gear has tangled with sparkier two-quid bottles. Faustino V's fruit, the devil take it, pathetically struggles to arrest the nose and strike the palate and hoarsely whispers where it should be ringing with a rich, fruity bellow. 10 points is about the most I can find within me to award it. Sorry, grandpa. Whatever else might be in my blood, nepotism, it would seem, runs thin.

But it runs. I cannot, I have to admit, leave out of this Tesco introduction Superplonk itself. Taking up an idea by Janet Lee and with the participation of the *Guardian* newspaper, I actually blended a red and a white wine of this name with *Weekend Guardian* readers in mind. The wines are widely on sale in the store (even if modesty has prevented me from including them in the Tesco entries which follow). How could I resist a once-in-a-lifetime challenge to create a Superplonk for readers of my column?

Wine writers are, after all, possessed of the same sort of playful egos as football supporters. We love to dream of the perfect team: that particular cabernet sauvignon added to that shiraz supported by that nebbiolo. The game is irresistible. Sometimes it's not just different grape varieties but different vintages of the same grape. At times, it's different grapes from different countries. When friends drop by for a casual supper on a day I've been tasting wine and I have several dozen bottles opened, I might mingle a Chilean merlot with a Clare Valley shiraz and add a splash of south Italian negroamaro and . . . the wine is all over the place. It's terrible – a sum of the parts which is never as good as each individual component wine.

My ideas on marrying one wine with another or mixing several grape varieties together do not, then, always work out. But Janet said have a go and have a go I did. My only stipulation was that the wine would end up on shelf at £2.99 or less. As the project progressed, and likely suppliers and countries of origin were canvassed, it quickly became apparent that I may not have a problem but suppliers had a big one: my price ceiling was a tough condition. Australia and South Africa, for instance, were both perfect for the quality of fruit I was after but they simply couldn't do it for the money. I wasn't so daft as to expect, for £2.99 the bottle, a world-class level of complexity, but I had to have supreme drinkability. Wines, a red and a white, which you could open and drink anytime for the sheer pleasure of the fruit.

In the end, the choice of country and potential supplier was narrowed down to Spain. Chile clamoured for inclusion right to the end but the price would have been closer to £3.99. So Spain it was, and one bodega in particular. I had admired its wines over the years for the vibrant quality of their fruit and their inoffensive price tags. When I visited them and spent time in the lab putting various grape varieties together I was impressed with their patience and their enthusiasm. Both wines are soft and attractively fruity with a strong hint of local character, and my aim has always been to make them unpretentious bottles I myself would like to open at the end of the day and enjoy either by themselves or with light foods.

But quite how Tesco managed to keep them below my £2.99 ceiling I do not know. When the father and son team who run the bodega faced Ms Lee across the negotiating table I was out of the room. I was spared, then, the spectacle of strong men sobbing.

But not, more's the pity, the sight of feeble men bitching. The idea of a wine writer putting together a couple of bottles of Superplonk for his newspaper's readers upset certain po-faced members of the wine-writing fraternity and the wine trade. But then I do several things which seem to grate with the old farts brigade.

One of which, of course, is this very book.

Tesco
Tesco House
PO Box 18 Delamare Road
Cheshunt
EN8 9SL

Tel 01992 632222
Fax 01992 644235

SEE STOP PRESS SECTION AT END OF BOOK FOR LAST-MINUTE ADDITIONS TO THIS RETAILER'S RANGE.

ARGENTINIAN WINE RED

Alamos Ridge Cabernet Sauvignon 1993

Flavour and style. Hints of tannin but this is deliciously melded with the fruit. Great with food.

Stowells of Chelsea Mendoza Red Wine (3 litre)

Delicious rounded fruit with a meaty edge. Good depth of flavour and style.

ARGENTINIAN WINE WHITE

Alamos Ridge Chardonnay 1993

Should be just coming on to shelf as this book hits the shops – and an engaging, fruity wine it is, with a soft medley of flavours handsomely expressed.

AUSTRALIAN WINE RED

Australian Cabernet Sauvignon, SE Australia, Tesco

Leathery, slightly exotic aroma. Full, soft, caressing fruit of a degree of complexity which is surprising at the price.

Australian Mataro, Tesco

Australian Shiraz, McLaren Vale, Tesco   16   C

Exceptionally, compulsively drinkable bottle. Has vivid fruit, velvety and rich, and a weightiness which makes it a great partner for cheeses and rich foods.

Baldivis Estate Cabernet/Merlot, 1992   12   E

Sweet simplicity. Not available in all stores.

Barossa Merlot 1992, Tesco   16.5   D

Highly aromatic, deeply complex, ripely fruity, engagingly soft and deep, this is a superb mouthful of firm fruit. Forward and all-embracing, its chutzpah will annoy the old farts, but young farts like me think it is pure magic. Top 70 stores only.

Barramundi Shiraz/Merlot   14   C

Vibrant, spicy, fun.

Best's Great Western Cabernet Sauvignon 1992   13   E

Silly price for good fruit which comes at a third of the price from elsewhere. Delicious . . . but. Luckily only 15 stores have it.

Best's Great Western Shiraz 1992   15   E

A roast chicken (one of Tesco's excellent free-range French) and this would be a marvellous combo. It has weight, texture and vigour. Only at 15 stores.

Bin 707 Cabernet Sauvignon, Penfolds 1989   14   G

Top 70 stores only.

Bleasdale Langhorne Creek Malbec 1990   13.5   D

Expensive for the style. Tasty and well-developed but those extra pennies tell. Top 70 stores only.

323

Brown Brothers Tarrango 1994

So ripe, luscious and downright juicy it can be spread on bread and given to children as a warning not to crush too hard otherwise there is no character in the wine.

Cabernet Sauvignon, Tesco

Lovely cuddly soft fruit. Very tongue-huggable.

Chapel Hill Cabernet Sauvignon 1991 `15` `E`

Rich and complex, meaty and full of well-textured fruit.

Chapel Hill McLaren Vale Shiraz 1992 `14` `E`

Smooth and flowing, beautifully executed, rich, finely textured. You wallow in it. Not at all stores.

Coonawarra Cabernet Sauvignon 1992, Tesco `14` `D`

Soft yet jammy – a jamminess richly counterpointed by a gentle tannic edge.

Cranswick Director's Reserve Shiraz 1992 `14` `D`

Plump and unathletic. By which I mean that it has lots of fat, rich fruit but can they run with food? Doubtful – unless soft pastas, quietly sauced.

Delatite Cabernet Merlot Devil's River 1992 `14` `D`

This is really what some critics find irksome in Aussie wine; for here we have flavour and fruit but will it stand up to food? Not beefy fodder, that's for sure, but light meat dishes will work. Not in all stores.

Goundrey Mount Barker Shiraz `16.5` `D`

So smooth and comforting, seductive and richly structured, it's a sin not to share it with friends – or not, as the case may be.

Hardys Nottage Hill Cabernet Sauvignon 1992 `15.5` `C`

Rich, leathery, satisfying wine.

Hardys Nottage Hill Cabernet Sauvignon/ Shiraz 1993 `16` `C`

Controlled soft spice laid on smooth blackcurrant fruit. Delicious, firm, well-styled.

Ironstone Cabernet/Shiraz 1992 `16` `D`

Something interesting to get your teeth into for not a lot of money. Rich tannins, gravy-edged fruit, and a deep delivery of flavour. Selected stores.

Kingston Estate Reserve Shiraz 1991 `12` `E`

Maglieri Shiraz, McLaren Vale 1992 `15.5` `D`

Controlled spicy fruit which is perfectly mature yet still with bags of energy and bite. Top 70 stores only.

McLaren Vale Grenache, Tesco `16.5` `C`

Just plain wonderful. Has rounded fruit with dry, gently tannic undertones and a sinfully soft, lingering finish. Brilliant fruit. Not at all stores.

McLaren Vale Merlot, Ryecroft 1993 `16` `D`

Beautifully integrated fruit and acid. A very soft, rich wine of stand-alone class and vibrancy. Only food will make it wobble. Choose light dishes – not those overspiced or oversauced.

Mick Morris Durif 1991 `16` `E`

Looks like ink, smells like port, textured like fresh tar, tastes like cassis (plus rich tannins of great depth), this is a very potent contender indeed. Try it with roast game (duck breast with cassis sauce would be wonderful). But be warned: a little goes a long way with this 15 per cent alcohol wine. Only at the top 70 stores.

Mitchelton Cabernet Shiraz 1993 `13` `C`

Not in all stores.

Old Penola Estate Coonawarra Cabernet Sauvignon 1989 `14.5` `D`

Mint and blackcurrant, edging towards middle age. Wonderful with cheeses and grilled vegetable tarts. Soft velvet texture. Top 70 stores only.

Orlando RF Cabernet Sauvignon 1992 `14.5` `C`

Touch of beefiness here and velvet tannins. Too soft? For claret die-hards, yes. Not for me.

Oxford Landing Merlot 1993 `16` `C`

Oodles of dry yet sweet-finishing fruit which is deep and very richly endowed. Pungent, potent, very purposeful.

Penfolds Australian Red, Shiraz/Cabernet Sauvignon, South Australia, Tesco `14` `B`

A ripe example of vivacious fruit. Brilliant value.

Penfolds Bin 128 Shiraz, Coonawarra 1990 `14` `D`

Very immediate soft fruit. Delicious with grilled sausages and meats.

Penfolds Bin 35 Shiraz Cabernet 1992 `15` `C`

Ripe, soft fruit with some development ahead of it. Smooth and palate hugging. Delightful. Attractive berry flavours, well-structured and balanced. Very drinkable now but a 17/18-pointer in 3/4 years.

Penfolds Kalimna Bin 28 Shiraz 1991 [14.5] [D]

Pewsey Vale Adelaide Hills Cabernet Sauvignon 1991 [15] [D]

Soft with delicate tannins which impinge but don't intrude. A tasty specimen but a nervous one. Don't frighten it with any food but the simplest. Top 70 stores only.

Rosemount Balmoral Syrah 1992 [14] [G]

Wonderful tannins here, soft and yet determined. This wine will get better and better over the next 5/6 years. Only from the top 15 stores.

Shiraz, Tesco [13] [C]

Excellent value, demurely fruity.

St Halletts Old Block Shiraz 1992 [14.5] [E]

Impressively structured. Ripe, full and deep. Mild food only, though – kidneys in red wine, for example, would annihilate this bottle. Selected stores only.

Stowells of Chelsea Shiraz Cabernet (3 litre) [14] [G]

Rich fruit with earthy undertones. Has a long, meaty finish with a firm, purposeful balance of fruit and acid.

Tarrawarra Pinot Noir Yarra Glen 1990 [13] [E]

Temple Bruer Cornucopia Grenache 1994 [D]

Delicious but so highly polished that it almost slips into the medium-dry category. Top 70 stores.

Temple Bruer Shiraz/Malbec 1989 [14] [D]

Dry, mature, serious, with a beautifully developed tannic softness. Top 70 stores only.

Tesco Australian Grenache

Rippling fruit, with depth and style. Plenty of flavour.

Tesco Australian Red, Shiraz/Cabernet Sauvignon S. Australia

Brilliant value. The shiraz and cabernet sauvignon grape varieties combine most attractively and offer a tarry aroma, excellent fruit with some cherry and plum, and a dryness which is not too spicy or sweaty. Outstanding value.

Wynns John Riddoch Cabernet Sauvignon 1991

What a price! But what a wine! You can taste it 5 minutes after the last drop has gone down the throat – it lingers like a Gioconda smile.

Yalumba Bushvine Grenache, 1993

Aromatic, softly tannic, figgy, blackcurranty, plummy – this is a lot of wine. Tremendous partner for casseroles.

Yalumba Shiraz 1991

Yarra Glen Pinot Noir 1993, Tesco

Still don't think a lot of this wine. Not in all stores.

AUSTRALIAN WINE WHITE

Australian Chardonnay, South East Australia, Tesco

Has oodles of fruit and finishes with a sly wink of lemonic acidity.

Australian Colombard/Chardonnay, Tesco

Great combo of grapes offering zest, fruit and acid. Lovely glass of wine. Very tasty.

Australian Sauvignon Blanc, SE Australia, Tesco

Dry yet with lots of friendly fruit which makes the wine palatable with salads or on its own.

Australian White, Rhine Riesling, SE Australia, Tesco

Flavour and fruit. Ignore the riesling you may know and hate – this example has the sun in it.

Australian White, Tesco

Twenty years ago this wine would have labelled itself Australian Hock.

Barramundi Semillon/Chardonnay

Rich, fruit-salad nose. Lots of pineapple acidity and great, swinging melon/mango fruit. Smashing wine to let the heart soar.

Best's Victoria Colombard 1994

Richly inviting aroma with the fruit well held up by the vigorous acidity. A wine of character for all sorts of fish and chicken dishes, salads and starters. Selected stores.

Brown Brothers Dry Muscat 1993

But with scallops with a minted pea puree, this rates 15 points. Not at all stores.

Brown Brothers Late Picked Muscat 1993

Delicious sweet aperitif: floral and summery.

Brown Brothers Late Picked Muscat Blanc 1993
`14` `D`

Humm. Aperitif? With pud? Nope. Try it with fresh grapes. Not at all stores.

Cape Mentelle Semillon/Sauvignon Blanc 1994
`17` `E`

Sublimely fruity and well-cut. Has an upper layer of creamy melon and a lower one of gooseberry. But this is not a stuff-yourself-full-of-calories slice of fruit cake; this is the product of a maitre patissier.

Chardonnay, Tesco
`12` `C`

Chateau Tahbilk Marsanne
`14` `D`

A rich yet fresh-to-finish concoction for grilled chicken and chilli pepper. Good with oriental food, especially Indonesian or Thai.

Clare Valley Riesling 1994, Tesco
`15.5` `C`

Utterly scrumptious. Imagine picking a fresh lime, gathering a fresh melon, squeezing them, full and ripe, into a glass, and then adding a splash of mineral acidity. Not at all stores.

Delatite Dead Man's Hill Gewurztraminer 1992
`12` `D`

An overpriced curiosity. Appealing rose-petal fruit but lacks bite and an easy-to-swallow price. Not available in all stores.

Fume Blanc, Hunter Valley, Rosemount Estate 1994
`13.5` `D`

Expensive – a touch. Sauvignon blancish – a touch. Not at all stores.

Hardys Australian Rhine Riesling, South Australia, Tesco 14 B

Elegant, ripe fruit with a touch of acidic butteriness. Good sound stuff. Brilliant with grilled fish.

Hardys Nottage Hill Chardonnay 1994 17 C

Best vintage yet. Lovely textured, oily fruit, never overdone or blowsy and a buttery, melony finish of surefooted delivery. Terrific value for such classy drinking.

Hunter Valley Semillon 1993, Tesco 14 C

Light, saucy, fresh. Quiet fruit without the usual punch of woodiness. Good with grilled chicken. Not at all stores.

International Winemaker Oaked Semillon/ Sauvignon Blanc 1992, Tesco 14 C

Big woody fruit of depth. Great with grilled chicken.

International Winemaker Semillon/ Sauvignon Blanc McLaren Vale, 1992 14 C

Delicious woody nose – a white Graves in all but name, but with a lush touch. Excellent food wine.

Ironstone Semillon/Chardonnay 1994 15 D

Fruity elegance with a fresh, lemonic edge. Delicious aperitif or with squid dishes. Also suits mild oriental food. Selected stores.

Jabiru Sauvignon Blanc 1993 13 C

Not a totally convincing wine. But then nor is the s.b. grape grown in Australia. Topical fish food label. Very minerally and fresh. To drink with shellfish and oily fish.

Kingston Estate Reserve Chardonnay 17 E

An outstanding specimen of breeding and pedigree style. Has

warmth and purpose, richness and flavour, yet lovely harmonious acids. Very fine. Not available in all stores.

Krondorf Show Reserve Chardonnay 1993   16   E

Potent, rich, purposeful, a real treat. Save it for Christmas Day smoked salmon. Not available in all stores.

Lindemans Chardonnay, Padthaway 1991   10   E

Lush woody aromas with distant echoes of butterscotch. The fruit reveals this olfactory blueprint in the flesh but with additional weight of sour melon.

Lindemans Padthaway Chardonnay 1992   15   E

A somewhat quiet chardonnay for an Aussie but don't mistake the purity of the fruit or the keenness of purpose.

McLaren Vale Chardonnay 1993, Tesco   15   D

Rich fruit gives an attractive acidic canopy. A well-structured wine for grilled or poached chicken. Has typical Aussie fatness but this is never too gross; rather, it is smooth, comforting and agreeably tasty. Not at all stores.

McWilliams Elizabeth Semillon 1989   13.5   D

Has typical sour fruit and some weight of woodiness, but with a lemony rich finish. This isn't as developed as a five-year-old ought to be. Not available in all stores.

Mitchelton Muscat Late-Picked, Victoria 1993   14   C

Definite aperitif wine. Has the acidity, too, for fish dishes with rich spicy sauces. Also good with spicy prawns. Top 70 stores only.

Mitchelton Semillon/Chardonnay Victoria 1993   13.5   C

Noble Semillon, Riverina 1992, Tesco (half bottle) `15` `D`

Echoes of lemon curd and ginger marmalade here. Drink it with a black mood and watch it lift. Top 70 stores only.

Old Triangle Semillon/Chardonnay 1994 `16` `C`

Not big but hugely delicious and stylish. A special occasion tipple – great with smoked salmon dishes. Melon and citric pineapple (very subtle) gracefully intertwined offer great fruit/acid balance. Where many a sem/chard combo in Aussie hands is leather-gloved, this one is all silk and lace. Multi-layered, individual, fine.

Penfolds Koonunga Hill Chardonnay 1994 `14` `C`

Still rich and fruity and mouth-filling as ever it was – though £4.99 is getting a bit too rich.

Penfolds Semillon/Chardonnay 1994 `15` `C`

This has lovely warfaring acidity and fruit which clash deliciously over the tastebuds. Not at all stores.

Pewsey Vale Rhine Riesling 1994 `14` `C`

Yes, it's riesling. But . . . swallow your prejudices and put a smile on your face – with smoked fish. Not at all stores.

Preece Chardonnay 1993 `13.5` `D`

Good but neither quirky nor as exciting as previous vintages.

Rhine Riesling, Tesco `15` `B`

Rich, oily and most attractively fruity. Great aperitif and also with fish. Interesting accompaniment to complex salads.

Rosemount Roxburgh Chardonnay 1992 `16.5` `G`

A point for every quid it costs – yet compared with so many white burgundies this wine is great value. It has extremely elegant wooded fruit, a highly luxurious texture and an imperious finish.

Rothbury Estate Verdelho, Hunter Valley 1994   16   C

Unusual style of wine with rewarding, dry apricot/peach fruit, slightly smoky. An attractive wine in superb form. Top 70 stores only.

Sauvignon Blanc, Tesco   13   C

Semillon, Tesco   12   B

St Halletts Semillon/Sauvignon Blanc   14   D

Superb style and flavour to the fruit, plus a lovely zest of acid. Very elegant.

St Halletts Semillon/Sauvignon Blanc 1994   15   D

Delicate ripe hints.

Stirling Estate Chardonnay 1993   15   D

Delicious. A gentle giant. Restrained woody fruit with hints of citrusy peach. Top 70 stores only.

Stowells of Chelsea Semillon Chardonnay (3 litre)   14   G

Presence and lift, style and purpose – this fruit knows where it's going. Good with food and mood.

Temple Bruer Botrytis Riesling (half bottle)   14.5   D

A blend of '92 and '93, this is a very rich wine which is good now with soft fruit desserts but kept for 10 years will be dazzling.

Tesco Australian Nouveau 1995   13   C

Tesco Australian Rose 1995

Barbie doll-flavoured but I dare say the kids will like it.

The Antipodean 1994

Mildly amusing but divertingly expensive.

Tim Adams Semillon 1994

As befits a wine which shows two men on its label scrubbing out a barrel, this is an expensive bottle (and available at a mere 14 branches). It has a gorgeous, soft, peachy (but dry) feel to it balanced by firm acids. Probably laid down for AD 2000.

Western Australian Chenin Blanc 1993, Tesco

Lovely rich edge to the fruit which makes it a wine to go with a dish like lemon chicken. Dry honeyed feel to the fruit is rather classy. Not at all stores.

Wildflower Ridge Chenin Blanc, Houghton, Swan Valley 1993

Seafood or nothing.

Yalumba Museum Show Reserve Rutherglen Muscat (half bottle)

Considering you get cough mixture, floor polish, oranges, cherries and herbal honey in your glass, the fact that the stuff in the glass has cost you £2.30 is probably a fair price. But it is an acquired taste – and strictly for deep-rich desserts and deep, rich pockets. (Adventurous souls, seeking perfumed feet, could try polishing up the floorboards with it.)

AUSTRIAN WINE RED

Winzerhaus Blauer Zweigelt 1993 `14.5` `C`

A superb wine, chilled, for rich fish dishes, chicken and oriental duck. A light, fruity, supple wine – much more attractive than the beaujolais it could easily replace.

Lenz Moser Blauer Zweigelt 1994 `15.5` `C`

The beaujolais of Vienna (but much better). A lovely supple, fruity wine of considerable charm and no little finesse. Great value and served chilled will please even those who say they prefer white to red. Top 70 stores.

Lenz Moser Siegendorf Rot 1993 `13` `D`

A pleasant, fruity experience for the palate. A slightly less engaging ride for the pocket. Top 14 stores only.

AUSTRIAN WINE WHITE

Austrian Dry White `14` `B`

Lovely pear, apple and peach fruit and controlled acidity. Quite delicious and superb value for money.

Lenz Moser Gruner Veltliner 1994 `13` `C`

Not offering such big thrills as previous vintages. Selected stores.

Lenz Moser Servus 1994 `10` `B`

Servus? No thank you awfully much.

Winzerhaus Gruner Veltliner 1993 15 B

Winzerhaus Pinot Blanc 1992 12 B

BRAZILIAN WINE RED

Brazilian Cabernet/Merlot, Tesco 12 B

Sweet, simple fruit. Not complex or rich or deep. But a friendly glass none the less.

BRAZILIAN WINE WHITE

Brazilian Chardonnay/Semillon, Tesco 14 B

Got softer and less gawky, this wine, as it's aged in bottle. Not at all stores.

Brazilian Pinot Noir, Tesco 12.5 C

Reasonable level of fruit. But with Brazilian on the label and such vibrant colours, it would be reasonable to expect a colourful, vibrant wine – especially at £3.99.

BULGARIAN WINE RED

Bulgarian Country Red, Tesco 13 A

**Bulgarian Cabernet Sauvignon Reserve
1989, Tesco** 15.5 B

An aromatic, rich, bright-fruit edged wine of impressive weight and class for the money. Soupy, ripe (yet dry-finishing) and excellent with roasted and grilled meats and vegetables.

BULGARIAN WINE   WHITE

Bear Ridge Aligote   `14` `B`

Lots of flavour here. A more multi-layered aligote (grape variety) than ever emerged from Beaujolais. Not in all stores.

Bear Ridge Bulgarian White 1993   `13` `B`

Sound, fruity, drinkable, technically correct. But wears a bowler hat rather than a baseball cap.

Bear Ridge Dry White   `12` `B`

Not at all stores.

Bear Ridge White Cabernet Sauvignon 1994   `13.5` `B`

Well, it's not every day you drink the claret grape so wan, but the fruit's all there – quirky and talcum-soft. Good with fish salads. Not in all stores.

Bulgarian Chardonnay Reserve, Tesco   `14` `B`

Bulgarian Country White, Tesco   `12` `A`

CANADIAN WINE   RED

Canadian Red, Tesco   `10` `C`

Niagara Peninsula Canadian Red Wine

Quirky, soft, aromatic, polished – and very odd. But this oddness disappears under food, as it would, for that matter, under the cataract which gives the wine its name. Not at all stores.

CANADIAN WINE WHITE

Canadian White, Tesco 13.5 C

Aromatic and tasty. The wine is a touch expensive at nigh on four quid.

Niagara Peninsula Canadian White Wine

Fresh and fruity. Not complex or grand, but acceptable. Not at all stores.

CHILEAN WINE RED

Caliterra Cabernet Merlot 1993 C

Dry and rich-edged. Good balance, slightly restrained but ultimately very satisfyingly fruity and very good value.

Caliterra Cabernet Sauvignon Reserve 1992 14.5 D

Classy feel here and some delivery of savoury fruit.

Canepa Cabernet Sauvignon 1992 C

The tannins cruise in behind the lush fruit which is crushed blackberry. Lovely wine. Top 70 stores only.

Canepa Oak Aged Cabernet Sauvignon 1992   14   C

Not a pound better wine than the store's own-label Chilean cabernet.

Canepa Oak Aged Zinfandel 1994   14   C

Jammy yet very dry with touches of rich tannin. Top 70 stores only.

Chilean Cabernet Sauvignon, Tesco   15.5   C

Gone up slightly in price but also gone up in my estimation. Superb assemblage of tannin, fruit and acid all marching sweetly yet drily together. Can be decanted and served to ignorant nobs who will coo over its immense charms.

Chilean Red, Tesco   15   B

Undistinguished aromatically but serious rich fruitiness of the blackcurrant variety (from the cabernet sauvignon in the blend) and a touch of dry tannicity (courtesy of the malbec). Very well priced.

Cousino Macul Merlot 1991   14   C

Well-matured, dry, and firmly structured.

Don Maximo Cabernet Sauvignon 1993   16.5   D

Gorgeous expression of South American controlled exoticism thinly overlaid with European style, polish and wit. Utterly scrumptious wine.

Errazuriz Merlot 1994   17   C

Wonderful fruit! Dances all over the tastebuds on little velvet clogs.

Merlot, Tesco   13   C

Attractive rich, savoury merlot.

Montes Alpha Cabernet Sauvignon 1990 | 13.5 | E

Age for 5/6 years. Good tannins.

Santa Rita Merlot, Maipo, Tesco | 14 | C

Delicious, soft and serious at one and the same time. Rich fruit firmly balanced.

Undurraga Pinot Noir, Maipo 1992 | 14 | C

Not highly aromatic, as classic pinots should be, but classy, flavoursome fruit of decent weight and quality. Will it develop in bottle over the next year? I fancy it might.

CHILEAN WINE   WHITE

Caliterra Casablanca Chardonnay 1994 | 16.5 | C

Superb rich edge to the final thrust of the elegant fruit. Impressive wine with gusto, flavour and real style.

Caliterra Sauvignon Semillon 1994 | 13 | C

A 17-point wine until this last spring when its whistle-clean potency of fruit began to lose its brilliance.

Canepa Oaked Chardonnay 1993 | 16 | C

Hints at rumbustiousness but doesn't, thankfully, quite pull it off. The punchy fruit (melon) is beautifully counterpointed by the acidity (pineapple), and the result is a lovely, good value tipple. Great with all sorts of fish and light fowl dishes.

Chilean Chardonnay/Semillon,Tesco | 15 | C

If only it was £3.99 (or less). Lovely rich edge to the fruit which is striking and modern – a bruiser with elegance – and it's good with rich fish dishes. Not at all stores.

Chilean Sauvignon Blanc, Tesco

Character, style, real class. Fruit and freshness. Flavour. Great stuff.

Chilean White, Tesco

Was £3.29 – now presumably cheaper. As good if not better (not only because of the price but also the concentration of fruit) than many a fancy sancerre. Freshness, flavour, bite – great stuff! Open-any-time-you-please wine. Bargain.

Cuvee Ryman-Montes Chardonnay 1993

Hugh, the winged Bordeaux-based Englishman, always makes wines which immediately impact on the nose and this wine is no exception. However, its hugely inviting aroma of ripe melon and fresh peach is all foreplay; I failed to reach a climax worth rating more than 10 points at this price. A muted, expensive chardonnay of little style.

Errazuriz Chardonnay 1994

Thirst-quenching yet complex. Has lovely ripe acids and rich fruit which together make for a truly beautiful beast.

Sauvignon Blanc Santa Rita 1991

CYPRIOT WINE RED

Keo Othello

Much ado about nothing.

CYPRIOT WINE WHITE

Keo Aphrodite Dry White `11` `B`

ENGLISH WINE WHITE

English Table Wine NV `13` `B`

FRENCH WINE RED

Anjou Rouge, Tesco `13` `B`

Some amusing fruit. Best drunk chilled with grilled salmon.

Beaujolais, Tesco `13` `C`

Light and fruity, the label says, and this is no lie.

**Beaume de Venise Cotes du Rhone
Villages 1993** `13` `C`

Bordeaux Chateau Michelet (2 litre) `11` `E`

**Bourgueil, La Huralaie, Caslot-Galbrun
1992** `15` `C`

Black cherries and raspberries richly mixed, very dry, very
chunky. Superb food wine. Coal-chewy, dark, and dank to
taste, it is hard and tannic, and it needs a little time to soften.
Could be brilliant by the time this book is published.

Burgundy, Henri de Bahezre, Tesco `12` `C`

Buzet 1991 13.5 C

Brisk fruit, edgily tannic.

Cabernet Sauvignon, Haute Vallee de l'Aude, Tesco 13 B

Excellent value for the family get-together with a roast on the table.

Cahors, Tesco 13 B

Good.

Carignan Daumas Garsac 1994 14.5 C

A rich, brisk brew with tannic presence modified by soft, ripe fruit.

Chardonnay Serge Dubois, Vin de Pays d'Oc 1992 13 C

Subtle, woody aroma with a gentle richness to the fruit. Classy in feel but not ultimately in the finish. Remarkable aperitif. Available through Tesco mail order only – two bottles per case.

Chartron La Fleur Bordeaux Rouge 1993 14.5 C

Bargain: savoury fruit, dry and a touch sulky but handsome tannins give it a final flourish of some style.

Chateau Bois Galant, Medoc 1990 13 D

Impressively well developed, the tannins in this wine. Very good with grilled lamb chops with rosemary.

Chateau Cantemerle, Haut Medoc 1987 13 F

Chateau Cote Montpezat, Cotes de Castillon 1993 14 D

Good, brambly fruit, good tannins. An austere wine but will

age for several years and will go now with roasts meats.

Chateau d'Arsac Haut-Medoc 1991 `11` `G`

Chateau de Beaulieu Coteaux d'Aix en Provence 1994 `11` `C`

Chateau de Caraguilhes, 1991 `15.5` `C`

Dry, but not austerely so in spite of an earthy edge. An immensely attractive wine of decided rustic stance but it fights with both fists – fruit and acid – and the result is a balanced wine of great food compatibility.

Chateau de Goelane 1992 `12` `D`

Weak finish to the performance lets it down a touch.

Chateau des Gondats 1992 `13` `D`

Serious tannins. Must have food, roast or raw.

Chateau du Bluizard, Beaujolais Villages `10` `C`

Almost charmless, but not quite. Top 70 stores only.

Chateau Guillon Graves Rouge 1992 `12` `C`

Chateau Haut Faugeres, St Emilion 1991 `13.5` `E`

Grasps at being impressive and classic and doesn't quite achieve it with the effortlessness of previous vintages.

Chateau Labegorce Margaux 1989 `13` `G`

Chateau Leon, Premieres Cotes de Bordeaux 1987 `12` `C`

Chateau Les Combes Saint Estephe 1990 `13` `E`

Chateau les Gravieres, St Emilion 1992

Light, dry, but will it repay cellaring? I think not.

Chateau les Valentines Bergerac 1989

Very dry and still developing flavour in bottle (will improve in 2/3 years). Has a meaty edge to blackberry fruit which is rather serious.

Chateau Lynch Moussas, Pauillac 1989

Chateau Marquis-de-Terme, Margaux 1988

There is a touch of beefiness about this grand margaux but I would prefer to wait a few years before I met it and it had softened.

Chateau Michelet, Bordeaux (2 litre box)

A hugely approachable, soft, friendly claret. Very drinkable and very smooth.

Chateau Patache d'Aux, Cru Grand Bourgeois 1991

Splendid little claret with depth of fruit and tannins, and of surprising class. Great roast lamb wine. Might be even better if you put it down for 3 years.

Chateau Pigoudet, Coteaux d'Aix en Provence 1991

Delicious chocolate-coated (yet dry) brambly fruit. Very tasty.

Chateau St Georges, St Emilion 1989

A lot of dosh but a lot of posh. Has classic tannin/fruit balance, with echoes of cedarwood, tobacco and dark chocolate. Lovely wine.

Chateau St Louis La Perdrix, Costieres de Nimes 1993, Tesco `14` `C`

Yes, it's earthy, but it has a lush fruity undertone which lingers longer than is respectable for so down to earth a wine.

Chateau St Nicholas, Fronsac 1987 `10` `D`

Chateau Toutigeac 1992 `14` `C`

Good, rich, balanced, well-structured.

Chateau Vieux Castel Robin, Saint Emilion 1990 `15` `D`

Soft and very thick with such accessible fruit you can eat it . . . I mean drink it . . . with a spoon.

Chateauneuf du Pape 1994, Tesco `13` `D`

Chateauneuf du Pape les Arnevels, Quiot 1992 `12` `E`

Touch flabby.

Chateauneuf-du-Pape Le Chemin des Mulets 1992 `13` `E`

Sweet fruit, unusually fresh and accommodating for a C-du-P.

Chinon, Baronnie Madeleine, 1990 `13` `D`

I think this wine is going through a closed stage and in 1/2 years time it will be much tastier.

Claret, Tesco `14` `B`

Lovely soft yet dry example of the genre. Excellent value for a superbly approachable bottle.

Clos de Chenoves, Bourgogne Rouge 1990 `12` `D`

Corbieres, Tesco 14 B

Bargain fruity fulfilment.

Cotes de Duras, 1993 10 B

Cotes de Duras, Tesco 13 B

Soft with faintly savoury fruit. Very good value.

Cotes de Provence, Tesco 13 B

Relatively smooth rustic plonk.

Cotes de Roussillon Rouge, Tesco 12.5 B

Cotes du Frontonnais 1990 13 B

Cotes du Marmandais Domaine Beaulieu-Saint Saveur 1992, Tesco 13 B

Cotes du Rhone, Tesco 12 B

Easy-going to the point of absurdity.

Cotes du Rhone Villages 1993 11 C

Cotes du Rhone Villages 1994, Tesco 13 C

Young and dry. Will soften in the months to come.

Couly Dutheuil Chinon, Baronnie Madeleine 1992 16 D

Lovely maturity (which will develop for a further 3/4 years). The cherry and raspberry fruit has fully integrated with the slate-like tannins and the result is a lovely dry, food-friendly wine (all meats and vegetables) as well as being superbly drinkable by itself – chilled.

Crozes Hermitage 1992 13 D

Domaine Cazelles-Verdier, Minervois 1990

Dry, smoky, fruity, rich. A lovely wine. Available through Tesco mail order only – two bottles per case.

Domaine de Conroy, Brouilly

I am compelled to report that this hammily fruity wine is not bad – even if it is expensive. Not at all stores.

Domaine de la Doline Fitou 1992

Soft, supremely drinkable, and very briskly fruity. Not at all stores.

Domaine de la Sansoure Corbieres, Les Producteurs du Mont Tauch 1995

Lovely bright cherry-edged wine with good solid hints of rustic warmth overlaid with a zingy modernity. Top 14 stores.

Domaine de la Source, Syrah 1994, Tesco

Dry and fruity. More a town than a country mouse.

Domaine de Lanestousse Madiran 1990

Shows the Aussies a clean pair of fruity, leathery, dry-soled heels and even chucks in a genuine, and unique, rustic edge. A deeply savoury, tannicky, velvety, lithe wine of superb character. Wonderful with all cheese dishes.

Domaine de Pauline Cotes du Rhone 1993

Good tannins here but well tamed by the frisky fruit which also offers excellent balancing acids. Good chilled, this wine. Selected stores.

Domaine de Prebayon, Cotes du Rhone Villages 1993

Some depth and flavour here.

Domaine de Trillol, Corbieres 1989 `14` `C`

Lively and bright with a heavy hint of smoker's cough to the fruit. Available through Tesco mail order only – two bottles per case.

Domaine des Baumelles, Cotes du Luberon 1993 `12` `C`

Domaine du Petit Chene, Corbieres 1990 `14` `C`

Attractive fruit of some depth. Not especially complex. Very deep fruit with a touch of spice. Dry. Available through Tesco mail order only – two bottles per case.

Domaine du Soleil Vegan Merlot, VdP d'Oc 1994 `14` `C`

Dry, leathery, very attractive.

Domaine les Hauts des Chambert, Cahors, 1988 `13` `D`

Domaine Maurel Fonsalade, Saint Chinian 1993 `15` `C`

Very dry with delicious soft fruity bits poking through. A great savoury beast for casseroles and cheese dishes. Only at the top 70 stores.

Domaine Saint James Viognier, Vins de Pays d'Oc 1994 `14` `C`

Quirky fruit (that's fresh, young viognier for you) – which has flavour and style. Must be drunk with fish dishes or perhaps Thai food.

Dorgan, Vin de Pays de l'Aude, Tesco `13` `B`

Has a few rough edges which a good bowl of pasta would soon smooth out.

Escoubes Rouge, Vin de Pays de l'Aude, Grassa, Tesco
14 | B

Brilliant value for sheer pizzazz of the fruit.

Fitou, Tesco
14 | B

An aromatic, richly endowed, smooth bottle of fruit.

French Cabernet Sauvignon, VdP de la Haute Vallee de l'Aude, Tesco
12 | B

Anyone who says they find cabernet sauvignon too austere will find a friend in this wine.

French Country Red, Tesco (1 litre)
13 | C

Fronton, Cotes du Frontonnais 1991
13 | B

Nice baked fruit.

Gamay VdP du Jardin de France, Tesco
13.5 | B

Light, bright, cherryish.

Gevrey Chambertin, Marchand 1992
10 | F

Some savoury fruit, but the price? Absurd.

Grand Carat, Vin de Pays du Comte Tolosan 1994
11 | B

Earthy as a gardener's welly-boot sole after an afternoon on the allotment.

Grenache Daumas Garsac 1994
13.5 | C

Needs softening. Will develop well over the next year?

Grenache, Tesco
16 | B

Terrific fruit, terrific price tag. Even Aussie wine-makers (who must remain anonymous) have raved about this dry yet vibrantly fruity wine. Rustic yet rich, smooth yet characterful, this is a stunning wine for the money.

Hautes Cotes de Beaune, Caves des Hautes Cotes 1992 `10` `D`

Top 70 stores only.

Hautes Cotes de Nuits, Caves des Hautes Cotes 1992 `12` `C`

International Winemaker Syrah Vin de Pays d'Oc 1992, Tesco `13` `C`

Big, dry, earthy fruit of some structure. Excellent food wine.

La Vieille Ferme, Cotes du Rhone, 1992 `13.5` `C`

Highly drinkable, soft and fruity. Exciting? No. But it is all there.

Laperouse Val d'Orbieu & Penfolds, VdP d'Oc 1994 `13.5` `C`

The fruit has a somewhat namby-pamby attitude to the tannins. Needs time to develop in bottle (6 months or more).

Le Bahans du Chateau Haut-Brion 1992 `12` `E`

Les Domaines Buzet, Domaine de la Croix 1989, Tesco `13` `C`

Tannins in evidence, herby and baked, and maybe it will get even better over the next 2/3 years.

Les Domaines de Beaufort Minervois 1993, Tesco `13` `B`

Cheery cherries.

Les Domaines des Baumeilles, Cotes du Luberon 1992, Tesco `13` `C`

Les Forts de Latour, Pauillac 1986 `10` `H`

Les Vieux Cepages Carignan 1994 `12` `B`

Les Vieux Cepages Grenache 1994 `13` `B`
Probably at its best with spicy food.

Louis Jadot Beaune Premier Cru 1990 `10` `F`
Only in the top 70 stores.

Margaux 1992, Tesco `12` `E`

Medoc, Tesco `12` `C`

Merlot, Vin de Pays de la Haute Vallee de l'Aude, Tesco `13` `B`
Don't put pepper on your sausages. Drink this wine with them instead.

Minervois, Tesco `13` `B`
Pleasant cherry fruit.

Morgon, Arthur Barolet 1994 `11` `D`

Organic Red, Chateau Vieux Gabiran 1990, Tesco `14` `C`

Pauillac 1990, Tesco `13.5` `D`
Dry, authentic claret.

Pavillon Rouge du Chateau Margaux 1990 `11` `G`

Red Graves, Tesco `12` `C`
Bit weedy, but respectably weedy. Overpriced.

Reserve du Reverend Corbieres Rouge 1990 `15` `C`

Delicious, savoury fruit of depth and style. Burnt fruit, very dry, herbs and black cherries. Brilliant for roasts. Available through Tesco mail order only – two bottles per case.

Saint Joseph, Verrier 1992 `10` `D`

Sancerre Rouge `12` `D`

Dull. Pricey. A pointless purchase. Only available in the top 57 stores.

Saumur 1991 `15` `C`

Saumur Rouge 1993 `13.5` `C`

An excellent bottle for those Spanish fish stews with chorizo.

St Emilion, Tesco `13` `C`

Attractive soft fruit finish to a stalwart British favourite.

Vin de Pays de Cotes du Tarn, Tesco `14` `B`

Delicious, modern, soft fruit. Fresh finish. Slightly nutty. Very good value.

Vin de Pays de l'Aude Rouge, Tesco `13` `B`

Has a pleasing lilt to its voice which recalls sweet cherry.

Vin de Pays de la Cite de Carcassonne, Tesco `13.5` `B`

Lots of flavour here.

Vin de Pays de la Gironde, Tesco `10` `B`

Vin de Pays des Cotes de Gascogne Rouge, Yvon Mau, Tesco `13` `B`

Some bouncy fruit in evidence here.

Vin de Pays des Cotes de Perignan, Tesco `14` `B`

Worth buying just for the Darling Grapes of September label.

Vintage Claret 1990, Tesco `13` `C`

FRENCH WINE WHITE

Alsace Gewurztraminer 1993, Tesco `13` `D`

Too expensive, Alsace wines. Even Tesco can't keep the price of this perfectly spicy and Chinese food-loving wine below £4.50 as it ought to be. Not at all stores.

Alsace Pinot Blanc, Tesco `11` `C`

Anjou Blanc, Tesco `13` `B`

Good value. Basic fruit.

Beaujolais Blanc 1993 `10` `C`

Blayais `10` `B`

Bordeaux Blanc de Blancs `13` `B`

Bordeaux Blanc, Tesco `15` `B`

Brilliant cheapie with lemon, lime and melon fruit softly and subtly put together.

Bordeaux Rose, Tesco `13.5` `C`

Excellent little wine for flirting with.

Cabernet de Saumur, Caves des Vignerons de Saumur, Tesco `14` `B`

A good, firm rose with dryish cherry and raspberry fruit.

Cepage Terret, Vin de Pays de l'Herault, Delta Domaines 1993 `13` `B`

If you want the classic earthy fruit of the terret grape, here it is.

Chablis 1993, Tesco `11` `D`

Chablis Premier Cru, Montmain, La Chablisienne 1991 `13` `E`

Chardonnay Domaine des Fontaines VdP d'Oc, Tesco (2 litre) `14` `E`

Box clever! Brilliant little well-made, richly fruited wine of style and class. Excellent fish wine.

Chardonnay Reserve, Maurel Vedeau 1994 `13.5` `C`

Good grilled fish wine with good depth of flavour. Top 14 stores.

Chardonnay, Vin de Pays d'Oc, Tesco `11` `B`

Chasan 1991, International Winemaker series `12` `B`

Some pleasant melon fruit to this Vin de Pays d'Oc.

Chateau de Beaulieu Coteaux d'Aix en Provence 1994 `13` `C`

Chateau de Carles Sauternes 1993 `12.5` `F`

Lot of money. Too much for this plonker. Top 70 stores only.

Chateau de la Colline Bergerac Blanc 1994 `14` `C`

Classy depth of fruit here with real flavour. Welcome to the

New World, Bergie! Although is this wine losing bite as it matures? In April when I first tasted it it seemed much fresher than it did when last tasted this September. But it's still a well-rated wine.

Chateau de la Colline Bergerac Rose 1994

Pear-drop and cherry ripe.

Chateau la Foret St Hilaire Entre-Deux-Mers

A touch of greater complexity here, for more money than your average vin de pays and so better with food.

Chateau Laquirou, La Clape, Coteaux de Languedoc Blanc 1991

Dull, doesn't live in the mouth. Will work with grilled fish only. Available through Tesco mail order only – two bottles per case.

Chateau les Marcottes St Croix du Mont 1990

Superb honeyed fruit. Only at Wine Advisor stores.

Chateau Liot Sauternes (half bottle)

Delicious honeyed beaut. Good with rich blue cheese and foie gras. Not at all stores.

Chateau Magneau, Graves 1990 [14] [F]

A hugely elegant, richly wooded wine of taste, flair and flavour. Marvellous with grilled fish with a complex sauce.

Chateau Malagar, Bordeaux Blanc 1994 [15] [C]

Classy and classic. Very serious, deep fruit, dry and haughty, but with a truly stylish finish. Great with grilled chicken and saucy fish dishes. Not at all stores.

Chateau Passavant Anjou 1993 `13` `C`

Delicious with smoked oysters on toast. (Really.) Top 70 stores only.

Chenin Blanc, VdP du Jardin de la France, Tesco `15` `B`

Has a delicious off-dry honey finish to a crisply conceived wine.

Clairette Daumas Garsac 1994 `12` `C`

Still dull.

Cotes de Provence, Tesco `11` `B`

Cotes de Roussillon, Tesco `12` `B`

Some pleasant fruit to this.

Cotes du Rhone Blanc 1994 `13` `C`

Severely earthy and bold and a touch underfruited. Not at all stores.

Cuvee Reserve Cotes du Rhone Blanc, Tesco `15` `C`

Tesco takes over the 100 per cent bourboulenc (grape variety) crown from Safeway. This is an unusual wine, unusually beautifully balanced, unusually good value for a Rhone white, and, most unusual of all, it's on sale in Britain. Undoubtedly, the wine-maker's New World experience has helped, for this is a modern wine, without being horribly tarty and obviously fruity, and very stylish with aroma, finish and class. Great with trout or salmon.

Domaine Chancel Rose 1994 `13` `C`

Flavour here.

Domaine de la Done, Rose Syrah 1993   `13.5` `B`

**Domaine de la Huperie, Muscadet de
Sevres et Maine Sur Lie 1993, Tesco**   `13` `C`

Musty and green but good with curried winkles.

Domaine de la Jalousie 1994, Tesco   `15` `C`

Exotic acids underpinning the round soft melon grapiness of
the style. Terrific, punchy, refreshing glug. Not at all stores.

**Domaine de la Jalousie Late Harvest VdP
des Cotes de Gascogne 1992**   `14` `C`

Must be tried with Thai and Chinese food. Or, like me, drink
it with pastrami coated in a mustard and sour cream dressing
between slices of rye bread. Not at all stores.

**Domaine de Montauberon Marsanne, VdP
d'Oc 1993**   `12` `C`

Dry. Too dry.

**Domaine du Soleil Chardonnay VdP
d'Oc 1994**   `13.5` `C`

Earthy fruit here.

Domaine Lapiarre Cotes de Duras 1993   `15` `C`

Attractive, almost NZ zest in the aroma of the wine which
contrives to grassy herbiness. The fruit is soft and melon,
not hugely bold but effective, and the finish is crisp and
flavoursome. An excellent wine by itself or partnered with fish
and salads.

**Domaine Sabagnere, VdP de Gascogne
1993**   `13.5` `C`

Zippy and bright. Not at all stores.

Domaine Saint Alain, Vin de Pays des Cotes du Tarn 1993, Tesco `14` `B`

Excellent fruit (analogous to nothing yet grown). Mysteriously delicious.

Domaine Saubagnere, VdP des Cotes de Gascogne 1993, Tesco `14.5` `C`

Very fresh and pineappley and full-built but, not surprisingly, very woody.

Domaines Saint Pierre Chardonnay, Vin de Pays d'Oc 1993 `12.5` `C`

Pleasant country flavour. What country? Oh, you know, a country far away where they speak drily and sunnily of rustic matters.

Dorgan White Vin de Pays de l'Aude `13` `B`

Dry Muscat. Vin de Pays des Pyrenees-Orientales 1993 `11` `B`

Entre Deux Mers, Tesco `15` `B`

Vividly fruity yet in the end a finely balanced specimen. Good with fish or a great quaffing wine. Perfect price.

Entre Deux Mers, Tesco `12` `C`

Escoubes, VdP des Cotes de Gascogne, Grassa, Tesco `14` `B`

A delicious pineapple wine with firm fruit lurking behind a fresh face.

Floc de Gascogne `14` `D`

Made from grape juice with armagnac tossed in to bring it up to 17 per cent. A simple peasant recipe and I enjoy its rusticity as a pick-me-up (or should I say as a pull-me-down?) after a hard day's wine tasting. The view of my household is that it is about as toothsome a proposition as old rugby boots pickled in treacle.

Fortant de France Grenache Blanc 1994 `15.5` `C`

A truly flavoursome glug as well as a rich wine with great food-loving traits.

Fortant de France Sauvignon Blanc 1994 `15` `C`

Lovely big wine with a subtly blistering attack of melon nicely subdued in the finish. Delicious.

French Chardonnay, VdP d'Oc, Tesco `13` `C`

French Colombard/Chardonnay, Tesco `13` `C`

So fruity it's medium dry.

French Country Wine, VdP des Cotes de Gascogne, Tesco (1 litre) `14` `C`

Delicious. Breezy and fruity and very good value.

French Semillon, Tesco `14` `B`

Good value, well-fruited, well-made.

Gaston Dorleans Vouvray Demi-Sec 1993 `12` `C`

Aperitif. Or try it with smoked oysters. Not at all stores.

Grenache Blanc, VdP de l'Herault, Tesco `12` `B`

Haut Poitou Sauvignon Blanc 1994 `13.5` `C`

Aromatic, fruity, fresh, gripping – good with grilled and poached fish dishes. Touch expensive for the style.

International Winemakers Blanc de Noirs/Cabernet Sauvignon Rose

14 B

A Vin de Pays de l'Aude of unusual frivolity and roseate deliciousness.

La Vieille Ferme Cotes du Rhone Blanc 1993

14 C

Some lean hungry fruit, hungry for flavour, but saved by the elegant acids and complexity. Good with fresh fish. Not available in all stores.

Laperouse Blanc Val d'Orbieu & Penfolds, VdP d'Oc 1994

14 C

Delicious. A marriage of sun and freshness which makes for an invigorating tipple.

Le Porcil Chardonnay 1992

14 D

Elegant, quiet, very attractive.

Les Domaines de la Source Muscat, Tesco

13 C

Pleasant aperitif.

Les Vieux Cepages Cinsault Rose 1994

10 B

Les Vieux Cepages Clairette 1994

10 B

This is dull and gawkily fruity and even, dare I say it, a touch cabbagey. Considering it's one of France's more exciting wines this is a surprise.

Louis Jadot Pouilly Fuisse 1993

11 E

Macon Blanc Villages 1993, Tesco

12 C

Meursault 1992

12 F

Has some flavour and edgy, class, but what a price tag.

Monbazillac Roc de St Laurent (half bottle)

Waxy, floor-polishy and only to be tackled with food (blue cheese).

**Montagny Premier Cru Oak Aged,
Buxy 1991**

Muscadet de Sevres et Maine

Don't think of it as muscadet. Think of it as very pleasant, fruity, uncomplicated wine.

Muscat Cuvee Jose Sala, Tesco

Toffee-nosed and less than £4? Aristocratic sweetness never came so cheap.

Muscat de Beaumes de Venise (half bottle)

Useful half bottle. Has a waxy finish along with the usual honey. Top 14 stores.

Muscat de Rivesalte (half bottle)

A light pud wine with soft citrus and subtle marmalade undertones. Excellent with grapes and hard cheese to make a complete meal. Honey with a raisin undertone. Delightful with hard-fruit tarts.

Muscat de Rivesalte, Les Abeilles

Refined, elegant, marmalade fruit. Rather hoity-toity in fact and perhaps too delicate to tackle rich desserts but fruit tarts would be okay.

Oak Aged White Burgundy 1994, Tesco

Very soft and friendly and the fruit is on pleasant terms with the wood.

363

Organic White, Entre Deux Mers, Chateau Vieux Gabiran 1994, Tesco
14 C

Very good fruit here (ignore its organic status). Drink it with non-spicy grilled vegetables. Not at all stores.

Petit Chablis 1993
12 D

Pouilly Fume, Cuvee Jules 1994
10 D

Premieres Cotes de Bordeaux, Tesco
11 B

Riesling, Tesco
14 B

True varietal vivacity of fruit and acid. Brilliant oyster wine.

Sancerre, Alphonse Mellot 1993, Tesco
12 D

Expensive for what the New World, with the same grape (sauvignon blanc) is doing better.

Saumur Blanc, Caves des Vignerons de Saumur 1991, Tesco
14 B

Touch of grassy, buttery fruit and a distant echo of honey in it – yet this is a very dry wine for all that.

Sauvignon Blanc, Tesco
13 B

Has some richness of tone but is it quite as crisp as it might be?

Sauvignon de St Bris, Tesco
12 C

St Romain, Arthur Barolet 1993
13 D

This has taste. It has fruit. It also has a price tag.

St Veran Les Monts, Co-Op Prisse 1993
13.5 D

Not at all stores.

Touraine Sauvignon, Tesco `13` `B`

Delicious, fresh, gooseberry aroma but then it fails to punch home the fruit on the finish. Quiet, understated fruit. Not shrieking with grassy overtones.

VdP de la Dordogne Co-Op Sigoules, Tesco `15` `B`

A modern, melony wine without being brash. Lots of fruit and flavour and balancing fresh acidity. Superbly drinkable.

Vin de Pays des Cotes du Tarn `11` `B`

Vintage Blend Chardonnay Aligote 1993 `0` `B`

This is the worst-labelled, worst-tasting white wine I've drunk in years. I would have preferred to introduce into my mouth wool moistened with ditchwater. Initially 0 points. After two hours of opening, however, it improves to 5 points.

Vouvray, Tesco `14` `B`

Touch of sweet fruit in an off-dry wine of great appeal. Supremely nice wine for the hock drinker looking for more finesse and food compatibility.

White Graves, Tesco `13` `C`

GERMAN WINE RED

Baden Pinot Noir 1990 `12` `C`

Has a cough-sweet quality you may find useful in darkest mid-winter.

Echo Hill Baden Pinot Noir 1993 `13` `B`

Called Echo Hill, presumably, because if you shout loud enough

GERMAN WINE

the sound is faithfully returned. Therefore I shout: 'More Fruit Please!' I await its return with eager anticipation.

GERMAN WINE — WHITE

Baden Dry, Tesco

There is a faint echo of sticky toffee in this dry fish 'n' chips wine. Good clean drinking.

Bereich Johannisberg Riesling Kabinett, Krayer 1993

Bernkasteler Kurfurstlay, Tesco

Try it instead of Lieb – much more of a generous wine. Not at all stores.

Binger Scharlachberg Riesling Kabinett Medium Dry, Villa Sachsen 1993

Perhaps the most eccentric German to reach these shores since Bert Trautmann played in goal for Manchester City. Brilliant marzipan-fruited aperitif. Not at all stores.

Bornheimer Adelberg Beerenauslese 1994 (half bottle)

Will taste at its best around 2010. Top 70 stores.

Devil's Rock Riesling 1994

Whatever happened to Klinsmannsovercrappenbergermeister-singer Trocken? The new world of label names sweeps across Germany, but not a new world of fruit in the bottle.

Dry Country German Wine, Tesco (1 litre)   `13` `C`

Dry Hock, Tesco   `13` `B`

Fresh and straightforward and good with fish dishes.

Echo Hill Baden Blanc 1994   `14` `B`

Most engaging fish and chips wine.

Grans Fassian Riesling Trocken 1993   `12` `D`

Strictly for riesling freaks and then, perhaps, not even for them
for 5/7 years. Touch pricey. Selected stores.

Hock, Tesco   `11` `A`

**Kreuznacher Riesling Spatlese, Anheuser
1991**   `12` `C`

Nice fruit. Needs a couple more years to develop. Everything
my wife hates in a German wine. But in 5 years?

Morio Muskat, Tesco   `15` `B`

A brilliant thirst-quenching guzzle with a marzipan dry finish
to its fruit. Great solvent for end-of-the-day blues.

Mosel-Saar-Ruwer Classic Riesling 1993   `13.5` `B`

Delightful fresh citric fruit. Try it with smoked fish. Will age
for 4/5 years.

Muller Thurgau, Tesco   `12` `B`

Niersteiner Gutes Domtal, Tesco   `12` `B`

**Piesporter Treppchen Riesling Kabinett,
1991**   `12` `C`

Not at all stores.

Rauenthaler Rothenberg Riesling Kabinett, Diefenhardt 1989 `14` `C`

Remarkable value for the year with the petal fruit beginning to emerge. Nice aperitif now but in 3/4 years will be even better.

Rheinpfalz Dry Riesling `12` `B`

Riesling Kabinett Brauneberger Kurfurstlay, Paulinshof 1993 `12` `D`

A baby. Keep it for years before you open it (in the next century).

Riesling Mosel, Tesco `13` `B`

A simple, pretty aperitif in the lightweight Moselle tradition.

Ruppertsberger Hoheberg Riesling Kabinett 1989 `13` `D`

This is a gentle riesling, well-mannered and dry (although it is officially a haustrocken) but it is only beginning to shrug off its youth and approach impressive middle-age. I'd lay it down for another 3/4 years.

Scharzhofberger Van Volxem 1990 `15` `C`

An elegant Moselle and a truly individual piece of work: full of fruit yet never sweet, with gently assertive acidity, it has some finesse granted it by virtue of the kerosene quality showing through. You could lay it down for years and it would develop.

Silvaner, Tesco `12` `B`

Slight muted quality to the fruit. Wants some freshness to it and assertiveness.

St-Johanner Abtei Kabinett Tesco `11` `B`

St-Johanner Abtei Spatlese Tesco `12` `B`

Steinweiler Kloster Liebfrauenberg Auslese `13.5` `C`

Blue-cheese wine (but not Roquefort). Not at all stores.

Steinweiler Kloster Liebfrauenberg Kabinett `13.5` `C`

Delicious as a home-coming tipple – before you dive into something serious. Not at all stores.

Steinweiler Kloster Liebfrauenberg Spatlese `13.5` `C`

Try it with a goat's cheese salad. Not at all stores.

Stettener Stein, Muller Thurgau `10` `C`

Trittenheimer Apotheke Riesling Kabinett, FW Gymnasium 1992 `14` `D`

Again, a German white for smoked fish or, better, left for another 7/10 years to more fully develop those pungent kerosene undertones.

Weissburgunder Dry White Wine `11` `B`

Weissburgunder, Tesco `13` `C`

Delicious earthy fruit bouquet, dry fruit of a vague melon character and a clean finish. Tough competition at £3.99. Good with fish dishes and especially an unspicy fish soup.

Wiltinger Scharzberg Riesling Kabinett, Moselle 1993 `14` `B`

Light, summer aperitif – good, rich yet subtle. Just undercut by firm, balancing acidity. Has a good peasant elegance about it. Not at all stores.

GREEK WINE · RED

Nemea 1992 `13.5` `C`

The smell of sun-baked Hellenic isles in every sip? Not quite.
But close. Very close. Top 70 stores only.

GREEK WINE · WHITE

Kretikos 1991 `12` `C`

HUNGARIAN WINE · RED

Merlot/Cabernet Sauvignon `10` `C`

Reka Valley Hungarian Merlot, Tesco `14` `B`

Touch old-sockish but great fun chilled with grilled salmon steaks,
or swigged at room temperature with sausage and mash.

HUNGARIAN WINE · WHITE

Chapel Hill Hungarian Irsai Oliver 1994 `13.5` `B`

Gentle, muscat-edged aperitif. Top 70 stores only.

Dunavar Prestige Chardonnay 1994 `14` `C`

Good depth to the fruit which is relieved by a gentle citric edge.
Good class in your glass for a fair sum of money.

Hungarian Chardonnay, Tesco `10` `B`

Oreghegyi Chardonnay `10` `C`

Reka Valley Hungarian Chardonnay, Tesco `8` `B`
Perfectly dreadful. Might go well with stale baked beans on toast. Not at all stores.

Tokaji Aszu 5 Puttonyos 50cl `16` `D`
Brilliant almond and orange marmalade wine with a gorgeous honey polish to the fruit. Wonderful with soft fruits.

ITALIAN WINE   RED

Barbaresco Viareggio `11` `D`

Barolo Giacossa Fratelli 1991 `14` `D`
Hints of typicity. Subdued ferocity rather than the full barolo roar. Not at all stores.

Cabernet Sauvignon del Veneto, Tesco `13.5` `B`
Very attractive with spicy meatballs. Not at all stores.

Cantina del Taburno 1994 `13.5` `C`
Oh so narrowly fails to make 14, I feel mean, cruel and curmudgeonly.

Carignano del Sulcis 1992 `13` `D`
Very limited availability and, Tesco tell me, only on sale with wine advisors on hand. This is so these ladies and gentlemen can explain why this £6 wine should offer £3 fruit.

Chianti 1992, Tesco   `13` `B`

Chianti Classico 1993, Tesco   `14` `C`

Smooth, very smooth. Like an Italian waiter hovering for a tip (and deserving one).

Chianti Classico Riserva 1989, Tesco   `14` `D`

Excellent.

Chianti Colli Senesi 1993, Tesco   `13` `C`

Bright and earthy.

Chianti Rufina 1991, Tesco   `15` `C`

Has the earthy edge of Rufina chianti but it's soft and gently spicy. Not at all stores.

Copertino Rosso 1991   `16` `B`

Light yet insistent, this cherry and plum wine is quite delicious (especially lightly chilled) on its own as a simple celebration of life. Not at all stores.

Fontanafredda Barolo 1991   `10` `E`

Lousy value.

Giacosa Fratelli Barolo 1988   `13` `D`

Italian Red (1 litre)   `11` `B`

Tetrapak. Fruit juice for red wine beginners.

La Vis Trentino Merlot 1993   `13.5` `C`

Soft and squashy with a tannic 'ping' dragging itself along in the background. Not at all stores.

Merlot del Piave, Tesco   `12` `B`

Monica di Sardegna, Tesco 　　　11　B

Might go well with tomato tartlets.

Montepulciano d'Abruzzo, Tesco 　　12　B

Petit Verdot Casale del Giglio 1995 　　14　C

Brisk, hints of depth (without really reaching it) and lots of brambly flavouring. Selected stores.

Pinot Noir del Veneto, Tesco 　　　12　B

Tastes like cough mixture (mild and soothing). Odd. Not at all stores.

Primitivo del Salento 1993, Tesco 　　15　C

A soft, easy-going wine at first and then it leaps on the tastebuds like a mad panther. Delicious, curious, maddeningly difficult to describe. Lots of electric hard fruit mingling with bright soft berries. Will undoubtedly develop over the next 2/3 years in bottle. Not at all stores.

Rosso del Lazio, Tesco 　　　　12　B

Rosso del Piemonte, Tesco 　　　12　C

Rosso del Salento, Tesco 　　　　15　B

Warm and sunny, simple yet gripping, this is a bargain fruit-packed bottle. Seductively jammy wine with a serious undertone. Not at all stores.

Rosso di Montalcino 1992, Tesco 　　14　D

None of your bruised, squashy fruit with this jammy beast. Delicious and soft as peach fuzz.

Salice Salentino Rosso 1987 　　　13　C

Very ripe. Good with rich foods.

Shiraz Casale del Giglio 1994

More accessibly sweet-natured and fruity than the previous year's vintage. But still a delicious red wine of style.

Sicilian Red, Tesco

Also comes in a useful 3-litre box for under £11 (equalling 45p a glass).

Viarengo Barbaresco 1986

Cherries, figs and blackberries. Lots of fruit, sweet and dry – delicious wine to drink by itself.

Villa Boscorotondo, Chianti Classico 1993

Real elegance and class under a fiver. Wonderful rich, soft fruit with a lingering, tannic edge of licorice which only deserts the teeth half a minute after the fruit has soothed the throat.

Villa Cerro Amarone della Valpolicella 1987

Like dilute cherry liqueur with a brisk edge. Superb fruit to go with cheesy risottos.

Villa Gaida Lambrusco Rosso DOC

Sweet and cherry-ripe.

Villa Pigna Cabernasco, 1991

Squashy black cherry, raspberry and plum fruit which is not top heavy on fat but dry, biscuity (in a subtle way) and very warming.

Villa Pigna Rosso Piceno 1990

Oh so close to 14 points! And it's not getting any younger.

Vino da Tavola Rosso, Farli `12` `A`

Vino de Tavola `14` `A`

Most attractive, soft, cherryade fruited wine for pasta lovers and pizza freaks.

ITALIAN WINE   WHITE

Bianco di Custoza, Barbi 1994 `12` `B`

Blanco del Lazio, Tesco `14` `B`

A fruit cake in Lazio! Tasty stuff. Not in all stores.

Blanco del Piemonte, Tesco `13` `C`

Good wine, lots of attractive fruit, but a touch pricier than it should be.

Chardonnay Alto Adige, E Von Keller 1992 `15` `C`

Good surge of buttered melon fruit, excellent acid balance. Good value. Relish.

Chardonnay del Veneto, Tesco `13` `B`

Works softly – like a cat burglar.

Chiaro Bianco della Bascilicata 1994 `12.5` `C`

Selected stores.

Colli Amerini, Tesco `14` `C`

Has an edge of near-coriander dryness and spiciness. Excellent with grilled chicken. Not in all stores.

Colli Lanuvini DOC, Tesco   `13` `B`

Excellent value, very fresh and light although not overloaded with fruit. Aperitif.

Colli Toscani 1993, Tesco   `13` `B`

Faustino V White 1989   `10` `C`

So dull as to be beyond belief. It struggles so hard to be aromatically interesting and fruity, it is exhausted by the time the wine gets anywhere near the organs of smell and taste.

Frascati 1994, Tesco   `13` `C`

Italian White (1 litre)   `10` `B`

Tetrapak. Easy to open and easy to close. The latter being the action I prefer with this dullish, too-respectable wine.

Italian White Wine, Tesco   `14.5` `B`

An unusual white – it is made from red merlot grapes. Delicious fruit of distinction and style, freshness and flavour. Only in the top 70 stores.

Nuragus di Cagliari, Tesco   `12` `B`

Not as bright and breezy a wine as it once was. Not at all stores.

Orvieto Classico Abboccato, Tesco   `13` `B`

Off-dry, but very pleasant fruit. Good aperitif.

Orvieto Classico, Vaselli 1994   `12` `C`

Pinot Grigio del Veneto, Tesco   `14` `B`

A pinot grigio with fruit! Alleluja!

Pinot Grigio, Tiefenbrunner 1993   `12` `C`

Prosecco del Veneto, Tesco | 13.5 | B

Fresh, nutty, attractive. A pleasurable glug by itself or with fish pie. Not at all stores.

Sauvignon Blanc del Veneto, Tesco | 12.5 | B

Not at all stores.

Sicilian White, Tesco | 14 | B

Warm, sunny, accommodatingly fruity. Great value. Not at all stores.

Soave Classico 1992, Tesco | 11 | C

Stowells of Chelsea Chardonnay (3 litre) | 13.5 | G

Some weight to the fruit, and balance. A pleasant glug.

Taburno Flanghia 1994 | 11 | D

Nothing like a soave or frascati, but a lot pricier.

Trulle Chardonnay del Salento 1994 | 15 | C

Bargain. Wonderful varietal warmth and depth of flavour for the money. Not at all stores.

Verdicchio dei Castelli di Jesi Classico 1994, Tesco | 13.5 | C

Tinged with not unpleasant fruit. Not at all stores.

Villa Cerro Soave Recioto 1992 | 14 | C

An interesting sweet aperitif. Good with hard fruit and a slug of cheese and Italian sweetmeats and cakes. Also almond biscuits.

Villa Pigna Chiara | 14 | B

Nutty – yet a suggestion of crispness.

Vino da Tavola Bianco

Fresh with a light finish of lemon. Delicious aperitif.

MEXICAN WINE RED

**Mexican Cabernet Sauvignon, L. A. Cetto
1990, Tesco**

A soft echo of menthol with this handsomely well-developed specimen. Tremendously soft and well-flavoured (even hints at cassis). Not at all stores.

MOLDOVAN WINE WHITE

Sauvignon Blanc Hincesti 1993

Excellent varietal style: fresh, keen, crisp but with with decisive touches of fruit showing through. Brilliant value.

MOROCCAN WINE RED

Moroccan Red

Raisiny and ripe: excellent with roast vegetables and meats.

NEW ZEALAND WINE RED

**Coopers Creek Cabernet Sauvignon,
Auckland 1990, Tesco**

Delicious ripe fruit.

New Zealand Cabernet Sauvignon/Merlot 1992, Tesco
`13` `C`

Curious marriage which isn't entirely convincing in spite of its respectable, if not over-exciting, rating.

Riverlea Wines Cabernet Sauvignon/ Merlot, Gisborne 1991, Tesco
`15` `C`

Amazingly well-integrated varieties with softness, smoothness and very effective final delivery. Delicious.

NEW ZEALAND WINE   WHITE

Chardonnay, Tesco
`14` `C`

Woody, rich and buttery, the fruit seems to fight on the tongue, in the mouth. Great with chicken and rich fruit dishes.

Coopers Creek Chardonnay, Hawkes Bay 1993
`15` `E`

Elegantly sour-puss fruit which has firmness, elegance and style. Delicious with shellfish or quiet solo drinking.

Dry White, Tesco
`12` `C`

Attractive all-round wine with plenty of rounded fruit. Might be better, in fact, with less fruit and more of that searing New Zealand grassiness.

Jackson Estate Sauvignon Blanc 1993
`14` `D`

New Zealand Chardonnay, Gisborne, Tesco
`13` `C`

Basic, touch expensive, and not greatly typical. Not at all stores.

New Zealand Dry White, Tesco | 13.5 | C

Simple, fruity, hints at real style rather than flaunts it. Not at all stores.

Nobilo Sauvignon Blanc, Marlborough 1992 | 10 | C

Riverlea Wines Sauvignon Blanc, Gisborne 1993, Tesco | 14 | C

Has the grassy edge of the species well controlled.

Sauvignon Blanc 1992, Tesco | 12 | C

Stoneleigh Marlborough Chardonnay 1993 | 13 | D

Top 70 stores only.

Stowells of Chelsea New Zealand Sauvignon Blanc (3 litre) | 13.5 | G

Keen, grassy aromas, good fruit, rather a quiet finish.

Timara Dry White | 12 | C

Villa Maria Chenin/Chardonnay 1993 | 12 | D

Villa Maria Sauvignon Blanc 1993 (half bottle) | 15 | C

They always get enough lift from the fruit here to balance out the grassy acids. Superb.

PORTUGUESE WINE   RED

Bairrada 1990, Tesco | 13.5 | B

Borba Alentejo `14.5` `B`

Terrific value. Lots of flavour and style and more concentration of fruit than comparatively priced vins de pays.

Dao 1991, Tesco `14` `B`

Country bumpkin wearing city togs. Tasty.

Dom Jose, Tesco `14` `A`

This rural masterpiece of peasant pulchritude has been likened to five-day-old lorry driver's socks, but the secret with this earthy fruit stew is to let it breathe for a bit before tackling it. Better, pour into a large earthenware vase (removing flowers first). It has been known to be specially promoted at £1.99 which is even more endearing.

Douro 1989, Tesco `13` `B`

Finishes like brambly apple.

Garrafeira Fonseca 1984 `12` `C`

I might reduce it to make a basis for a mushroom sauce but I wouldn't drink it without the dish for company. Top 70 stores only.

Garrafeira Red 1983 `12` `C`

J.P. Barrel Selection 1991 `15.5` `C`

Has the lot: acid, fruit, tannins, well-structured and properly finished off. Has richness, softness and bramble-fruited depth. Bargain. Not at all stores.

Periquita Portuguese Red 1991 `13.5` `C`

Light yet gruff-voiced. Top 70 stores only.

Quinta da Cardiga `13` `B`

Brilliant value.

Tinta da Anfora 1990 `13` `C`

Coffee, catering chocolate and figs up front which fade as they hit the throat. Doesn't quite deliver the punch its aromatic and primary palate complexity suggest.

Tinto Velho 1988 `13` `C`

Velho Reguengos de Monsaraz 1987, Tesco `16.5` `C`

Rich, chocolatey, chewy, tangy, swirling with fruit and double cream. Bargain fruitiness.

PORTUGUESE WINE · WHITE

Bairrada 1993, Tesco `13` `B`

Can't argue with this once fried fish is plonked beside it.

Cova da Ursa Chardonnay 1990 `13` `D`

Lemon on the pleasant fruity aroma, butter and almonds in the mouth, some staying power to the finish. An unusual and attractive chardonnay.

Dao Branco 1993, Tesco `13` `B`

Douro Branco 1993, Tesco `14` `B`

Softness of the fruit makes it plump and giving but there's a lean, lemony quality to the acidity and this gives the wine a two-fisted attack. Excellent value.

Dry Portuguese Rose, Tesco `12` `B`

Joao Pires Moscato 1993 `15` `C`

I love this wine. It is aromatic, spicy and mixes hot pears with cool melon – edgily exotic; it is wonderful as an aperitif or brilliant with scallops with a pea and mint puree.

ROMANIAN WINE RED

Classic Pinot Noir 1990

Brilliant cherry fruit, dry, bright and weighty without being overripe.

Romanian Cellars Pinot Noir

Dry cherries with a blackcurrant tang. Lush, fruit-centred glug with a dryness well suited to partner food.

Romanian Cellars Pinot Noir/Merlot

Enchanting. Brilliant value. The East Europeans seem to make a habit of successfully marrying unlikely grape varieties and this bottle is no exception. Top 70 stores only.

SOUTH AFRICAN WINE RED

Backsberg Merlot 1993

Still acidically evolving in bottle. Good with light food but in a couple of years great with rich food. Top 14 stores only.

Cape Pinotage 1992, Tesco

Sweet, elegantly smoky and rubbery fruit, like a drier style of beaujolais but tastier.

Cape Red

Tetrapak. Soft and ripe with a lushly polished soft fruit middle.

Delicious chilled for picnics or outdoor sporting events (or indoor slurping).

Charles Back Gamay 1995 `12` `C`

Runs so quickly over the tongue that you scarcely catch the fruit. But I believe it is delicious – if you can hold on to it.

Clearsprings Cape Red (3 litre) `14` `E`

Good cheering glug: bright, breezy, bouncy.

Fairview Merlot Reserve 1992 `15` `D`

Leathery, aromatic, serious yet wonderfully gluggable. Classy, striking, yet ineffably modest and self-effacing. Top 70 stores only.

Fairview Shiraz 1992 `14` `C`

Soft, delicious, not over-spicy. Rather pleased-with-myself quality to the fruit. Not available at all stores.

Kanonkop Pinotage 1993 `14` `D`

Soft and simple style here – unusually. Top 14 stores only.

Leopard Creek Cabernet Sauvignon/Merlot 1993 `C`

Flavour, ripeness and vibrancy.

Oak Village Vintage Reserve Stellenbosch 1993 `C`

Most attractive. Almost very attractive.

Paarl Cabernet Sauvignon, Tesco `13` `C`

Fiercely brisk and cheekily fruity. Denture wearers be warned! Not at all stores.

Robertson Shiraz Cabernet 1994, Tesco

Sweet and jammy.

Rustenberg Pinot Noir

Aromatically intriguing. Fruit compares with a modern Nuits-St-Georges.

South African Cabernet Sauvignon/Merlot Winemaker, Tesco

Mouthy and rich, fresh to finish.

South African Red, Tesco

Excellent value. Bit standoffish at first, but has a firm handshake of fruit and a warm, friendly finish.

Stellenbosch Merlot, Tesco

Good fruit. A pleasant, dry plonk.

Stellenzicht Block Series Shiraz 1993

A 20-point wine by AD 2000 if we're lucky. But drinkable, by golly, today. It's smooth, rich and deeply flavoured (and anything can happen in the next 4 years).

Stellenzicht Shiraz Reserve 1993

Jammy, dry yet rich, this has flavour and it needs FOOD!!

Stowells of Chelsea Pinotage (3 litre)

Soft, not as vivacious – nor with as big a finish – as some, but attractive and well-balanced.

Winemaker Cabernet Sauvignon Merlot, Tesco

Lovely brandy fruit – really jammy and delicious. Rich and full of flavour.

SOUTH AFRICAN WINE   WHITE

Barrel Fermented Chenin 1995   14.5   C

Tasty, rich-edged, pleasurably quaffable as well as strangely favoured (and flavoured) to go with chicken dishes.

Boschendal Grand Cuvee 1992   13   D

Good but not exciting.

Cape Chenin, Tesco   14   B

Fruity and fine with it.

Cape Colombar, Tesco   15   B

Aromatically a marriage of eau de cologne and apple and pear. The fruit is a medley of flavours: pawpaw and ripe melon being the most prominent. Not a serious wine but a joy of gluggability.

Cape White   13.5   B

A brilliant zingy white for picnics in the easy open/easy close cardboard Tetrapak.

Danie de Wet Chardonnay Green Label 1994   12   C

Dewetshof Riesling 1994   11   C

Stick to chardonnay, Danie.

Fleur du Cap, Noble Late Harvest 1990 50cl   12   C

Searingly sweet, treacle-tartish wine with not enough solid botrytis (i.e. noble rot) complexity and concentration of fruit. This is what that word noble in the name means, referring as it does to the technique of allowing grapes to rot on the vine and to become infected with the botrytis fungus before picking them so that there is less water in the fruit and the grape-sugars develop.

Goiya Kgeisje 1995

Delicious and getting more serious year after year. This '95 isn't as vibrantly fresh as previous years.

International Winemaker South African
Sauvignon Blanc, Tesco

Superb s.b. of freshness and flavour and creamy, nutty, rich-edged fruit. Terrific shellfish beauty. Delicious style.

La Motte Sauvignon Blanc 1994

Leopard Creek Chardonnay 1994   14 C

Milder than you would expect from a leopard but tasty and attractive.

Oak Village Sauvignon Blanc 1994   13 C

Robertson Chardonnay 1994, Tesco   15 C

A beautiful chardonnay (for £3.99) of deft fruit, deep purpose, and subtle yet persistent structure. Under £4, one of the most attractive chardonnays around. Not big or blowsy, over-wooded or overripe; just understated elegance. Not at all stores.

Robertson Chardonnay/Colombard
1995, Tesco   13.5 C

The best white wine its English wine-maker, John Worontschak, has yet made.

South African Cape Dry White (3 litre)   14.5 E

Vivid soft fruit with a clear finish. A brilliant crisp solvent to wash away those cares at the end of the day – and an excellent-value box. Has real sunny fruit on the finish.

South African White, Tesco 15 C

Brilliant melony (deep and vivid) and pear-drop wine with a fresh acid cut and an almond finish. Delish aperitif. Quite a tastebud-awakener. Excellent muscat-touched fruit.

Stowells of Chelsea Chenin Blanc (3 litre) 14 F

Comes out bright and clean – here is fruit and zip and real style.

Swartland Sauvignon Blanc 1993, Tesco 13 C

Has some elegant restraint but isn't as impactful as it might be.

Van Loveren Blanc de Noir Muscadel 15 B

Bite, flavour, style. Good rich-edged fruit. Fresh, cool, firmly built.

Van Loveren Blanc de Noirs 14 B

The slightest blush you've ever seen! Delicious aperitif with raspberry and strawberry fruitiness. Great fun.

SPANISH WINE RED

Berberana Monastrel 1994 13.5 B

Respectable, fruity, all above board.

Campillo Gran Reserva, Rioja 1982 11 E

Fading on the finish – the fruit, that is. The tannins, though soft, are still around. Top 14 stores.

Cinco Casas Red, Tesco

Lots of fresh young fruit and flavour. Delicious price.

Cune Rioja Reserva 1988

Only 14 stores have it! What a shame, but I'm rating its lovely mature, sweet yet dry-finishing fruit – not its comparative exclusivity.

Don Darias

The Old Don seems a bit thinner than when I last encountered him but he's still hale and hearty and full of vanilla-ey fruit.

Gandia Merlot

Gran Don Darias

Marques de Caceres Rioja 1991

Calm, polished, dry, very attractive. Not a coarse note anywhere.

Marques de Chive, Tesco

Dry, mature, raspberry fruit, rather light but eminently glugworthy.

Marquis de Grinon Petit Verdot 1994

Brilliant texture, weight, balance, fruit and style. Has rich, dusky, almost exotic fruit with a hint of dry allspice and a deep, lingering, tannin-edged finish. Superb price for such all-embracing flavour and sheer chutzpah. Will age well to AD 2000. Move over, cab sauv! Petit Verdot has arrived! Top 14 stores.

Marquis de Grinon Syrah

If only it was £3.99 it would rate 16 but it's £7.99 and rates less. It's a handsome beast, though. Top 70 stores.

Ochoa Tempranillo 1990   `14.5` `D`

Rioja Reserva 1987, Tesco   `17` `C`

Baked fruit and herb bread aroma, assertive soft fruit with no unwelcome intrusion from the wood, and a lush sweet fruit finish. Utterly delicious. A very controlled production from beginning to end.

Rioja Vina Mara Reserva, Tesco   `13.5` `D`

Yes, it's a more-together specimen – the style is mature and fruity – than the non reserva – but not £1.50's worth of togetherness. Not at all stores.

Rioja Vina Mara, Tesco   `13.5` `C`

Santara Red 1993   `14` `B`

Even manages to sneak in some tannin amongst the meaty fruit. Not at all stores.

Senorio de los Llanos 1989   `13` `C`

Spanish Red (1 litre)   `14.5` `B`

Tetrapak. Great value here for a big soup-plate of flavours and textured fruitiness.

Stowells of Chelsea Tempranillo La Mancha (3 litre)   `15` `F`

A bright, cherry/plum dry wine of really good fruit, balance and a really attractive finish.

Toro 1990, Tesco   `14.5` `C`

Captivating softness and ripeness. Flavour, fruit, firmness – a memorable mouthful. Not at all stores.

Torres Coronas 1991

Valhondo Country Red

Not a harsh note struck anywhere here. Soft, full, dry, fruity, firmly structured. Not at all stores.

Vina Ardanza Rioja Reserva 1987

Needs food like a crutch – it limps without it. And it's an awful lot of money. Top 14 stores.

Vina Mara Rioja Alavesa, Tesco

Has hints of tannin and deep, ripe, delicious, bustling fruit bursting with flavour.

Vina Mayor Ribero del Duero 1991

Aromatic, chunky edge to fruit which is elegant and soft.

SPANISH WINE WHITE

Castillo de San Diego 1993

Well, they have to do something with sherry grapes.

Cinco Casas White, Tesco

Highly pleasing little wine of delicious soft fruit with a dash of muted lime.

Don Darias

With a spicy fish stew or curry, this is the wine.

Galician Albarino 1992

An unknown wine and one of Iberia's great seafood partners. It lacks zip but the fruit has some power and will really shine with a complex spicy fish stew or paella.

Gandia Chardonnay 13 B

Good varietal character without the sun. Quiet, pale, unfussy.

Marques Caceres White Rioja 1994 12.5 C

Marques de Chive White Wine, Tesco 12 B

Vanilla, coconut and fruit which don't quite marry up. But great with Thai food.

Marquis de Grinon Durius Sauvignon Blanc 1994 13.5 C

Has some molar-shaking flavour but seems a mite expensive for the effect. Only in the top 70 stores.

Moscatel de Valencia, Tesco 15 B

Just under £3 makes this a honey of a bargain. And with it, your Christmas pudding goes down with a broad smile on its face.

Rioja, Tesco 13 C

Rueda 1991, Tesco 12.5 C

Funny old thing. Rustic as hob-nailed wellingtons. Not at all stores.

Rueda, International Winemaker Series 1992, Tesco 11 B

Superior Rioja Vina Maria 14.5 C

Tasty and most sanely balanced. Compares, would you believe, with certain New World whizz kids.

Torres Sangredetoro 1991 15.5 C

Licorice!? Very dry, starts well. Drink it in an hour – it fades.

Valhondo Country White

What a pity! The finish lets it down; otherwise this wine would score much higher. It pales at the sight of goal having set itself up so nicely, and fails to strike the balls cleanly. Not at all stores.

Villa del Vero Chenin Blanc 1994

You don't see Spanish chenin blanc every day. This could be one of the reasons.

Vina del Castillo 1992

White Rioja, Tesco

Mute, a touch, and curiously inexpressive for a rioja at this price. It seems a good style but not an exciting one.

USA WINE   RED

Californian Cabernet Sauvignon, Tesco

Lovely touches of eucalyptus, soft, unhurried, delicious, to a firmly fruity and solidly structured specimen. Terrific value for the money.

Californian Red, Tesco

Interesting what went through the label designer's mind when (s)he designed this curious blue and somewhat incongruous townscape on the bottle. Maybe too much of this wine perhaps? Very audacious. The wine only surprises by being soft and dry and quiet-mannered.

Californian Zinfandel, Tesco

More cabernet in this new blend. Excellent. Sweaty armpit

aroma. Lovely rich, smooth fruit (plums and black cherries, touch of spice). Good rich finish. Great glug.

Glass Mountain Cabernet Sauvignon 1991   16   D

Delightful pure fruit sweetness. Not a harsh edge anywhere. Available at regional stores only.

Tesco Californian Pinot Noir   10   C

Dullest pinot noir I've tasted in a coon's age.

Washington State Red   12.5   C

USA WINE   WHITE

August Sebastiani's White Zinfandel 1994   12.5   C

Sweetish fruit but fair flavour. Rated at £2.99 only. Not worth £3.99.

Californian Chardonnay, Tesco   15   D

Not on the store's shelves until early 1996, this suffers only from being a quid more than it should be.

Californian White, Tesco   12   C

Glass Mountain Californian Chardonnay 1992   15   D

Some real elegance here and rich style without blowsiness or intemperance. A delicious bottle to enjoy solo. Divertingly delicious fruit. Available in regional stores only.

Oregon Chardonnay 1993, Tesco   13.5   C

Some richness and flavour here.

Quady Elysium Black Muscat 1993
(half bottle)

Cassis-like. Try it with blackcurrant fool.

Washington State White

This I found hard to dislike but equally difficult to enthuse over. It seems loose to me – and the components weren't knit properly.

FORTIFIED WINE

10-Year-Old Tawny Port

Australian Aged Tawny Liqueur Wine,
Tesco

Wonderful figgy, raisiny, bottle-softened warrior. To fight with fruit cake.

Dow's 20-Year-Old Tawny Port (half bottle)

A gorgeous, raisiny, ripe, sweet tipple for cheese and biscuits – but available only in Tesco's top 25 stores.

Fine Old Vintage Character Port, Tesco

Ripely fruited and rich – a well-priced alternative to vintage port. Good with rich cheeses. Not at all stores.

Finest Madeira, Tesco 14 D

Brilliant with fruit cake. Not at all stores.

Graham's Malvedos 1979 Vintage Port 16.5 F

Wonderful sweet finish on the ripe fruit. Only at Tesco's top 25 stores.

Graham's Six Grape Port   `14` `E`
Delicious forward fruit. Sweet. Only at Tesco's top 25 stores.

LBV Port 1989, Tesco   `15` `D`
A delicious bottle for festive feast endings (cake, cheese, conversation). Not at all stores.

Superior Manzanilla, Tesco (half bottle)
Brilliant value. Saline, elegant and very dry. A nutty world-class aperitif. Or drink with grilled prawns.

Superior Oloroso Secco, Tesco (half bottle)
Just by itself and *Coronation Street*. Heaven!

Superior Palo Cortado, Tesco (half bottle)   `17` `C`
Rich, very dry camomile fruit, nutty undertone. For drinking alone with literature – or a superb aperitif. It revives even the most jaded tastebuds – lovely dry fruit.

Tesco Tawny Port   `13.5` `D`
Finishes sweet. Not at all stores.

Warre's 1968 Colheita Tawny Port   `13` `H`
Only at Tesco's top 25 stores.

Warre's 1980 Vintage Port   `17` `G`
Just overwhelmingly fruity and rich. Beautiful, round and smooth. Quite exceptional. Only at Tesco's top 25 stores.

Warre's Traditional LBV 1981   `15.5` `F`
Rich and ripe. Very smooth and polished.

SPARKLING WINE/CHAMPAGNE

Asti Spumante, Tesco   10 C

A sweet muscat wine of little personality. Tesco's Moscato is
much better value.

Australian Sparkling Brut, Tesco   15 C

Lovely feathery feel and terrific fruit and acid balance making it
impressively elegant in the mouth. Under a fiver it is outstanding
value for money.

Backsberg Brut 1990 (South Africa)   13.5 C

Only a touch (a little fruit) behind £4.99 cavas.

Blanc de Blancs Champagne, Tesco   13 G

Blanquette de Limoux, Tesco   13 D

Soft, attractive bubbly. Only a weak finish prevents it scoring
much higher.

Cava, Tesco   15 C

Very elegant. Tasty fruit, clean and firm. Not at all stores.

Champagne Premier Cru 1983, Tesco   11 H

Champagne, Tesco   13 F

Chardonnay Frizzante, Tesco   10 B

Chardonnay Spumante   15 D

Great-value sparkler with a great touch of Italian bravura on
the typical chardonnay fruit.

Chevalier de Moncontour Mousseux Brut `10` `D`
Bony, sterile, about as thrilling as a smack in the kisser from a wet sock.

Cremant de Bourgogne 1989, Tesco `18` `D`

Cremant de Loire Rose, Cave des Vignerons de Saumur `12` `D`

Deutz (New Zealand) `12` `E`
Just like Deutz champagne from the well-known Rheims company.

Freixenet Brut Rose (Spain) `14.5` `D`
A delicious, summery rose of style and flavour.

Grand Duchess Brut Sparkling Wine, Russia `10` `C`
Comradely, but only just.

Henri Mandois Champagne `12` `F`

Jansz Tasmanian Sparking `12` `E`

Lindauer Brut `13.5` `D`
New Zealand's champagne copy.

Loridos Espumante 1987 `11` `D`

Louis Massing Grand Cru Blanc de Blancs `16` `E`

Michel Arnould Champagne `12` `G`

Moscato d'Asti, Guilio Alfero 1992 `15` `C`

Moscato Sparkler, Tesco `12` `A`
A 5 per cent junior wine for senior tipplers.

Moscato Spumante, Tesco · 13 · C

Muscat flavour all the way through. Good fun aperitif.

Paul de Villeroy Brut Champagne 1989 · 14 · G

A deliciously light, elegant, subtly lemon-edged bubbly of class.
Top 70 stores.

Premier Cru Brut Champagne, Tesco · 14 · F

Classy, delicious and very well made. Knocks many a grand
marque into a cocked hat.

Prosecco Spumante, Tesco · 14 · C

Delicious peachy/strawberry aperitif. Great fun.

Rose Cava, Tesco · 15 · C

Subtle raspberry here and fruit hints in this brilliant value-for-
money bubbly.

Salinger 1989 · 12 · G

Seppelts Salinger Sparkling Wine (Australia) · 15 · F

Mature yet fresh-finishing. Some elegance. Dry.

Seppelt Sparkling Shiraz (Australian) · 16 · E

Wonderful bittersweet fruit of emulsion-like thickness and rich,
blackberry flavour. Great fun with game birds. Not available in
all stores.

Soave Classico Spumante · 13 · D

South African Robertson Sparkling, Tesco · 13.5 · D

Fresh and perky. A youthful bubbly for youthful occasions
(christenings, etc).

South African Sparkling Sauvignon Blanc
1993, Tesco   15 C

Sparkling Chardonnay, Tesco (France)   14 C

Very soft. Very very soft. Certainly not for classicists but I like
it. Top 70 stores only.

Tradition South African Sparkling   15 D

Well-formed, fruity, fresh, classy – well put together and
infinitely better than many sparkling wines at twice the price.

Vintage Cava 1991, Tesco   13 D

Yalumba Cuvee Sparkling Cabernet
Sauvignon   15 E

Utterly ravishing stuff. Dry fruit, soft to finish. Great fun. Eat?
Nothing. Drinks by itself.

Yalumba Pinot Noir/Chardonnay, Australia   16 E

Absolute stunner for the money: rich and biscuity, great
balancing acidity and an overall style hinting refinement and
class. Rheims quakes in its Gucci boots!

WAITROSE

Is this the year Waitrose comes out of the closet? It's been rattling around inside the thing listening to its own noise, and believing that its own ethos and prevailing sense of piety would stand steadfast against the angry hordes outside, but this inwardness has proved a faulty basis for growth during the febrile years of a recession which it never seemed would end. The good news is, of course, that it won't ever end. Thus we can be assured of cheaper and better wines for years to come, and fiercely competing supermarkets will maintain their defiance of the Chancellor's whims and the teetotal lobby's sneers by continuing to unearth terrific bargains for under three quid. These are to be found at Waitrose but in spite of this the store basks in the image of being the minor public school supermarket catering to those who do not put low prices as the major reason for choosing the place at which they shop but instead the perceived quality of the merchandise. Earlier this year *Which?* magazine rated the store as one of the most expensive in a supermarket survey of prices.

Waitrose is an 111-branch enigma (or maybe 116 by the time this book is out). It used to be one wrapped up in mystery but the mystery has dissipated to reveal a modern streak of retailing instinct which, had it been exhibited years ago, would have meant Sainsbury's and Tesco had something more to worry about than each other. It has had problems coming to terms with the modern electronic age and only this year has every branch in the chain had check-out scanners put in (when its bigger competitors have had them humming away for a decade). It has at last made up its mind about Sunday opening, too, after everyone else defied Sabbath custom and threw open their doors – though I believe less than a quarter of Waitroses now do open on our official day of rest. It's also put in a new, more streamlined distribution system for its wines. It's even opened its first petrol station (somewhat behind Tesco, for example, which is the nation's largest independent petrol retailer) and this is to be found at a new Waitrose store concept called 'Food & Home' in Southend of all places. This is, as its name suggests, a department store and food shop combined. Another one is expected to open this year. None of these things, however, matters so much to the store as obtaining the Royal Warrant in 1994 (its mail order wine subsidiary, Findlater Mackie Todd, already had one).

However, to return to my first question. The answer to which, in spite of the heretical activity detailed above, is no – not completely. Waitrose has poked its nose outside the closet and taken note of what the rest of the world is doing but it hasn't yet fully emerged and still to some extent breathes its own stale air. Waitrose continues to be the one wine retailer the wine-buying department of which is exclusively staffed at buying level by Masters of Wine (due to its manager being a board member of the Institute of MWs) and it is still nervous of people like me who like to peep into closets to find the truth within. MW after a buyer's name may well be no more guarantee you will be delivered of a great bottle of wine than MD after a doctor's is a promise you will be relieved of the pain in your neck. Yet the wine department has been remarkably consistent. Julian Brind is its urbane manager and he is charm and self-effacing intelligence personified. I feel at times that he must wince as he reads some of the more exotic descriptions I apply to his wines and I suspect he would love to be dealing in wine in a world free of vulgar wine writers. His is the only department well-mannered enough to have ever rung me up to ask my permission to use a favourable *Superplonk* review of a Waitrose wine for publicity purposes, and he is the only wine buyer to have replied to the questionnaire I sent all retailers asking questions about their business that 'we are not supposed to give out this sort of information' and, further, that 'I trust you will not pass it on.' Such an enigmatic response indicates the presence of an outsider rattling the doors of its closet and feeling ruffled, but politeness demands a reply and so, however reluctantly compiled, the document was returned to me properly filled out.

But I am a wine journalist. Information, as an aid to insight, is my lifeblood. My questionnaire said quite plainly that it was seeking information which would be of help to readers of the *Superplonk* book and so pass it on I must. The modesty of Mr Brind, who would be superbly cast as a rather too good-looking mathematics don who solves, reluctantly at first but then with growing enthusiasm, the criminal conundrum baffling the college authorities in some BBC-TV Oxbridge melodrama, or perhaps playing M in an Ian Fleming mystification, does him credit.

Thus I can tell you that Waitrose's top half-dozen best-sellers do not number amongst them a fifteen-year-old first growth Medoc or a couple of ancient halves of port but somewhat less fancy fare. And each is somewhat of a bargain – which does, as I have long suspected, throw into serious question the belief that Waitrose customers are not concerned with value for money. Where these six wines are concerned, value-for-money is as good as printed in electric colours on the price ticket:

1. Waitrose Good Ordinary Claret (£3.25).
2. Les Trois Couronnes, Vin de Pays de l'Herault (£2.59).
3. Hock, Deutscher Tafelwein (£2.49).
4. Waitrose Cotes du Rhone (£3.15).
5. Bulgarian Cabernet Sauvignon (£2.95).
6. Hardy's Southern Creek Semillon/Chardonnay (£3.79).

What can we deduce from this list of preferences? That Waitrose customers are, as Mr Brind himself believes (and states as such in my questionnaire), from those three camps which socio-economists list as the most wealthy in the land: A, B and

C1. Quite patently, wealth is not to be equated with money to burn; however much the store's customers may spend on food, where wine is concerned they are as canny as the next tippler.

And in this respect Waitrose is as good a place as anywhere to fill your trolley – as the entries which follow this introduction demonstrate.

What, however, of the future? And what of that crippling closet? Well, as far as sourcing the wines is concerned, there is no doubt that Waitrose knows exactly which countries will provide the most exciting additions to the store's range over the next few years and the closet's doors will be flung wide. In answer to a question about where the wines of the future will be coming from, Mr Brind replied as follows:

1. South Africa.
2. Chile.
3. France (non-Appellation Controlee areas).
4. Eastern Europe.
5. Spain and Portugal.
6. Italy.

This is an interesting list. I couldn't have compiled a better one myself – certainly not if volume is a consideration. If it isn't, then I would have also included merlots from Washington State and New Zealand, sparkling wines from New Zealand, and I would have added Argentina and Western Australia to the list.

It does, though, need pointing out that the country at the head of that list would have been on it a long time before apartheid vanished. Waitrose was happy to list South African wines when the country was a pariah with other supermarket wine buyers, and the harsh critic might say, so what's new? Shows loyalty if nothing else. And if I were to try to characterise the overriding feature of the Waitrose wine department, loyalty would be it.

It has always showed loyalty to its customers (for surely they've had a taste for good ordinary claret for generations but never perhaps paid, comparatively, so little for it), loyalty to wine-makers' own presentations (the store doesn't muck about with own-labels to the extent its competitors do), loyalty to old-established regions with a small but determined following at the store (like mature German rieslings from Kabinett to Auslese levels), and even loyalty to wine writers. There are those of this latter persuasion whom Mr Brind prizes highly; not for their publicity potential nor for their ability to turn out a winning phrase which can be borrowed and stuck on a shelf; he treasures them because they wrote about the excellence of Waitrose's range of wines in the old pre-Maggie days before Cloudy Bay and Chilean Cabernet Sauvignon were ever dreamt of – and the idea of the flying wine-maker and the armed policewoman would have been met with incredulity – and these scribes of the vine turn up every year to enjoy their lunch at the annual Waitrose wine tasting as if nothing had changed.

For, in many respects, little has changed at Waitrose. In an era when so much change has been seen, with hindsight, for the fool's gold it really was, maybe Waitrose, cheerfully ensconced in its closet, has the secret: do what you do best, only do it better each time.

I agree with that one hundred per cent.

Waitrose Limited
Customer Service Department
Southern Industrial Area
Bracknell
Berkshire
RG12 8YA

Tel 01344 424680
Fax 01344 862584

Findlater Mackie Todd & Co Limited (Waitrose Direct)
Freepost London SW19 3YY

Tel 0181 543 0966
Fax 0181 543 2415

ARGENTINIAN WINE   RED

**Santa Julia Malbec/Cabernet Sauvignon,
Mendoza 1993**   `13` `C`

ARGENTINIAN WINE   WHITE

Mendoza White Wine (3 litre)   `15.5` `F`

Here you get a winebox containing the equivalent of 4 bottles
of wine for £12.93 (or £3.23 a bottle) and the contents are
delightful. The wine has a lush melon aroma leading to rounded
fruit, also melony, yet cut with sufficient acidity to provide
balance, freshness, style and modernity. Its zippy personality
easily rates the 15.5 points.

Santa Julia Torrontes, Mendoza 1994   `13` `C`

Also available by mail order through Findlater, Mackie Todd.

**Stowells of Chelsea Mendoza Dry White
(3 litre)**   `13` `G`

Some soft melony edge to the fruit. Not exciting, but sound.

AUSTRALIAN WINE   RED

**Angove's Nanya Malbec/Ruby Cabernet
1994**   `14` `C`

Soft, squashy summer fruits, vibrantly flavoursome.

Angove's Nanya Malbec/Ruby Cabernet 1994, Waitrose `12` `C`

Weeps with juice when it also needs a cough or two to give it more balance.

Berri Estates Cabernet/Shiraz 1992 `15` `C`

Rich, soft, lots of character yet simple to swallow. Also available by mail order through Findlater, Mackie Todd.

Brown Brothers Tarrango 1994 `11` `C`

So ripe, luscious and downright juicy it can be spread on bread and given to children as a warning not to crush too hard otherwise there is no character in the wine.

Browns Shiraz/Malbec, Padthaway 1994 `12` `D`

Chateau Reynella Basket Press Shiraz 1992 `16` `D`

Spicy, deep and so full of flavour you wonder for a moment – could grapes really be squeezed to yield fruit so rich?

Coldstream Hills Cabernet/Merlot 1992 `11` `E`

Daft price for such juicy, £4-level, Italian-style fruit.

Goundrey Langton Cabernet/Merlot 1992 `13` `D`

Bit too giving and childlike for the money but hugely quaffable.

Hardys Southern Creek Shiraz/Cabernet 1994 `15.5` `C`

Rolling soft fruit well supported by acids and tannins: firm, delicious, decisive.

Jacob's Creek Dry Red, Shiraz/Cabernet 1993 `15` `C`

Fun, yet serious fun. Great with the usual meaty things.

Leasingham Shiraz, Clare Valley 1992 `17` `D`

Brilliantly orchestrated fruit and tannins in rich voice together. Superb depth, complexity and flavour.

Oxford Landing Cabernet/Shiraz 1993 `14` `C`

By a whistle the fruit holds off the acidity at the finish to get it to 14 points.

Penfold's Rawson's Retreat Bin 35 Cabernet Sauvignon/Ruby Cabernet/Shiraz 1993 `12` `C`

Soft and rather expressionless.

Penfolds Bin 2 Shiraz/Mourvedre 1992 `15` `C`

Plum and black cherries, muted spice. Delicious! Will develop and get even better.

Penfolds Bin 35 Shiraz Cabernet 1992 `15` `C`

Ripe, soft fruit with some development ahead of it. Attractive berry flavours, well structured and balanced. Very drinkable now but a 17/18-pointer in 3/4 years.

Peter Lehmann Cabernet Sauvignon 1992 `16.5` `D`

True class, quiet power, weight of fruit and decisive balance.

Yaldara Grenache, Whitmore Old Vineyard 1994 `15` `C`

Delicious: yoghurt-rich edge to the impossibly soft fruit.

AUSTRALIAN WINE
WHITE

**Angove's Nanya Estate Riesling/
Gewurztraminer 1994** `12.5` `C`

**Arrowfield Show Reserve Chardonnay
1992, South East Australia** `13` `E`

**Arrowfield Show Reserve Late Harvest
Riesling 1993 (half bottle)** `13` `E`

Lots of money but oodles of ravishing sweet fruit. Great with fruit tarts.

Baldivis Estate Chardonnay 1993 `12` `E`

Hair-raising price, too.

**Brown Brothers King Valley 1993 Rhine
Riesling, Victoria** `13` `D`

Lay down for 3 years? Good stuff, packed with biscuity, lemon-sherbet fruit but expensive for drinking now. Needs time.

**Currawong Creek Semillon/Chardonnay
1992** `13` `C`

Hardys Nottage Hill Chardonnay 1994 `16` `C`

Controlled soft spice laid on smooth blackcurrant fruit. Delicious, firm, well-styled.

**Hardys Southern Creek Semillon/
Chardonnay 1994** `12` `C`

**Houghton Wildflower Ridge Chenin
Blanc 1994** `13` `C`

Mitchelton Reserve Marsanne 1992 `15.5` `D`

Lots of ritzy acidity underpinned by rich fruit. Also available by mail order through Findlater, Mackie Todd.

Moondah Brook Verdelho 1994 `14` `C`

Good firm fruit – for scallops.

Nanya Estate Riesling/Gewurztraminer 1994 `12` `C`

Curious.

Oxford Landing Chardonnay 1994 `15` `C`

Rich, nicely buttered and broad. Lots of character.

Oxford Landing Sauvignon Blanc 1994 `13.5` `C`

Some good sauvignon fruit here. Also available by mail order through Findlater, Mackie Todd.

Penfolds Bin 202 South Australian Riesling 1993 `14` `C`

Superb, rich aperitif. Delicious.

Penfolds Bin 21 Semillon/Chardonnay 1993 `15` `C`

Fresh and lively yet a dollop of pineappley melon keeps intruding. Delicious, refreshing wine. Also available in half bottles.

Penfolds Koonunga Hill Chardonnay 1993 `13` `C`

**Villa Maria Private Bin Chardonnay,
Gisborne 1994** `14` `D`

**Wakefield White Clare Crouchen/
Chardonnay 1991 Clare Valley, South
Australia** `14` `C`

Not as deeply wooded as previous vintages but still a wine in
fighting form.

BULGARIAN WINE RED

Bulgarian Cabernet Sauvignon/Merlot 1991 `14` `B`

Cabernet Sauvignon Russe 1990 `14` `B`

Dry, serious-edged, yet friendly and food-compatible.

Cabernet Sauvignon/Merlot, Iambol 1994 `15` `B`

Lovely biscuity fruit with chewiness, yet in the final flourish
softness and flavour.

Iambol Reserve Cabernet Sauvignon 1990 `13` `B`

Also available by mail order through Findlater, Mackie Todd.

Merlot/Gamza `13` `B`

Oriachovitza Barrel-aged Merlot 1994 `13.5` `B`

Only a surrender to the acidity in the finish ranks this fruit
lower than it might be. More guts, more points!

**Stowells of Chelsea Cabernet Sauvignon
(3 litre)** `14` `F`

Dry, very good, rich, savoury-edged fruit – good with food.

CANADIAN WINE   RED

Harrow Estates North Shore Red, Ontario 1994

Juicy, but too juicy. We need more than juice.

CHILEAN WINE   RED

Concha y Toro Merlot 1994

Almost too smooth for its own good but as the blackcurrant fruit swirls so sveltely over the tastebuds a ripple of dry tannins take the throat. Super stuff in the end.

Cono Sur Cabernet Sauvignon 1993

Really flavoursome fruit here of depth and gravity yet with that ineffable Chilean touch of gently exotic multiplicity of soft fruit tastes. One of the Wines of the Month for December 1995 – 12 bottles for the price of 11.

Cono Sur Pinot Noir Reserve 1994 | 13.5 | D |

Expensive cherry fruit. Exceedingly drinkable but not sufficiently complex for the money to justify a higher rating.

Montenuevo Zinfandel, Maipo 1994 | 12 | C |

Valdivieso Merlot, Lontue Region 1993 | 15.5 | C |

Gripping, rich, assertive, well plotted from start to finish. A good thriller.

CHILEAN WINE — WHITE

Caliterra Chardonnay 1994 `13` `C`

Montenuevo Chardonnay 1994, Maipo `14` `C`
Handsome richness of fruit here.

Montenuevo Sauvignon Blanc 1994, Maipo `12` `C`

Valdivieso Barrel-fermented Chardonnay, Lontue 1993 `15` `D`
Meursault too scrawny and overpriced for you? Try this instead.

Valdivieso Chardonnay, Lontue 1993 `13` `D`

ENGLISH WINE — RED

Chapel Down Epoch I West Sussex 1993 `12.5` `C`
A drinkable, rateable English red wine! Has soft dry fruit with some style to it.

Denbies Surrey Gold 1992 `13` `C`
Decently made, well structured – you might say as much of a pre-fab.

ENGLISH WINE — WHITE

Chapel Down Epoch V East Sussex 1993 `13` `C`

Chiltern Valley Medium Dry 1991   8   C

Perfectly revolting wine.

Priory, Lamberhurst Vineyards   14   B

Woolly fruit, attractive, subtle. Very pleasant wine at an excellent price.

Rock Lodge Outige & Muller-Thurgau 1993, Waitrose   12   C

Finish mars the performance – it beats the whole of the defence then slips in the mud as it sees the goal yawn. Pity.

FRENCH WINE   RED

Baron Villeneuve du Chateau Cantemerle, Haut Medoc 1990   13   E

California-style claret. Delicious stuff now, but liquid velvet in 5 years' time.

Beaujolais Villages Jean-Marc Anjoux 1994   11   C

Bergerac Rouge AC 1994   12   B

Cabernet Sauvignon, VdP d'Oc Hugh Ryman 1993   13.5   C

Polished, well-mannered. Good with mild stews.

Cabernet Sauvignon, Vin de Pays d'Oc 1992   12   C

Cahors Cuvee Reserve 1992   13   C

Touch austere. Like a nine-year-old smoking a pipe and reading Wittgenstein.

Chateau Biston-Brillette, Moulis 1990 `14` `E`

Delicious, pricey but delicious: soft, rich, lovingly well-built.

Chateau Blanzac, Cotes de Castillon 1990 `14` `D`

Keep it for another 5 years.

Chateau d'Arche, Haut-Medoc 1990 `13` `E`

Chateau de Nages Costieres de Nimes AC 1993 `14.5` `B`

Very food-friendly. Dry, charcoal-edged fruit – has good tannins which will soften.

Chateau Haut d'Allard Cotes de Bourg 1993 `15` `C`

Lovely meaty aroma, soft fruit with a sophisitcated, classic edge and a lingering finish. Good price.

Chateau Les Moulins des Calons, Montagne St Emilion 1993 `14` `D`

Leave it for a couple of years yet. It'll put on points.

Chateau Lestage-Simon, Haut Medoc 1990 `12` `F`

Splendid in feel, outrageous in price.

Chateau Lyonnat Lussac St Emilion AC,1989 `13` `D`

Chateau Maine-Bonnet, Graves 1990 `13.5` `D`

Good bourgeois claret.

Chateau Marseau, Cotes du Marmandais 1993 `12` `C`

Some mild tannic presence. The fruit is mild at heart.

Chateau Moulin de Madaillan, Bordeaux
1994   `13` `B`

Good value for what can call itself a proper claret – if that still means anything these days.

Chateau Segonzac Premier Cotes de Blaye
AC, 1993   `13.5` `C`

Distant cherry echo to reedy blackcurrant fruit.

Chateau St Maurice Cotes du Rhone 1993   `14` `C`

Tasty and well-developed. Soft fruit to go with lamb casserole.

Chateau Vieux Robin, Medoc 1990   `12` `E`

Interesting tannins – maybe in another couple of years?

Chateauneuf-du-Pape, Delas Freres 1993   `13` `E`

Chorey-les-Beaune, Domaine Maillard Pere
et Fils 1992   `12.5` `E`

Cotes de Ventoux AC 1992   `14` `B`

Cotes du Rhone 1994, Waitrose   `13` `B`

Good finish here. Very meaty. Also available in half bottles.

Cotes du Ventoux Les Oliviers 1994   `15` `B`

Great value here – real Rhone character but softer and riper and at a humble price.

Crozes-Hermitages Cave des Clairmonts
1992   `13.5` `D`

Soft but an austere edge – smoky fruit which will improve in bottle.

Domaine de Cantemerle, Cotes du Rhone Villages 1994 `14` `C`

Soft, not a lot of cloddish earth. Fruity.

Domaine de la Fourmone, Vacqueyras Tresor de Poete 1993 `14` `D`

This poet stuck to mere couplets: plums and blackberries (sprinkled with tannin).

Domaine de la Rose Merlot/Syrah, VdP d'Oc 1994 `13.5` `B`

Juicy and simplistic.

Domaine de St-Macaire, Vin de Pays de l'Herault `11` `B`

Domaine des Fontaines Merlot, Vin de Pays d'Oc 1994 `13.5` `B`

Soft, gently leathery.

Domaine Ste Lucie Gigondas 1994 Waitrose `13.5` `D`

Lucie is, as a matter of interest, the sainted patroness of those suffering from eye diseases. I myself am myopic. But I am not so shortsighted that I fail to recognise that seven quid, as near as dammit, is far too much for this thoroughly decent (and much underrated) village in the southern Rhone. At £3.99 this wine would rate 15 or more in a year.

Ermitage du Pic St Loup, Coteaux du Languedoc 1994 `13` `C`

A syrah/mourvedre blend – exclusive to Waitrose, this is an easy-drinking wine of surprising softness and simplicity.

Fleurie AC 1993 (half bottle)   `13` `B`

Foncalieu Cabernet Sauvignon Vin de Pays de l'Aude 1994   `13.5` `B`
Likes food and fast company.

Gamay Haut-Poitou 1993   `12` `C`
Very juicy.

Gamay/Syrah, VdP de l'Ardeche 1994   `13.5` `B`
Very attractive soft fruit – with a characterful edge.

Good Ordinary Claret Bordeaux, Waitrose   `13` `B`
A bargain – also available in a magnum for six quid odd. It's as good as its name and better than ordinary (thus offering us the only understatement ever made by a supermarket own-label bottle).

Graves AC Ginestet 1994   `13.5` `C`
Some agreeable tannic friskiness to the fruit. Good with meat (rare).

Hautes Cotes de Beaune, Tete de Cuvee, Caves des Hautes Cotes 1990   `10` `E`

La Roseraie de Gruaud Larose, St Julien 1992   `12.5` `E`

Le Secret Vin de Pays de Vaucluse 1994   `14` `B`
Soft, bright, gluggable to the enth degree.

Les Tuguets Madiran 1993   `13` `C`
Soft edge to rustic heart.

Macon Superieur Les Epillets, Cave de Lugny 1994   `12` `C`

Margaux 1990 13 E

Lovely classic drinkable margaux.

Margaux AC Ginestet 1994 12 E

Masquerade, VdP de l'Aude 1994 14 B

Juicy, fresh, cherry-edged. Great pasta wine.

Mercurey AC La Framboisiere, Faiveley 1992 13 E

Some initial flutterings of the heart which don't quite reach the soles of the feet.

Merlot/Cabernet Sauvignon, VdP d'Oc 1994, Waitrose 15.5 B

Oh, Madame Moulin, what a stunning wine you have bottled for the money! It has earthy touches, to be sure, but these grace rather than coarsen the soft ripe fruit and the result is characterful and delicious.

Minervois AC 1994 13.5 B

Dry, plum-centred.

Morgon Duboeuf 1994 (half bottle) 12 C

Not bad. Actually has some claim to cru typicity.

Morgon Duboeuf 1994, Waitrose 11 C

An experience the price renders almost absurd.

Oak Matured Bordeaux 1993 12 C

Pinot Noir Red Burgundy (Oak Aged), J. C. Boisset 1993 12 C

One of the Wines of the Month for December 1995 – 12 bottles for the price of 11. Also available in half bottles.

Prieure de Fonclaire Grande Reserve, Buzet AC 1993

`13` `C`

Claret toughness. Also available in half bottles.

Saint Joseph, Caves de Saint-Desirat, 1991

`14` `E`

A big, juicy, lovely glug – touch pricey – but great with mushroom risotto.

Special Reserve Claret, Waitrose 1989

`13` `C`

St Emilion

`13` `C`

Syrah Galet Vineyards 1994

`14.5` `C`

A handsome, rugged beast softened by rich tannins of some gentility and a warm, savoury finish. A delicious, soupy wine for all sorts of lamb dishes.

Terrasses de Landoc Grenache, VdP de l'Herault 1994

`14` `C`

Rustic but dry and approachable. Try it with cheese and roast vegetables.

Waitrose Special Reserve Claret, Cotes de Castillon 1993

`14` `C`

Good weighty Castillon value here. Decant 2 hours before drinking.

Winter Hill VdP de l'Aude 1994

`15.5` `B`

Tasting brilliantly. Deep, dark and savoury.

FRENCH WINE   WHITE

Beaune E. Delaunay & Fils 1992

`11` `E`

**Beblenheim Gewurztraminer d'Alsace
Cuvee 1993 (half bottle)** `12` `B`

Also available by mail order through Findlater, Mackie Todd.

Blanc de Mer `14` `B`

Now also in a magnum, for under six quid, this is the wine for large gatherings of the British chapter of The Bouillabaisse Club.

Blaye Blanc 1994 `13` `B`

Bordeaux Blanc, medium dry `11` `B`

Bordeaux Rose Francois de Lorgeac 1994 `13` `C`

Good and dry.

Chablis 1993 Gaec des Reugnis `12` `D`

Chablis Premier Cru AC Beauroy 1991 `13` `E`

Chardonnay Vin de Pays d'Oc, 1993 `13` `C`

One of the Wines of the Month for December 1995 – 12 bottles for the price of 11.

**Chateau Bastor-Lamontagne Sauternes
1990 (half bottle)** `14` `E`

Zippy marmalade edge to the burnt honeyed fruit.

Chateau Carsin 1993 Cuvee Prestige `15` `D`

Class and style, fruit and acid, deliciously serious.

Chateau Chaubinet 1992 Bordeaux AC `12` `C`

Chateau Darzac Entre Deux Mers 1994 `13` `C`

Great with fresh shellfish.

Chateau la Caussade 1991 Ste Croix du Mont AC

Chateau La Jalgue, Cuvee Prestige Bordeaux 1993

Gently woody fruit with very aristocratic acidity propping it up – a firmly built wine.

Chateau Roumieu-Lacost, Sauternes 1990

Good but pricey.

Chateau Terres Douces Bordeaux 1994, Waitrose

Lovely creamy wood (subtle but persistent) to the fresh, dry fruit make this an attractive fish wine.

Chateau Tour Balot 1990 1er Cotes de Bordeaux AC

Curious marzipan undertone to this wine. Good aperitif if well chilled.

Domaine de Raissac Vermentino, VdP d'Oc 1994

Unusual wine – an Italian grape grown in Oc. Very tasty.

Domaine des Fontanelles Sauvignon Vin de Pays d'Oc 1993

Domaine des Fontanelles, Syrah Rose VdP d'Oc 1994

A thoroughly respectable rose of real style and good dry fruit.

**Domaine Gibault, Sauvignon de Touraine
1993** `13` `C`

**Domaine Petit Chateau Chardonnay, Vin
de Pays du Jardin de la France 1993** `14` `C`

**Fortant Chardonnay, Vin de Pays d'Oc
1993** `13` `C`

**La Fontaine Chardonnay VdP d'Oc 1994,
Waitrose** `14` `C`

Good value. Solid, balanced, ripe fruit with a dry, mature
edge.

**Laperouse Blanc Val d'Orbieu & Penfolds,
VdP d'Oc 1994** `15` `C`

Rounded fruit flavours energetically supported by the elegance
of the acids.

Le Pujalet Vin de Pays du Gers 1993 `14` `B`

Bright, modern, fresh, inoffensive and very good value. Fish 'n'
chips would suit it admirably.

Macon Lugny, Les Charmes 1992 `12` `D`

Macon-Villages Chardonnay 1993 `13.5` `C`

Some character here.

Muscadet 1993, Waitrose `10` `B`

**Pinot Blanc d'Alsace AC 1992 Blanck
Freres** `12` `C`

**Pouilly Fume AC, Masson-Blondelet
1994** `10` `D`

Premieres Cotes de Bordeaux `13` `C`

A pud wine. But the pud needs to be very light.

Roussanne Ryman VdP d'Oc 1994 `14` `C`

Interesting flavour and richness of fruit. Great with smoked salmon. Also available by mail order through Findlater, Mackie Todd.

Saint Veran Duboeuf 1993 `10` `D`

Sancerre 1993 `11` `D`

Sancerre La Vraignonette 1993 `13` `D`

A touch of NZ grassiness here!

Sauvignon de St Bris Jean-Marc Brocard 1993 `12` `D`

Sauvignon Haut-Poitou 1993 `12` `C`

Terret/Chardonnay, VdP des Cotes de Thau J&F Lurton, 1994 `14` `B`

Cheap, delicious drinking – good with shellfish.

Tokay Pinot Gris d'Alsace 1993, Cave de Beblenheim (half bottle) `12.5` `C`

Vin de Pays du Jardin de la France Chardonnay 1993 `12` `B`

Viognier Chais Cuxac, VdP d'Oc 1994 `15` `C`

Oooh – lovely! Banana and peach softness plus rich nutty acids. Great style here.

Vouvray, Domaine de la Robiniere, 1993 `11` `C`

Waitrose Bordeaux Sauvignon AC 1994 `14.5` `B`

Excellent. Lively, dry, nuttily finished. Excellent price for such class.

Waitrose Gewurztraminer d'Alsace, Beblenheim 1993 `13` `D`

One for gewurz fans.

White Burgundy Chardonnay, AC Bourgogne 1993 `13` `C`

Winter Hill VdP de l'Aude 1994 `16` `B`

A blend masterminded by western Australians near Carcassonne in Southern France. It is full of flavour and style with a fresh edge to subtle rusticity. Splendid glug.

GERMAN WINE WHITE

Avelsbacher Hammerstein Riesling 1989 `15` `E`

Avelsbacher Hammerstein Riesling Spatlese, Moselle 1989 `13` `D`

Kerosene nose, oiliness to the fruit which is attractively deep.

Bad Bergzaberner Kloster Liebfrauenberg Auslese 1992 `14` `C`

A superb aperitif, with a glittering touch of honey.

Baden Dry `14` `C`

Dexheimer Doktor Spatlese, Rheinhessen 1993 `13` `C`

Erdener Treppchen Riesling QbA, Monchhof 1984 `15` `C`

Deliciously intriguing mineral/fruit bouquet, perfectly mature ripe fruit with an echo of petrol and acids and an overall lovely disposition. Bargain for the age. Try it with Thai seafood.

Erdener Treppchen Riesling Spatlese, Monchhof 1989 `14.5` `D`

Lovely acidic structure and persistence. Deliciously weighted, extremely elegant aperitif. Stun your guests with it.

Hochheimer Reichestal Riesling Kabinett 1993 `10` `C`

10 points now but it will rate 15 in 5 years' time.

Hochheimer Reichestal Stahleck Riesling Kabinett 1993 `14` `E`

Expensive – and rewarding to drink now as a black-mood-raiser but kept for 6/7 years it will be ambrosial.

Kirchheimer Schwarzerde Beerenauslese, Zimmermann-Graeff, Pfalz 1993 `14` `C`

Big-hearted sweetie which would be best left to develop over the next 10 years. Lay it down for the children's entrance to University?

Morio Muskat 1992 `15` `B`

Ockfener Bockstein Riesling QbA 1993 `14` `C`

Elegant, highly civilised, fruity, delicious – but all of these things apply to summer drinking in the garden.

Pinot Blanc Trocken 1992 `13` `C`

Riesling 1993, Waitrose (1 litre)   `13` `C`

GREEK WINE WHITE

Kouros Patras 1993   `13` `C`
Rich, oily flavours here – good with fish soup.

HUNGARIAN WINE RED

Sopron Cabernet Sauvignon 1994   `14.5` `B`
Inexpensive claret for the young lovers of the stuff.

HUNGARIAN WINE WHITE

Chapel Hill Irsai Oliver 1993   `13.5` `B`

Deer Leap Sauvignon 1993   `13` `C`

Disznoko Tokaji Furmint 1993   `12` `C`

Lakeside Oak Chardonnay 1993   `15` `B`
Some interesting complexity here for the money: gentle woodiness and fruit. Very attractive.

Szeksard Chardonnay 1993   `10` `B`

Tokaji 1983 Aszu 4 Puttonyos (50 cl)   `12` `E`

ITALIAN WINE   RED

**Amarone della Valpolicella Classico,
Campagnola 1990**   `13.5` `E`

Expensive but mildly entertaining. Also available through
Findlater, Mackie Todd.

Barolo Vigneto Castellato, Gigi Rosso 1991   `12` `E`

Eight quid's worh of wine? Nope.

Campo ai Sassi, Rosso di Montalcino 1992   `13.5` `D`

A quid cheaper and it'd rate a whole point more.

Carafe Red Wine, Waitrose (1 litre)   `13` `C`

Adds pizzazz to any pizza.

**Chianti Classico Riserva, Rocca delle
Macie 1990**   `13` `D`

Chianti Classico, Rooca delle Macie 1993   `13` `C`

**Dolcetto Vino da Tavola del Piemonte,
1993 Gemma**   `13.5` `C`

Soft, squashy, a hint of dryness. Good pizza wine.

Grifi 1989, Avignonesi   `15` `E`

Very cultured fruit on offer here.

**Merlot, Vino da Tavola del Veneto Vallade
1994**   `13` `B`

Juicy, fruity, fun.

Monica di Sardegna DOC 1993   `14` `B`

Lovely rich fruit here of surprising vibrancy for such a price.

Montepulciano d'Abruzzo, Umani Ronchi 1993 `15` `C`

Big yet not intimidating – soft and friendly and goes out of its way to smile. Brilliant value for such flavour and depth. Great with casseroles.

Salice Salentino Riserva, Taurino 1990 `15.5` `C`

Ripe, figgy fruit of great mature flavour. Smashing.

Teroldego Rotaliano DOC, Gaierhof 1992 `13` `C`

Waitrose Chianti 1993 `12.5` `B`

Soft, simple style.

ITALIAN WINE WHITE

Carafe White, Waitrose (1 litre) `13` `C`

Excellent value for a well-balanced dry white.

Chardonnay, Vino da Tavola delle Tre Venezie, Vallade 1994 `14` `B`

Good fruit bargain.

Frascati Superiore, Villa Rufinella 1993 `13` `C`

Very drinkable – for a frascati.

Lugana DOC 1994 Villa Flora, Zenato `14` `C`

Elegant, classy. Also available through Findlater Mackie Todd.

Orvieto Classico Secco, Cardeto 1993   `13` `C`

Passito di Pantelleria, Pellegrino 1993   `15` `D`
Try it with fruit cake. Delicious!!

Sauvignon Friuli Grave, Biduli 1994   `14` `C`
Good expression of the grape – with the added excitement of
lingering fruitiness.

Soave Classico, Zenato 1994   `13` `C`
Clean, fresh fruit.

**Verdicchio dei Casteli di Jesi DOC 1992
Villa Pigna**   `10` `C`

**Waitrose Nuragus di Cagliari DOC,
Sardegna 1993**   `14` `B`
Delicious welcome-home-from-work glug.

LEBANESE WINE   RED

Chateau Musar, Gaston Hochar 1988   `13` `E`
Not the great wine it once was. Geting too juicy and one-
dimensional (and expensive).

NEW ZEALAND WINE   RED

Montana Cabernet Sauvignon 1993   `13` `C`

NEW ZEALAND WINE WHITE

Cook's Chardonnay, Gisborne 1993

Jackson Estate Sauvignon Blanc 1994, Marlborough

Remarkably elegant. A fine, complex, balanced fruit and acid double act with a soft, subtle honey touch on the dry finish.

New Zealand Dry White Wine, Gisborne 1994

Flavoursome grilled chicken wine.

Villa Maria Private Bin Sauvignon Blanc 1994, Marlborough

Delicious grassy fruit. Would be superb with mackerel. Also available through Findlater Mackie Todd.

Wairau River Sauvignon Blanc 1993, Marlborough

PORTUGUESE WINE RED

Bairrada Reserva 1989, Dom Ferraz

Soft plum fruit of some attractiveness but not as excitingly boisterous a mouthful as previous vintages.

Periquita 1991 Jose de Maria da Fonseca

Dry, figgy fruit.

Ramada Tinto, Estremadura 1994

Good fruit here, juicy, straightforward; on its own or with vegetable salads or pies.

Tinto da Anfora 1990

Hairier, more severely tannic, than previous vintages. Put down for 2/3 years and it will be great.

PORTUGUESE WINE WHITE

Ramada Estremadura 1994

Lively, fruity, balanced, clean. Terrific for moules mariniere.

ROMANIAN WINE RED

Samburesti Pinot Noir 1994

Aromatic, rich-edged, dry, brambly yet soft and roundly finishing in the mouth.

Vat 4 Cabernet Sauvignon, Samburesti 1993

Wonderful rich dry fruit gently brushed by tannins which give the wine superb depth, flavour and character.

SLOVENIAN WINE WHITE

Labor Chardonnay 1993, Koper Region ☐12☐ C

SOUTH AFRICAN WINE   RED

Avontuur Cabernet Sauvignon/Merlot 1994   `13` `C`

Also available by mail order through Findlater, Mackie Todd.

Avontuur Pinotage, Paarl 1993   `16` `C`

Delicious! So delicious!! So so delicious!!!

Cape Dry Red, Paarl 1993   `16` `B`

Delicious polish to the berries and herbs. Great glug.

Clos Malverne Pinotage Reserve, Stellenbosch 1994   `15.5` `D`

Shows how brilliant this grape can be: has serious yet soft tannins and utterly captivating, velvet fruit.

Culemborg Pinotage, Paarl 1993   `13.5` `B`

A juicy pinotage of simple charms.

Delheim Cabernet Sauvignon, Stellenbosch 1992   `13` `D`

Fairview Shiraz Reserve, Paarl 1994   `15` `D`

The reserve of the label is on the back. The fruit, however, shows no such diffidence. It's exciting, dry, bold, soft, enticingly fruity.

Klein Constantia Cabernet Sauvignon, Constantia 1990   `12` `D`

Stellenzicht Cabernet Sauvignon, Stellenbosch 1992   `14` `C`

Great value: brisk, plummy fruit with flavour and depth.

Stowells of Chelsea Pinotage (3 litre) `13.5` `F`

Soft, not as vivacious – nor with as big a finish – as some, but attractive and well balanced.

SOUTH AFRICAN WINE — WHITE

Cape Release Chenin Blanc 1995 `14` `B`

Has a sunny, vibrant edge to its rich, creamy fruit. Delicious.

Avontuur Chardonnay 1993, Stellenbosch `14` `C`

A firm, delicious wine of style and class.

Avontuur Chardonnay 1994, Stellenbosch `13.5` `C`

A white wine with tannin? Surely not – but this wine has unusual texture and flavour.

Cape Dry White, Paarl 1994 `14` `B`

Good value here – better value, certainly, than most sancerres.

Clear Springs Colombard/Chardonnay 1994 `13` `B`

Good bargain fruit here – great with fish and chips.

Culemborg Chenin Blanc, Paarl 1994 `13` `B`

Delheim Chardonnay 1994 `14` `D`

Rich, creamy, woody and seemingly assertive, this wine is described as (sic) voluptious on its back label – this can only be an amalgam of voluptuous and meretricious for it flatters to deceive. It is rich but this richness is superficial. It will not take to highly flavoured foods.

Klein Constantia Chardonnay 1993   13.5   D

If only it would finish more briskly this wine would be ace. Has the pong but not the panache. And food will kill the flavour's intensity.

Simonsvlei Chardonnay Reserve, Paarl 1994   12.5   C

Stellenzicht Chardonnay, Stellenbosch 1994   16   C

Excellent value for money. Finely balanced touches of rich fruit and a good finish.

Stowells of Chelsea South African Sauvignon Blanc (3 litre)   13   F

Quiet but sound. Not a lot of zip but subdued soundness.

Van Riebeeck Cape Dry White 1993   13   B

White Jerepigo 1979   16   D

Wonderful with a slice of Christmas cake – it can only be rated on this basis.

SPANISH WINE   RED

Agramont Navarra 1991   14   C

Controlled vanilla edge. Lush centre. Good with serious roasts.

Cosme Palacio y Hermanos Rioja 1991   15   C

Dry and bruisingly fruity – wonderful with hearty stews.

Don Hugo `14` `B`

Turns out regularly for Spain's first eleven, though finicky aficionados complain at its lack of finesse, but poured into a common-sense glass and held under a common-sense nose there is no grumbling at the lush aroma and evident fruitiness.

Fuente del Ritmo, La Mancha 1993 `16` `C`

Ribera del Duero 1991 Callejo `14` `C`

Stowells of Chelsea Tempranillo La Mancha (3 litre) `15` `F`

A bright, cherry/plum dry wine of really good fruit, balance and a really attractive finish.

Torres Gran Coronas 1990 `12` `D`

I feel this wine needs a little time in bottle to be as exciting as it will be.

SPANISH WINE   WHITE

Don Hugo `15` `B`

Full, creamy, banana-ey, oaky, coconut-rich fruit, yet not boiled or blowsy but surprisingly fresh and pleasant to roll across the molars. Perfect for watching flavourless food programmes on television but equally superb with paellas and fish curries.

Banda Oro Rioja 1990, Waitrose `12` `C`

Castillo de Liria Moscatel, Valencia `15.5` `B`

Brilliant pudding wine for the money. Also, well chilled, an effective aperitif.

Don Hugo Rose

An excellent value-for-money rose with cherry and melon fruit.

Su'era Jerezana Dry Oloroso, Waitrose

When would you drink it? At funerals. Dull, decaying fruit which is half in heaven, half in hell.

USA WINE RED

Cartlidge & Browne Zinfandel NV

Fetzer Valley Oaks Cabernet 1992

Rich, characterful, classy, dry, very savoury.

Fetzer Vineyards Pinot Noir, Santa Barbara 1993

Deliciously inviting, classic aroma of pinot – truffley and mature. Fruit rather basic with only an echo of the classic touch of wild strawberry and farmyard compost.

Waitrose California Zinfandel/Gamay 1993

Simply not overwhelmed by this – like seeing Bobby Charlton in a netball skirt. Doesn't gel, this wine – the two grapes don't like one another.

USA WINE WHITE

Canyon Springs Pinot Noir Rose, California 1994

What a pity! What sounds an exciting idea turns out like going to the theatre, only to be seated behind a pillar.

Cartlidge & Browne Chardonnay, California 1993 | 15 | C

Stylish, forward, very attractive. Delightful oily, fruity chardonnay of interest to grilled chicken.

Fetzer Sundial Chardonnay, California 1993 | 13 | D

Sunny, rich California fruit – you can almost see it stretched out by the pool.

Stowells of Chelsea California Blush (3 litre) | 10 | F

Barbie-doll fruit, great for Barbie dolls.

Villa Mount Eden Chardonnay 1992 | 13.5 | D

Also available by mail order through Findlater, Mackie Todd.

FORTIFIED WINE

Starboard Batch 88 | 13 | E

Superb with berried tarts.

SPARKLING WINE/CHAMPAGNE

Angas Brut Rose (Australian) | 15 | C

One of those New World sparklers which deliciously tickle the nose and only lightly tickle the pocket but send shivers up the spine of champagne-makers.

Anna de Cordoniu Chardonnay, Spain 1990 `14` `E`
Stunning sparkler of great character: complete, full, elegant, classy.

BB Club Sparkling Chardonnay (Hungary) `12` `C`
Ageing a bit, this bottle, but a name to watch.

Blanquette de Limoux, Waitrose `13` `D`
Very attractive.

Cava Brut, Waitrose `15` `C`
Excellent value. Terrific dry, classic style.

Champagne Brut Blanc de Noirs, Waitrose `14` `F`
Delicious. Classic stuff.

Champagne Rose, Waitrose `15` `F`
The closest the poor teetotaller can come to grasping the flavour of this scrumptious article is by chewing a digestive biscuit spread thickly with crushed rose petals and drinking Perrier water with a microscopically thin slice of lime zest.

Champagne, Waitrose `14` `F`
One of the best supermarket champagnes you can buy.

Chapel Down Cuvee Sec (English) `12` `D`
Peachy but clean.

Clairette de Die Cuvee Imperiale (half bottle) `13` `C`
Sweet peachy aperitif.

Clairette de Die Tradition 1992/93 (half bottle) `13` `D`

Cremant de Bourgogne Blanc de Noirs, Lugny $\boxed{15}$ $\boxed{D}$

Refinement, class, style. At half the price of a comparable champagne. Also available by mail order through Findlater, Mackie Todd.

Cremant de Bourgogne Brut Rose, Cave de Lugny $\boxed{13}$ $\boxed{D}$

Diamantina Brut; Provifin, Brazil $\boxed{13}$ $\boxed{E}$

Not bad, not bad at all. But not in the class of a £5 cava.

Duc de Marne Champagne $\boxed{13}$ $\boxed{G}$

Rich biscuit fruit – delicious with smoked fish but expensive and too hearty, perhaps, for most bubbly fans. Also available through mail order.

Green Point Vineyards Brut, Australian 1992 $\boxed{13.5}$ $\boxed{F}$

Just like champagne. Surprised? I'm not.

Krone Borealis Brut 1993 (South African) $\boxed{12.5}$ $\boxed{D}$

Le Baron de Beaumont Chardonnay $\boxed{14}$ $\boxed{D}$

Excellent value for a delightful little sparkler.

Santi Chardonnay Brut, Italy $\boxed{11}$ $\boxed{D}$

Saumur Brut, Waitrose $\boxed{13}$ $\boxed{D}$

Seaview Brut $\boxed{15}$ $\boxed{D}$

Where available for under £5, one of the best sparklers on the market: stylish, refined, and quite delicious.

Seppelt Great Western Brut $\boxed{14}$ $\boxed{C}$

Light and breezy.

Waitrose Blanc de Blancs   `14` `G`

Expensive, but it is lean, lissom and roller-blade smooth.

Waitrose Champagne Brut Rose   `14` `G`

Scrumptious.

Waitrose Extra Dry Vintage 1989   `14` `G`

Surprising, such a decent rating for such an expensive wine. But it is very beautiful.

Yalumba Cuvee One Pinot Noir/Chardonnay
Prestige   `14` `D`

STOP PRESS

ASDA

AUSTRALIAN WINE   RED

**Hunter Cellars Bin 31 Night Harvest
Australian Red 1994**

Fruit juice. Pricey for such sweet, basic fruit.

**Peter Lehmann Barossa Cabernet
Sauvignon 1993**

Lashings of flavour from this gently leathery fruit.

AUSTRALIAN WINE   WHITE

**Goundrey Western Australia Unwooded
Chardonnay 1995**   16 C

Better without any wood. The sheer opulence of the fruit comes
shining through uncosmeticised. It will develop deliciously in
bottle over the next year but is superb now.

CHILEAN WINE   RED

Alto Plano Chilean Red

Tough, dry and a bit coarse, this rates in the respectable teens
because it is superb with casseroles.

Magnificum Canepa Cabernet Sauvignon 1991 | 11 | E |

Rather a lot of money for this fruit – delicious it may be but a tenner must buy really exciting complexity.

CHILEAN WINE — WHITE

Alto Plano Chilean White | 11 | B |

A Chilean soave.

Rowanbrook Sauvignon Blanc Reserve 1995 | 14 | C |

A delicate, aromatic aperitif.

Santa Helena Chilean Rose 1995 | 16 | B |

New vintage. Fruity, firm, perfectly balanced. Likely as not the most highly rated rose in this book. For the money, it may be capable of claiming this status in the world.

FRENCH WINE — RED

Cotes du Rhone Villages, Domaine de la Beluge 1994 | 14 | C |

Not in the traditional earthy Rhone mould but still has good fruity character.

GERMAN WINE WHITE

Ruppertsberger Hofstuck Riesling Kabinett 1993 `15` `B`

Delicious demonstration of whistle-clean fruit without a touch of sweetness or rawness of acidity. Brilliant aperitif. Great with smoked fish.

PORTUGUESE WINE RED

Pedras do Monte Portuguese Red 1994 `14` `B`

Cheap and cheerful – nothing old sockish about it – but it has an earthy character and its final flourish on the finish is eccentric. Still, it's great with pasta dishes.

SOUTH AFRICAN WINE RED

Fairview Estate Zinfandel/Cinsault 1995 `17` `C`

Astonishing maturity and finely knitted structure for such youth. Floods of spicy fruit, aromatic, very rich and deep and lingering. Brilliant value!

Kanonkop Bouwland Red 1994 `14` `C`

This estate Kanonkop is in love with fruit and this example is full of its obsession, with its expression as a soft, deep, loving mouthful of deliciousness.

Landskroon Estate Cabernet Franc 1995 `15` `B`

Lovely price for such texture, fruit, structure and winning bursts of flavour as it disappears down the gullet.

STOP PRESS

Stellenzicht Block Series Zinfandel 1995

What a winner with all sorts of food: roasts, casseroles, cheeses, game, etcetera. A smooth yet robust wine of distinctive character.

SOUTH AFRICAN WINE WHITE

Van Loveren 'Spes Bona' Chardonnay 1995

New vintage. On the edge of being classy for it is determined to please with its 'drink-me-again' fruit and this quiet enthusiasm is elegant and never overstated.

SPARKLING WINE/CHAMPAGNE

Asda Cava

New blend. A brilliant, elegant, classic bubbly of gentle fruit, no hint of yesteryear's earthiness, and fresh, whistle-clean finish. Superb for the money for which it gives the finest champagne a run.

Cordoniu Chardonnay Brut (Spain) 16 D

Delicious, classy, lively aperitif or to be drunk with smoked fish.

KWIK SAVE

BULGARIAN WINE RED

Merlot/Cabernet Sauvignon, Liubimetz 1994 `15` `B`

Lovely lingering meaty fruit which is staggering for the money. Classy bargain.

Suhindol Cabernet Sauvignon Reserve, Vinenka 1990 `15.5` `B`

Perfect age and maturity of fruit: dark, savoury, seriously well-textured and fruited and it's a huge bargain.

Suhindol Gamza Reserve 1991 `14` `B`

Has a woodiness which hits the back palate rather coarsely but upfront it's fine, and this niggling criticism does not apply when the wine is drunk with food.

BULGARIAN WINE WHITE

Khan Krum Riesling-Dimiat `14` `A`

Cheeky price, cheeky aperitif with a hint of muscat.

FRENCH WINE RED

Domaine Trianon, St Chinian Virginie 1994 `14` `B`

Very ripe and rich with a soft tannic shroud which goes chewy
on the finish. Excellent casserole wine (to marinate both meat
and molars in).

HUNGARIAN WINE WHITE

Hungarian Pinot Gris, Neszmely 1994 `15` `B`

A serious pinot gris for £2.89? Doesn't seem possible but this
is a beauty for the money. Lovely restrained apricot fruit.

ITALIAN WINE WHITE

Cadenza White `10` `B`

Dull wine. Exciting label. You could use the bottle as an elegant
doorstop.

Marks & Spencer

FRENCH WINE RED

Corbieres, Chateau de Seranc 1994

Meaty, savoury, subtly rich, very agile (leaps over casseroles and stews with ease) and has character without coarseness. And being sealed with a synthetic cork, no more dud fruit! So it gets an extra half point for this.

SPANISH WINE RED

Castillo del Ebro Navarra, AGE 1991

What a delightful wine! Wood and fruit delightfully yet assertively hand in hand. Lovely dry plum fruit with echoes of blackcurrant and raspberry.

SAFEWAY

ARGENTINIAN WINE WHITE

Argentina Chenin Blanc, Mendoza 1995

Fruity and flavoursome with a good crisp finish: splendid glug and fish wine.

AUSTRALIAN WINE RED

Australian Dry Red, Safeway

A really excellent little food wine with brisk, clean, plummy fruit.

H. G. Brown Bin 60 Shiraz/Ruby/Cabernet 1995

Light but very drinkable: fruity, soft, simple but effective.

Hardys Coonawarra Cabernet Sauvignon 1993

Good, rich, developing tannins.

Hardys Private Bin Cabernet Sauvignon 1995

Sweet fruit and very easy-going.

Hardys Private Bin Oaked Shiraz 1995 `14` `C`

SAFEWAY

AUSTRALIAN WINE · WHITE

Hardys Private Bin Oaked Chardonnay 1994

Meaty, rich, textured, classy, polished, excellent with chicken and fish. Excellent price.

Monty's Hill Chardonnay/Colombard 1995

Doesn't come down quite as effectively as it goes up, but it'll work well with food.

CHILEAN WINE · RED

Carmen Grande Vidure Cabernet 1994

Smooth, rich, classy – very good price for such accomplished fruit.

Tocornal Cabernet/Malbec 1994

Soft and cherry-edged. Good with food and cheering company.

Tocornal Chilean Red 1994

Bright and breezy cherry and plum, and very cheerful. Good with food, good without.

FRENCH WINE · RED

La Baume Cuvee Australe Syrah/Grenache VdP d'Oc 1994

Easy to quaff with its soft-edged plummy fruit.

453

SOUTH AFRICAN WINE RED

Kleindal Pinotage 1995

New vintage. Superb rich fruit which is never so heavy it cannot be enjoyed by itself nor so light it will not go with food. Lovely hammy fruit, slightly smoky but highly polished and smooth. Beautiful layers of flavour with a soft velvet finish.

Landskroon Cinsault/Shiraz 1993

Very tasty blackberry fruit with a burnt edge of dryness and flavour. Delicious.

Rosenview Cabernet Sauvignon 1995

Beautiful aroma of deep rich fruit and this is fully realised in the fruit itself. Frisks softly, ripely, satisfyingly.

Simonsvlei Pinotage Cabernet Reserve 1994

New vintage. Dry yet soft and gently tannic.

SOUTH AFRICAN WINE WHITE

Danie de Wet Chardonnay Sur Lie 1995

New vintage. Delicate (fruit will bruise it), lovely, quiet fruit with a gently citric finish. Civilised tippling for the bookworm.

SPANISH WINE WHITE

Monopole Barrel-fermented Rioja 1993   14 D

Expensive and purely for food (the wood is weighty but it overpowers the fruit). Grilled chicken great!

SPARKLING WINE/CHAMPAGNE

Maison la Motte Chardonnay 1993 (France)   14 D

Elegant bubbly for the money.

SAINSBURY'S

ARGENTINIAN WINE WHITE

Mendoza Country Rose Wine, Sainsbury's
Selected stores.

AUSTRALIAN WINE RED

**Tarrawingee Grenache, Barossa Valley,
Sainsbury's**
Top 75 stores. Wonderful rich flavour. Raspberry-tinged and
delicious.

**Tyrrells Cabernet Merlot, South Australia
1994**
Selected stores. Flavoursomeness of the kind which reminds the
well-travelled boozer of odd parts of Bordeaux rather than Oz –
but it does have a softness on the finish uncharacteristic of the
former region.

AUSTRALIAN WINE   WHITE

Allandale Chardonnay, Hunter River Valley 1994   `16.5`   `D`

Wine Direct only – not in store. Ripe and luscious fruit which teeters on the edge of full-blooded richness but the pineapple acids hold it back. A lovely wine of flavour and character. Superb with rich fish dishes.

Mick Morris Liqueur Muscat, Rutherglen (half bottle)   `15.5`   `C`

Top 36 stores. Liquid corduroy impregnated with honey and soft fruits. A textured miracle of thickness and deep deep flavour.

Wynns Coonawarra Chardonnay 1993   `14`   `D`

Top 80 stores only. Not a rich wine but a fruity one in a quiet but determined way. Touch expensive.

BULGARIAN WINE   RED

Yantra Valley Cabernet Sauvignon 1990   `14.5`   `B`

Selected stores. Real flavour and style here with the dry coating nicely counterpointing the soft rich middle fruitiness.

BULGARIAN WINE WHITE

Bulgarian Oak-fermented Chardonnay, Slaviantzi 1994

Selected stores.

CHILEAN WINE RED

Chilean Merlot, Sainsbury's

Rich and rampant, very dry and will soften quickly in bottle over the next few months.

Santa Carolina Cabernet Sauvignon Reserva, Maipo 1991

Top 75 stores. Quietly stylish and nicely fruity.

FRENCH WINE RED

Cabernet Sauvignon VdP d'Oc, Caroline de Beaulieu 1994

A touch unfriendly at the moment but rating highly because it will, within a few months, soften dramatically and be a really seriously deep, rich wine.

Chateau de la Tour, Bordeaux Rouge 1994

Selected stores. Real frisky claret with lingering fruit.

Chateau Saint Bonnet, Medoc 1990

Selected stores. Real hints of class here. Will improve for a few years yet or drink now with roast lamb.

Clos Magne Figeac, Saint Emilion 1992

Top 75 stores. Muscled, robust, dry, rich-edged and attractively savoury. Classy touches.

Domaine de Pujol Minervois, Cave de la Cessanne 1993

Good savoury shroud to the vaguely blackcurrant fruit. Has rustic character but is well-mannered and charmingly direct.

Fleurie, Georges Duboeuf 1994

Grenache Syrah, Cave de la Cessanne 1994

Top 75 stores. Rusticity and vigour with the fruit and it will soften and develop well over the next year. Maybe over the next 2/3 years.

Nuits St Georges Premier Cru Les Damodes 1993

Top 20 stores from January 1996.

Sainsbury's Classic Selection Margaux 1993

Selected stores.

Santenay Premier Cru, Clos Rousseaux 1989

Vin de Pays des Bouches du Rhone, Sainsbury's

FRENCH WINE WHITE

Meursault Les Perrieres, Premier Cru 1987 `10` `G`
Selected stores.

Viognier VdP d'Oc, Pere Anselme 1994 `14` `C`
New vintage, top 75 stores. Dry, polished, hinting at apricot fruit without fully grasping, but a poised mouthful of fruit nevertheless.

GERMAN WINE WHITE

**Bernkasteler Badstube Riesling Spatlese
Von Kesselstatt 1988** `14` `D`
Selected stores. Rich hints of fruit, vivid acidity, good balance and finish. Expensive but classy aperitif.

ITALIAN WINE RED

Merlot Atesino, K. Milne 1994 `12.5` `B`
Top 75 stores.

Squinzano Mottura 1994 `14` `B`
Top 75 stores only. Flavour, ripeness, gluggability – and a perfect pasta partner.

Terre del Sole Sardinian Red Wine `14` `B`
Selected stores. Serious fruit here which never descends into farce – though it is great fun to drink with rich Italian dishes.

ITALIAN WINE WHITE

Chardonnay del Salento, Vigneto di Caramia Puglia 1994 `14.5` `D`

Top 75 stores. Vigorous fruit of decided class and style. Great with grilled chicken.

Cortese del Piemonte 1994 `14` `C`

Selected stores. Rich and flavourful but not overdone. Touch expensive.

Sauvignon Blanc delle Tre Venezie, Sainsbury's `16` `C`

Selected stores. 'You'd never guess it was Italian,' says Sainsbury's Italian wine buyer, and he's hit the nail on the head. A beautifully structured, fresh, whistle-clean, classy wine. Lovely delicacy of flavour.

Terre del Sole Sardinian White Wine `14` `B`

Selected stores. Very clean, crisp and refreshing.

SOUTH AFRICAN WINE RED

Fairview Cabernet Sauvignon, Paarl 1994 `14` `D`

Top 75 stores. Tongue- and teeth-hugging tannins which should soften well over another year in bottle to reveal real classy fruit.

Fairview Pinotage, Paarl 1995 `15` `C`

Top 75 stores. Rubbery fruit of high polish, flavour and depth. Great food wine – casseroles, roasts, risottos.

Rustenberg Cabernet Sauvignon, Stellenbosch 1991

Top 25 stores. Old-style South African wine which is oxidised and dirty. Must have rich food to be remotely palatable.

South African Cabernet Merlot Reserve Selection 1994, Sainsbury's

Top 75 stores. Superb balance of elements, dryness and fruitiness, persistence and real classy flavoursomeness. Lovely polished wine of great fruit and class.

South African Pinotage, Sainsbury's

Swirling fruit which never gets giddy or out of balance. Great pasta plonk.

SPANISH WINE RED

Jumilla, Sainsbury's

Curiously delicious finish to the deep dry fruit. Most appealing wine – and good with casseroles and roasts.

Orobio Rioja Reserva 1988

Selected stores. Lovely flowing fruit with hints of vanilla woodiness.

Santara Cabernet Merlot, Conca de Barbera 1993

Top 75 stores. Velvety, polished, deep, lashings of flavour.

Sierra del Sol Tinto Vino de Mesa, Sainsbury's

Selected stores. Like baked apples.

SPANISH WINE   WHITE

Marques de Caceres Rioja Blanco
Crianza 1990

Top 25 stores. Terrific with grilled chicken or spicy fish dishes and oriental food. Not so hot without.

FORTIFIED WINE

Dow's Single Quinta Bomfim 1984

Top 20 stores. Lovely figgy, raisiny fruit which is like velvet (stretched).

Warre's Traditional LBV 1982

Selected stores. Pricey but luxurious.

SPARKLING WINE/CHAMPAGNE

Chardonnay Brut Methode Traditionelle,
Sainsbury's (France)

Selected stores. Elegant yet with hints of richness. As drinkable as many a champagne priced three times more.

TESCO

AUSTRALIAN WINE   RED

Kingston Estate Shiraz 1993   `14` `D`

Lovely rich fruit and light tannins. A meaty wine of great
softness and flavour and subdued spiciness. Selected stores.

Ruby Cabernet, Tesco   `14` `C`

Rich and fruity with a ripe edge softened by a smokiness and
cool depth. Delicious red wine.

AUSTRALIAN WINE   WHITE

Stirling Estate Chardonnay 1995   `15` `D`

New vintage, available at top 14 stores. Lovely rich ripe fruit
which careers off the tastebuds like liquid melon and slides down
the pocket of the throat.

FRENCH WINE   RED

St Estephe 1993, Tesco   `15.5` `E`

Has ripe blackcurrant overtones, no crude tannins, and rich,
warm, savoury fruit. Superb.

St Julien 1993, Tesco

A superbly well-balanced, fruity, delightfully dry claret of real class. Has a softness which is handsomely coated in good tannins. Delicious. Selected stores.

FRENCH WINE — WHITE

Chateau Passavent Anjou Blanc 1994

New vintage. Delicious aperitif and Chinese food wine – almost medium sweet but not truly or madly or deeply. Delicious. 14 stores only.

NEW ZEALAND WINE — RED

Coopers Creek Merlot 1994

Top 15 stores only. Soft, rich, rivetingly fruity depth with a texture which encourages the wine to slip down like brushed velvet.

New Zealand Cabernet Sauvignon, Tesco

Soft, ripe, juicy, friendly as a teddy bear.

NEW ZEALAND WINE — WHITE

Coopers Creek Chardonnay 1995

New vintage, top 70 stores only. Not cheap at eight quid but a beautifully crafted wine of elegant fruit with balance, youth and invigorating flavour.

SOUTH AFRICAN WINE RED

Beyers Truter Pinotage, Tesco 16 C

Superb fruit with good spiciness and plum/blackcurrant flavours, baked but not overbaked and wonderfully soft and deep in the throat. A brilliantly versatile wine, good with meats and chilled with fish.

SOUTH AFRICAN WINE WHITE

Cape Bay Semillon/Chardonnay 1995 14 C

Good fish wine with some style and freshness. Drink it young. It won't keep.

Franschoek Semillon, Tesco

A lovely ripe yet fresh glug with the bite and character, though always modern and zippy, to go with rich fish and chicken dishes.

Overgaauw Chardonnay 1995 14 D

Hints at exotic richness without going over the brink into blowsiness: controlled, subtly ripe, elegant in the modern mould.

SPANISH WINE RED

Marquis de Chive Reserva, Tesco

Selected stores. Lovely, soft vanilla edge to the ripe fruit. Good with mild Indian food.

Spanish Merlot 1995, Tesco   15.5 C

Selected stores. A gorgeous bottle of lovely, textured, soft, rich, gently leathery fruit.

SPARKLING WINE/CHAMPAGNE

Champagne Nicolas Feuillate Brut Premier Cru   15 G

A point for every pound. A beautiful, stylish, quietly haughty bottle of bubbly.

Sparkling Chardonnay, Tesco (Australia)   15 D

Lovely soft fruit, never too soft but sufficiently so to coat the tastebuds in flavour without numbing them into submission.